Missions
Accomplished?

Missions Accomplished?

The United States and Iraq since World War I

PETER L. HAHN

New York   Oxford
OXFORD UNIVERSITY PRESS

Oxford University Press, Inc., publishes works that further Oxford University's
objective of excellence in research, scholarship, and education.

Oxford New York
Auckland   Cape Town   Dar es Salaam   Hong Kong   Karachi
Kuala Lumpur   Madrid   Melbourne   Mexico City   Nairobi
New Delhi   Shanghai   Taipei   Toronto

With offices in
Argentina   Austria   Brazil   Chile   Czech Republic   France   Greece
Guatemala   Hungary   Italy   Japan   Poland   Portugal   Singapore
South Korea   Switzerland   Thailand   Turkey   Ukraine   Vietnam

For titles covered by Section 112 of the US Higher Education Opportunity Act,
please visit www.oup.com/us/he for the latest information about pricing and
alternate formats.

Published by Oxford University Press, Inc.
198 Madison Avenue, New York, New York 10016
http://www.oup.com

ISBN   978-0-19-533338-1 (paper)

9 8 7 6 5 4 3 2 1

Printed in the United States of America
on acid-free paper

This book is dedicated to
Ken, Phil, Kate, Pat, Karen, and David
From the wonder years to the present day, you have been the greatest!

CONTENTS

MAPS   ix

ACRONYMS   x

PREFACE   xi

Introduction   1

Chapter 1   Legacies of Empire: The Emergence of U.S.
Relations with Iraq, to 1958   7

Chapter 2   Cold War Challenges: The Pursuit of
Stability in Revolutionary Iraq,
1958–1979   38

Chapter 3   From Tension to Rapprochement:
U.S.–Iraqi Relations in a Turbulent
Decade, 1979–1989   67

Chapter 4   Reversing Iraqi Conquest: The Gulf War of
1990–1991   87

Chapter 5   The Enduring Menace of Saddam Hussein:
U.S. Containment of Iraq in the 1990s   113

Chapter 6   **The Downfall of Saddam Hussein: George W. Bush and the March to War in Iraq, 2001–2003**   136

Chapter 7   **The Quest for Stability: The Occupation of Iraq, 2003–2010**   164

Conclusion: Missions Accomplished?   203

BIBLIOGRAPHY   207

INDEX   217

MAPS

Map I-1   The Middle East during the Cold War Era, 1945–1991   4

Map 1-1   Distribution of Religious and Ethnic Groups in Iraq in the late Twentieth Century   9

Map 1-2   League of Nations Mandates in the Middle East after World War I   13

Map 2-1   Political Map of Iraq   42

Map 2-2   Kurdish Areas in the Middle East and Soviet Union   59

Map 4-1   Operation Desert Storm, February 1991   103

Map 4-2   Dissident Areas in Iraq after the Gulf War   107

Map 5-1   "No-Fly" Zones in Iraq   118

Map 5-2   Iraq's Oil Infrastructure   122

Map 5-3   Kurdish Areas of Northern Iraq   127

Map 6-1   Invasion of Iraq under Operation Iraqi Freedom, 2003   151

ACRONYMS

AWACS	Airborne Warning and Control System
CENTCOM	U.S. Central Command
CIA	Central Intelligence Agency
COIN	Counterinsurgency
CPA	Coalition Provisional Authority
CW	Chemical weapons
IIA	Iraq Interim Authority
IGC	Iraq Governing Council
INOC	Iraq National Oil Company
IPC	Iraq Petroleum Company
ISG	Iraq Study Group
KDP	Kurdistan Democratic Party
NATO	North Atlantic Treaty Organization
NSC	National Security Council
ORHA	Office of Reconstruction and Humanitarian Assistance
PUK	Patriotic Union of Kurdistan
UAR	United Arab Republic
UNMOVIC	U.N. Monitoring, Verification, and Inspection Commission
UNSCOM	U.N. Special Commission
WMD	Weapons of mass destruction

PREFACE

Iraq has figured prominently in U.S. foreign policy since the late 20th century and, since 2003, it has posed one of the most daunting foreign policy challenges facing the U.S. government. President George W. Bush's decision to wage a preemptive war against the regime of Iraqi Premier Saddam Hussein resulted in a smashing U.S. military victory and the overthrow of Hussein. The U.S. battlefield victory soon gave way, however, to a prolonged and costly occupation, a consequence of poor postwar planning by officials in Washington and unintended and unexpected repercussions of Hussein's downfall. For the remainder of the first decade of the 21st century, Iraq dominated the thinking of policy makers in Washington who were responsible for safeguarding U.S. interests in the volatile Middle East.

The war that began in 2003 marked the culmination of 2 decades of sharply rising U.S. involvement with Iraq. Saddam Hussein's seizure of power in Baghdad in 1979 and his invasion of Iran the next year—a move that sparked 8 years of bloody warfare between Iraq and Iran—attracted the attention of top U.S. foreign policy makers who were determined to preserve U.S. interests in the Gulf region. Despite some reservations about the qualities of Hussein's regime, U.S. leaders sided with Iraq because of their greater contempt for the government of Iran. Within 2 years of the end of the Iran–Iraq War, however, Hussein resumed a belligerent foreign policy, capped by the military conquest of Kuwait in August 1990, and the U.S. government moved to stop him. President George H. W. Bush led a multinational military operation that liberated Kuwait in early 1991. Bush and President William Clinton enforced legal, military, and economic restrictions designed to contain the Hussein regime until it moderated its policy or declined in power.

The U.S. military involvement against Iraq in the 1990s–2000s was preceded by decades of diplomatic and economic interaction with the government in Baghdad. Carved from the remnants of the Ottoman Empire mostly to serve British imperial interests, Iraq was generally viewed by the U.S. government as a British political responsibility from the end of World War I through the end of World War II. During that era, however, U.S. officials competed with the British for economic interests in Iraq and neighboring areas and they intervened directly in the internal politics of Iraq during World War II, when they feared that the country lurched toward a partnership with Nazi Germany. After 1945, when the Soviet Union loomed as a menace in the thinking of Western powers, U.S. officials engaged with Iraq on a variety of political, military, and economic initiatives to align the state with the Western alliance and to prevent it from slipping into Moscow's orbit.

This book is the first analytical synthesis of U.S. diplomacy toward Iraq during the 9 decades after that state was established at the end of World War I. It identifies and evaluates the various missions that officials in Washington pursued in Iraq, missions including crafty diplomatic initiatives to preserve friendly governments in Baghdad, military partnerships to preserve Western security imperatives during global conflicts, economic and military assistance to prevent the collapse of Iraq under Iranian pressure, and military action to contain the Hussein regime and, eventually, to depose it. Over the 90 years since Iraq became a defined political entity, that state emerged gradually from the shadows of the British Empire to become one of the most daunting foreign policy challenges facing the U.S. government. Along the way, various presidents, secretaries of state and defense, and other U.S. officials conceived of missions in Iraq designed to enhance U.S. interests in that state and across the Middle East or beyond. This book measures the degree to which those missions were accomplished.

This book provides students, scholars, and other general readers with a concise, analytical overview of U.S. diplomacy in Iraq. As the first synthesis on this topic, it is based on a broad range of declassified government documents, newspapers, memoirs, and secondary sources. The existing literature on U.S. policy toward Iraq includes relatively few works on the 20th century and an abundance of books on the early 21st century. *Missions Accomplished?* is the first study to place the relationship in a balanced, long-term historical perspective. Its text follows a lively pace through the early years, when the official relationship was distant and muted. Coverage becomes progressively more focused in the most recent decades, when U.S.–Iraqi relations became complicated. A full chapter is devoted to the Gulf War of 1990–1991 and two chapters examine the U.S. invasion and occupation of Iraq that started in 2003. The narrative flows at a pace appropriate to the importance and complexity of the actual historical events under scrutiny.

Missions Accomplished? was composed primarily for undergraduate students and for citizens interested in the history of a complicated foreign policy issue. The text was organized and crafted with brevity, clarity, and accessibility as high priorities. It aims to provide sufficient historical, global, and regional contexts surrounding U.S. diplomacy in Iraq so that readers can grasp the essential features of the story and the causes of conflict and change without encountering excessive detail. I deliberately avoided scholarly jargon. The book is recommended for students in such courses as the history of U.S. foreign policy, recent U.S. history, modern Middle East history, and international relations. I hope that graduate students and other scholars seeking a balanced and concise summary of the topic will also find this study beneficial. The book is also intended for interested and concerned citizens who seek to understand the history behind the headlines of recent years or those who struggle to define or comprehend an ideal future for Iraq.

This book takes a traditional approach to the study of U.S. foreign relations history. That is, it focuses on the exercise of power, the conduct of diplomacy, the practice of international politics, the interest in domestic politics and public opinion, and the application of military strength by U.S. government officials who calculated the national interests and formulated policies designed to achieve those interests. This approach reflects my convictions that such dynamics form the heart of international relations and that a traditional narrative provides a foundation for other modes of scholarly exploration. Although the book touches episodically on cultural features of the U.S. relationship with Iraq, I refrained from exhaustively exploring such matters on behalf of my aim to keep this synthesis concise. I welcome other scholars to explore such cultural aspects of U.S. relations with Iraq as gender, race and ethnicity, and religion.

I also aimed to incorporate significant material that revealed Iraqi history and perspectives. Although unable to exploit troves of Iraqi government documents, I relied heavily on the secondary literature in a quest to paint wholesome landscapes of Iraq's political structures and social institutions that shaped its foreign policy toward its neighbors and toward the United States. As a specialist on U.S. foreign policy history, I remained committed to capturing as much information as possible about the Iraqi factors that influenced the formulation of U.S. policy and thereby qualitatively shaped the relationship between Washington and Baghdad.

Each chapter in this book opens with a vignette about an individual American citizen who experienced a first-hand, significant encounter with Iraq. The six men and one woman portrayed include two ambassadors to Baghdad, an assistant secretary of state, a Navy captain, an Air Force pilot, an Army general, and an Army private who made the ultimate sacrifice for his country. The vignettes were devised to grasp the reader's attention, to illustrate how policy decisions made in Washington were actually implemented on the ground in Iraq, and to show the human face of U.S. policy. If these vignettes fulfill their aims, readers will find them colorful, dramatic, and poignant.

The text is also lavishly illustrated with maps and photos. The maps were selected to provide students and other readers with a geographic grounding that is an essential part of a common understanding of the U.S. experience in Iraq. The photos were chosen to complement the printed word by providing pictorial images of some of the major players and events described in the text. I hope that the illustrations provide an additional layer of meaning that will augment learning.

ACKNOWLEDGMENTS

I am indebted to several colleagues who assisted in the preparation of this book. Research assistants Daniel Vandersommers, Ryan McMahon, Katie Magee, James Helicke, Anna Hahn, David Hadley, Robert Denning, Michael Carrozzo, and

Joe Arena provided invaluable service in gathering sources, reviewing the literature, proofreading, and compiling maps and photographs. Professors Melvyn P. Leffler of the University of Virginia and Robert J. McMahon, Peter R. Mansoor, and Georges Tamer of Ohio State University each read an early draft of the entire manuscript and made excellent suggestions for improvement. Several referees recruited by Oxford University Press—Camron Amin, University of Michigan–Dearborn; Carol Bargeron, Texas State University; Michael Bracy, Oklahoma State University; Andrew Buchanan, University of Vermont; David Foglesong, Rutgers, The State University of New Jersey; Thomas Jodziewicz, University of Dallas; Michael Latham, Fordham University; Nicole Phelps, University of Vermont; and Samer Shehata, Georgetown University—also provided superb suggestions and critiques of this work when it was first conceived and presented in a prospectus and again when a full draft of the narrative was completed in the summer of 2010. I extend heartfelt thanks to each of these individuals for their significant contributions to this book.

I am also appreciative to the staff of Oxford University Press for the opportunity to publish this study. My special thanks to Senior Editor Brian Wheel, who recruited me to the project and who provided sage advice as the chapters took shape. Editorial assistant Sarah Ellerton guided the manuscript from my rough assembly of chapters and illustrations to a cohesive final product and production editor David Wharton guided it to press.

Finally, I acknowledge the support of my family. As usual, Cathy and our children, Anna, Ben, Paul, and Mark, provided steady encouragement as I examined the documents and toiled away at my computer. I also came to appreciate the interest in my professional work shown by my wonderful brothers and sisters: Kenneth Hahn, Dr. Philip Hahn, Katherine Asbeck, Patricia Minden, Karen Rizk, and David Hahn. Years ago we collectively experienced a remarkable voyage of growing up together in middle America. Today, we nurture a deep bond built on love, mutual support, and magnificent family adventures. In grateful recognition of the ties that bind our hearts, I dedicate this book to my sisters and brothers.

Introduction

On May 1, 2003, President George W. Bush flew in a Navy warplane from a naval air station in San Diego to the USS *Abraham Lincoln*, an aircraft carrier sailing some 30 miles to the west. The president, who had flown F-102 fighters for the Texas Air National Guard in 1968–1973, reportedly took the controls of the S-3B Viking aircraft and made a few maneuvers en route. Upon reaching the *Abraham Lincoln*, the pilot, Commander John Lussier, made a "tail hook" landing, in which a steel cable stretched across the deck brought the plane from a landing speed of 150 miles per hour to a sudden stop, over a mere 400 feet of deck space. This first-ever carrier landing by a U.S. president was conducted flawlessly and in front of a live television audience. When the president emerged from the Viking bedecked in a flight suit and helmet, hundreds of sailors, heading home after 10 months at sea in support of U.S. combat operations in Afghanistan and Iraq, cheered wildly for their commander in chief.[1]

Soon after landing on the carrier, President Bush delivered an upbeat televised address about the rapid success of U.S. and allied military forces in occupying Iraq and ousting Premier Saddam Hussein. Standing beneath an enormous banner proclaiming "MISSION ACCOMPLISHED," the president triumphantly declared that "major combat operations in Iraq have ended. In the battle of Iraq, the United States and our allies have prevailed. And now our coalition is engaged in securing and reconstructing that country." Paying tribute to the men and women of the U.S. armed services, Bush added, "Your courage, your willingness to face danger for your country and for each other, made this day possible. Because of you, our Nation is more secure. Because of you, the tyrant has fallen, and Iraq is free." While acknowledging that "we have difficult work to do in Iraq," Bush revealed no inkling that the ensuing occupation of Iraq would outlast his two-term presidency or that it would result in more than 4,300 U.S. military fatalities beyond the 139 deaths incurred in the invasion.[2]

Photo I-1
President George W. Bush addresses sailors aboard the USS *Abraham Lincoln*, at sea off the coast of California, May 1, 2003. The prominence of the "MISSION ACCOMPLISHED" banner suspended behind the president caused political controversy in ensuing years. SOURCE: AP Photo/J. Scott Applewhite.

Photo I-2
Bedecked in a flight suit, President George W. Bush waves to the crew of USS *Abraham Lincoln* moments after landing aboard the aircraft carrier in a Viking S-3B jet on May 1, 2003. At right is Commander John Lussier, who piloted the Viking jet to the carrier. SOURCE: AFP/Getty Images.

Photo I-3
President Bush enjoys a moment of casual repose with sailors aboard the USS *Abraham Lincoln*, May 1, 2003. SOURCE: U.S. Navy photograph by Photographer's Mate 3rd Class Tyler J. Clements (released).

President Bush had solid grounds for paying tribute to the U.S. soldiers who had conducted the invasion of Iraq that he had ordered on March 19. In a campaign of some 500 hours, U.S. and allied troops had completely demolished and scattered the Iraqi army of some 400,000 soldiers, occupied the country, destroyed the government, and driven Saddam Hussein into hiding. The capture of Baghdad on April 9 and the toppling of the towering statue of Hussein in al-Firdos Square had signaled the end of his brutal regime after 24 years in power. Given the overwhelming military success of the invasion, President Bush's implicit declaration of "mission accomplished" elated millions of Americans.[3]

The "mission accomplished" message soon emerged, however, as one of the most controversial presidential declarations in modern U.S. history. Many Americans who harbored deep doubts about the wisdom, legality, or morality of the president's decision to invade Iraq in the first place took little satisfaction in the military conquest. Further complicating the situation, the euphoria of the military victory quickly evaporated in the swelter of the ensuing military occupation, like water in a desert sun. As U.S. military and civilian occupation authorities in Iraq encountered numerous complications, including a pernicious and deadly insurgency, many Americans were left confused about the mission in Iraq and increasingly convinced that Bush's May 1 declaration of accomplishment was at best premature, if not completely wrong. Even President Bush eventually

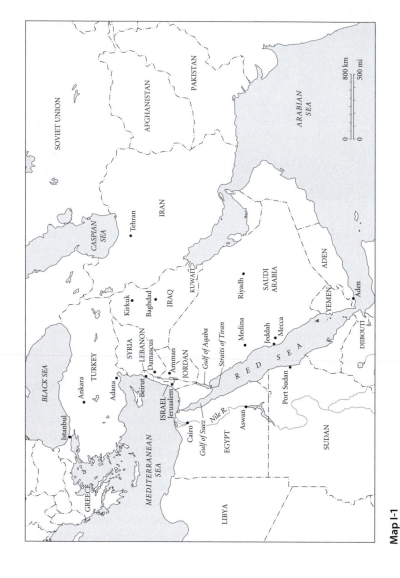

Map I-1

The Middle East during the Cold War Era, 1945–1991. From *Caught in the Middle East: U.S. Policy toward the Arab–Israeli Conflict, 1945–1961*, by Peter L. Hahn. SOURCE: Copyright © 2004 by the University of North Carolina Press. Used by permission of the publisher.

acknowledged that the "mission accomplished" banner proved to be a "big mistake" because it implied that the work in Iraq had been completed. "It looked like I was doing the victory dance," he later wrote, "that I had warned against."[4]

To shed light on the contemporary American experience in Iraq, this book analyzes the history of the relationship between the two countries from the creation of Iraq at the end of World War I to the present day. It emphasizes the formulation of U.S. policy toward Iraq in its political, strategic, military, and economic dimensions; it examines the influence of domestic politics and public opinion on that policy; and it assesses the public discourse on the controversial aspects of U.S. diplomacy. To establish the international context of U.S. diplomacy, the book considers the political situation in Baghdad; regional developments including the Arab–Israeli conflict, intra-Arab rivalries, and Iraqi–Iranian tensions; and global dynamics such as decolonization and the Cold War. The individuals who occupied key policy-making positions in both Washington and Baghdad are scrutinized.

Since the modern state of Iraq was founded during the World War I era, the United States has generally pursued a basic goal of promoting stability and U.S. security interests in that country. The precise U.S. mission changed and evolved over the 20th century, however, as global and regional political dynamics developed and as both the United States and Iraq gained in power and stature. What began as a relationship between an increasingly powerful Western state lacking official interests in the Middle East (the United States) and a relatively impotent mandate of the British Empire (Iraq) evolved through several stages including cooperation, intense conflict, and war. As circumstances, opportunities, and interests shifted on both sides of the relationship, U.S. policy makers adopted, modified, and abandoned various goals in Iraq. Some missions were accomplished; others were not.

The seven chapters that follow explain the diverse missions identified by the United States over time and assess the consequences and effectiveness of U.S. policies. Chapter 1 notes that from World War I through 1958 the United States shifted from its initial reliance on the British Empire to manage the Middle East toward an acceptance of greater responsibility for securing the region against external threats and internal instability. The rise of Nazi and then Soviet threats and the concomitant decline of Britain's ability to project power compelled U.S. leaders to become more active in Iraq. By the 1950s, the United States and Iraq forged a friendship and a security partnership. Chapter 2 illustrates that from 1958 to 1979, a period of political instability in Baghdad, U.S. leaders monitored Iraq from a distance, aiming to deny any inroads by Soviet-backed communism and to prevent any flare-ups in violence between Iraq and its neighbors. Iraq became more of a concern to U.S. officials in the decade after Saddam Hussein took power in Baghdad in 1979, the subject of Chapter 3. Although Hussein's invasion of Iran in 1980 generated turmoil across the Middle East, the United States and Iraq, sharing a common adversary in Tehran, began to reconcile their differences by the mid-1980s.

Chapter 4 explains that the U.S.–Iraqi rapprochement soon ended when Hussein launched an invasion of Kuwait in August 1990. Suddenly fearing that Iraq posed a serious threat to U.S. security interests across the region, President George H. W. Bush contested Iraq's conquest, leading to the Gulf War of 1990–1991 in which U.S. and allied forces expelled the Iraqi military from Kuwait. Bush allowed Hussein to remain in power in Baghdad, however, and thus had to formulate a new policy of containing the Iraqi dictator. Chapter 5 analyzes the containment policy that Bush and his successor, President Bill Clinton, practiced over a decade and explains how the revival of Iraqi power complicated the mission.

The final two chapters assess the approach to Iraq taken by President George W. Bush after 2001. Alarmed by the terrorist attacks of September 11, 2001, and the potential for even more lethal future assaults, Bush formulated a mission of preemptively demolishing the threat that Iraq seemed to pose to U.S. national security. The president ordered an invasion of Iraq in March 2003 that enjoyed considerable short-term success, as U.S. and allied firepower promptly wrecked the Hussein regime beyond repair. But the occupation of Iraq also earned the United States the responsibility of figuring out how to stabilize and govern the country in the post-Hussein era. The complications of that undertaking created serious doubts about whether the United States accomplished its latest mission in Iraq or even comprehended it.

NOTES

1. "Commander in Chief lands on USS Lincoln," May 2, 2003, http://www.cnn.com/2003/ALLPOLITICS/05/01/bush.carrier.landing/ (accessed June 30, 2010).
2. Bush, "Address to the Nation on Iraq from the U.S.S. Abraham Lincoln," May 1, 2003, *Public Papers of the President, 2003* (Washington: USGPO, 2003): 1: 410–13.
3. Keegan, *Iraq War*, 1–7, 127–203.
4. Bush, *Decision Points*, 257.

CHAPTER 1

Legacies of Empire
The Emergence of U.S. Relations with Iraq, to 1958

On April 2, 1941, U.S. Minister to Iraq Paul Knabenshue experienced the most dramatic day of his 28-year career in the Foreign Service. A native of Toledo, Ohio, Knabenshue had joined the State Department in 1914 and served for 18 years in junior positions in Cairo, Beirut, and Jerusalem before being appointed as Minister Resident and Consul General in Iraq in August 1932. After several years of relative quietude in Baghdad, he eventually faced political tensions connected to the origins and onset of World War II. By 1940–1941, as Nazi Germany tightened its grip on Europe and threatened to overwhelm Britain, Knabenshue warily eyed a political challenge by anti-British Iraqi politicians and military officers against the pro-Western Iraqi monarchy, ruled by regent Abdul Ilah on behalf of his 5-year-old nephew, King Faisal II. In January 1941, Knabenshue endorsed a move by the regent to force the resignation of Rashid Ali al-Gailani, a leading anti-British nationalist who had served for 10 months as prime minister. On April 1, however, al-Gailani and four army colonels launched a *coup d'état* against Prime Minister Taha al-Hashimi and reportedly issued an order to capture or kill the regent.

On the following morning, the regent suddenly showed up at the U.S. legation. He appeared, Knabenshue later reported, "in native woman's dress covering dressing gown and pajamas" and seeking U.S. protection. Within hours, the U.S. Minister loaded the regent into his official car, bedecked with the Stars and Stripes, and drove him to the safety of the British air base at Habbaniya, "accompanied by my wife as camouflage" and with the regent "lying on floor at back covered by [a] rug" and armed with a pistol. The daring ploy worked: the minister's car slipped without incident through several Iraqi Army checkpoints, "which were stopping and searching other cars." Delivered from peril in Knabenshue's limousine, the regent would return to control of his country on June 1, after British military forces crushed the al-Gailani revolt. For his part, Knabenshue would die in Baghdad on February 1, 1942, from tetanus contracted during a medical operation.[1]

Minister Knabenshue's adventure with the regent proved to be a crucial episode in the maintenance of Western security interests in Iraq during World

Photo 1-1
U.S. Minister to Iraq Paul Knabenshue, who in 1941 conducted the first recorded U.S. physical intervention in the internal politics of Iraq. SOURCE: Library of Congress, Prints & Photographs Division, NYWT&S Collection, LC-USZ62–137712.

War II. It followed a gradual rise in cultural and economic activity by American citizens in the Middle East region and marked the beginning of a gradual transition from Britain to the United States as the dominant Western power in the area. It also foreshadowed the security concerns that would emerge as dominant features of American policy after World War II. Knabenshue's intervention marked the first recorded physical U.S. intervention in the internal politics of Iraq. It would certainly not be the last.

Having become deeply involved in Iraq in the early 20th century, the British government remained intent on blocking Nazi inroads into Iraq. It was also unknowingly approaching a period of profound decline in its capabilities in the Middle East after 1945. A comparative latecomer to the region, the U.S. Government soon would be equipped and determined to practice a similar policy of preserving Western interests in Iraq by containment of the Soviet Union, although it would discover that nationalism and other factors internal to Iraq made the task difficult. This chapter will examine how the United States, the heir of the British imperial legacy, defined and pursued its first official mission in Iraq during and after World War II.

ORIGINS OF MODERN IRAQ, TO 1945

The modern state of Iraq occupies territory once known to the Western world as Mesopotamia—Greek for "land between the rivers," in reference to the basin between the Tigris and Euphrates. (The British formally named the territory Iraq after World War I.[2]) Baghdad, which originated in the 8th century, sits on the Tigris, which flows south from Turkey. Flowing east from Syria, the Euphrates joins the Tigris just north of Basra, forming the Shatt al-Arab ("River of the Arabs"), which marks the modern Iran–Iraq border and empties into the Persian Gulf. Iraq possesses only some 26 miles of seacoast, and the Shatt al-Arab is its only navigable inlet. The north of the country is mountainous, and much of the west is a vast swath of the Great Syrian Desert. Iraq's 2007 population, estimated at 27.5 million, included Arabs (75–80 percent), Kurds (15–20 percent), and Assyrians, Turkomans, and other ethnic minorities (5 percent). Ninety-seven

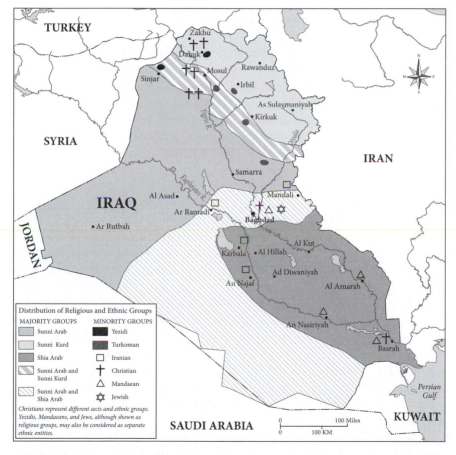

Map 1-1

The distribution of Iraq's religious and ethnic groups in the late 20th century is depicted in this map produced by the Central Intelligence Agency in 1978. SOURCE: Courtesy of the University of Texas Libraries, The University of Texas at Austin.

percent of Iraqis were Muslims, with Shiites outnumbering Sunnis at approximately a 2 to 1 ratio (3 to 1 if Kurdish Sunnis were excluded).[3]

Iraq claims a long history. The Tigris and Euphrates provided fresh water and trade routes that spawned the early development of human society and culture. Ancient civilizations included the Sumerians, who dominated Mesopotamia in the 3rd millennium BCE and who invented writing. A millennium later, the Babylonians ruled southern Mesopotamia; they were known for scientific discovery, for developing a complex legal code, and for inventing the concept of keeping time in intervals of 60 seconds, 60 minutes, and 24 hours. The Assyrians concurrently ruled northern Mesopotamia, building a militaristic culture distinguished by ruthlessness toward enemies. Around 1850 BCE, Abram (later Abraham) began a divinely inspired migration from Ur to Canaan, giving foundation to ancient Israel and its Jewish faith. Cyrus the Great conquered Mesopotamia in c. 500 BCE, opening 11 centuries of rule by Greeks, Persians, Parthians, and Romans.[4]

The rise of Islam had a profound and enduring influence on Iraq. The Prophet Muhammed (570–632 CE) founded the religion and established a political federation among tribes of the Arabian Peninsula, and in 637, Arab Muslims defeated the Persians and conquered Mesopotamia. Eventually, however, tribal rivalries and theological and political differences rent the cultural unity of Islam. A struggle ensued over dynastic succession after soldiers assassinated Uthman, the third caliph ("successor" to Muhammed), in 656. Ali, the fourth caliph, was assassinated in 661. Power passed to Muawiya, who founded the Ummayad dynasty. But devotees of Ali, known as the Shia ("partisans of Ali," also known as Shiites), refused to yield to the Sunni elite. They venerated Ali's tomb at Kufa and built the holy city of Najaf around it. Upon the death of Muawiya in 680, Ali's son Husain made a bid for power but his small band was brutally defeated and Husain was beheaded. Ultimately, the Ummayad dynasty was beset by internal strife and collapsed in 749–750, except for a small remnant that survived in southern Spain.

The Abbasid dynasty (750–1258) next governed Mesopotamia and other lands ranging from North Africa to Afghanistan. That dynasty embraced aspects of Persian culture and made notable achievements in medicine, geography, mathematics, astronomy, chemistry, and literature—enjoying the so-called "Golden Age of Islam." Founded in 762, Baghdad emerged by the 9th century as the most advanced city in the world, spanning 2 miles in diameter, protected by massive walls, and supported by an elaborate agrarian economy based on complex irrigation systems.[5]

Baghdad abruptly lost its grandeur in 1258, when the Mongol horde conquered the city. Within days, hundreds of thousands of people were killed and the vast city was laid to waste by systematic looting and destruction. A Muslim army halted the Mongol advance near Nazareth in 1260, but Baghdad never recovered from the invasion. Over subsequent centuries, Shiites and Sunnis of Mesopotamia developed a culture of dominance over and revenge against each other as Shiite Persians and Sunni Turks battled for control of the land. The Ottoman Turkish conquest of Baghdad in 1638 brought to Mesopotamia a relative stability destined to last nearly 3 centuries. The Ottomans defined the modern, western border of Persia; divided Mesopotamia into the three *vilayets* (provinces) of Basra, Baghdad, and Mosul; and, by the 19th century, exercised a distant, city-based authority. In the hinterland, local elites and warlords garnered power through tribes, clans, and families, planting the seeds for the eventual growth of an Iraqi–Arab identity. Although the Ottomans considered the three provinces of Mesopotamia separate entities, by the late 19th century the elites of the provinces knitted cultural and social connections and they began to resist certain dictates of the Ottoman central government. These dynamics planted a foundation on which Iraqi nationalism would emerge in the 20th century.[6]

Britain first became interested in Mesopotamia in the 19th century. Determined to protect its lines of communication to India and to contain French and Russian expansionism, Britain sought official and commercial interests in the Persian Gulf region. In a complicated diplomatic balancing act known as the Eastern Question, British officials sought to preserve the Ottoman Empire, not because they admired it, but because they calculated that its demise would spark imperial wars over its spoils. By the early 20th century, Britain seized control of the oil industry in Iran, probed Ottoman lands for additional such resources, and competed with German firms for mineral rights concessions across modern Iraq.[7]

World War I spawned massive changes in the political landscape of the Middle East in general and Mesopotamia in particular. On the regional scale, the Ottoman Empire's decision to ally with Germany and Austria-Hungary set the stage for its military defeat and political collapse. Britain solidified its presence in Egypt and, with its tribal Arab allies, liberated Palestine (including Transjordan) and Syria from Ottoman control, enabling postwar European control of those territories. To stabilize Arabia, Britain recognized Hussein, the grand sheriff of Mecca, as guardian of the Muslim holy places at Mecca and Medina. British imperial forces also invaded and occupied Mesopotamia. Motivated by a desire to protect Persian Gulf oil resources, the British landed an Indian force along the Shatt al-Arab in November 1914 and soon occupied Basra. The Ottomans repulsed an early thrust on Baghdad and surrounded and destroyed an entire British army (composed mostly of Indian soldiers) at Kut al-Amara in 1916, but a larger British army captured Baghdad in December 1917. Britain "push[ed] on with campaigns," the scholar Elizabeth Monroe aptly noted, that were "relatively cheap in human life and valuable in terms of British power."[8]

British officials moved quickly to consolidate their hold on Mesopotamia. In 1915, an interdepartmental government committee identified the area as a potentially valuable postwar prize, a place of opportunity for Indians and British colonists in India, and, if properly irrigated, a grain producer. Basra was considered the key asset, with Baghdad and Mosul desired for security against Russian encroachment. Indications of oil resources in Mosul and a desire to protect the province's Nestorian Christians, who had rebelled against the Ottomans in 1916, provided additional incentives to control the north. The British India office advocated annexation of Mesopotamia on the rationale that Britain could not allow the Turks to reoccupy it nor cede the conquest to Russia or France. Under the Sykes–Picot agreement of May 1916, France recognized British control of Basra and Baghdad provinces and Britain yielded Mosul to local Arab control (under French economic influence). Generally, British officials believed that they had earned such spoils through their military victories and the sacrifices of their soldiers. Lt. Colonel Arnold Wilson, who became acting civil administrator in May 1918, arranged a plebiscite that exaggerated popular support for British rule. He also adopted a government modeled on British administration in India, appointed Indians to second-tier administrative positions, imported the Indian currency (the rupee) and legal code, and criticized U.S. President Woodrow Wilson's call for self-determination as a threat to the stability of the territory.[9]

Britain consolidated its military gains through crafty postwar diplomacy. Soon after the Ottomans signed the Armistice of Mudros in October 1918, British and French leaders declared that they jointly sought to establish independent Arab states across the region. But such words were a mere nod to the principle of self-determination and a smokescreen to shroud imperial ambitions. At the Paris Peace Conference of early 1919, British Prime Minister David Lloyd George and French Premier Georges Clemenceau together resisted Wilson's liberal ideals for postwar settlements. By the end of 1919, London and Paris agreed to a revision of the Sykes–Picot agreement that transferred Mosul from the French to the British, gave France a 25 percent share of the Turkish Petroleum Company, and authorized Britain to construct oil pipelines from Persia through the French zone to the Mediterranean. At the San Remo conference of April 1920, the two powers agreed that Britain would govern Iraq and Palestine as mandates (officially under the League of Nations) and that France would act likewise in Syria and Lebanon.[10]

Britain's imperial scheming stimulated the growth of nationalism and some political resistance among the peoples of the three former Ottoman provinces grouped together as the mandate of Iraq. At the end of the Ottoman era, those peoples were divided by cultural and ethnic identities (Arab Sunnis, Arab Shiites, and Kurdish Sunnis); by rural–urban dynamics, with urbanites tending to have more education and wealth; by historic tribal patterns; and by the legacy of the separated provincial administrations of the Ottoman period. The lumping of the three provinces into a single entity and the imposition of imperial controls over it, however, stimulated a sense of pan-Iraqi identity and resistance. As early as the summer of 1919, Iraqi nationalists who had fought with Faisal in Syria and returned home angry at British duplicity launched attacks on British soldiers, killing a small number. A more general uprising erupted in the summer of 1920. Organized bands of Iraqis overran exposed British garrisons and assassinated British officials in towns and cities. By August, the rebels announced a provisional government of Iraq and the revolt spread across the whole country, with the exception of fortified cities and the southern Tigris Valley. A burst of nationalism overcame traditional ethnic, cultural, and geographic divisions among the Iraqi people, the scholar Hanna Batatu observed. "For the first time in many centuries, Shi'is joined politically with Sunnis, and townsmen from Baghdad and tribesmen from the Euphrates made common cause."[11]

Britain ruthlessly suppressed the revolt, gaining short-term success but planting the seeds of long-term trouble. Under the command of General Aylmer L. Haldane, British and Indian ground troops backed by British air power killed rebel leaders and demolished rebellious villages. By March 1921, when the rebellion was crushed, some 2,000 Anglo-Indians and 8,000 Iraqis died in the fighting. General Haldane later recorded that he sought to "teach the insurgents the price thay [they] had to pay for throwing down the gauntlet to the British Empire. The punishment had of necessity to be exemplary." As the scholar Elie Kedourie notes, such a military victory came at a price because the British incubated an Iraqi political culture of instability and violence, generated deep anti-British nationalism, and centralized local power in a small elite that lacked checks or balances.[12]

While suppressing the revolt within Iraq, British authorities also used diplomatic muscle to impose their objectives over alternatives favored by local elites. In March 1920, an elected congress met in Damascus and proclaimed the independence of Syria, including Palestine and Lebanon, with Faisal as king. Local leaders in Iraq similarly declared independence and announced a union with Syria. These steps reflected deep local resentment of the French and disappointment in

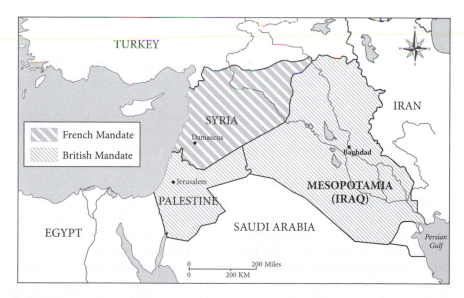

Map 1-2
The Middle East mandates developed by Western powers through the League of Nations in the aftermath of World War I.

British violations of wartime promises. But France and Britain, in coordinated replies, nullified the local actions on the grounds that the assemblies were not recognized by the international community and that their actions violated international diplomatic conferences. Britain removed Abdallah from Baghdad and named him emir of Transjordan (separated from Palestine), and then enthroned Faisal, expelled from Syria, as king of Iraq. British officials met in Cairo in March 1921 to affirm Faisal as king, to approve "Iraq" as the formal name of the mandate, and to replace costly ground forces with air power as the foundation of British authority in the country.[13]

To consolidate its internal control of Iraq in the 1920s, Britain governed in a partnership with local elites and established a façade of Iraqi sovereignty. King Faisal was authorized to preside over certain civil affairs. He in turn empowered Sunnis—who, although members of an ethnic minority, tended to be more urbanized, better educated, and wealthier—to administer the state apparatus and to transition it away from Ottoman legacies. Faisal entertained some nationalist ambitions to achieve true independence, but ultimately calculated that cooperation with Britain would both ensure Iraqi security and integrity and enhance his own personal interests within the Iraqi political order. Thus, Faisal recognized that the British High Commissioner in Iraq bore substantial authority. In 1924, British officials and King Faisal signed a 20-year alliance, and in 1925, Britain allowed elections for a two-chamber Iraqi parliament to ratify the treaty, although it had to suppress a movement demanding full independence. In 1930, a 25-year defense pact was signed, providing Britain with air bases at Habbaniya (50 miles west of Baghdad) and Shaiba (near Basra) and providing Iraqi troops with British military training. In 1932, Britain formally recognized Iraqi independence, although it maintained control of oil assets and the air bases. British officials insisted on keeping the air bases they deemed vital to the security of India and other imperial interests. Some Iraqi nationalists vocally objected that these arrangements perpetuated British influence over their country, but they lacked the political power to alter the outcome.[14]

Britain gained international affirmation of its authority over Iraq in diplomatic conferences in the early 1920s. The League of Nations affirmed the Middle East mandates in 1922. At the Uqair Conference of 1922, Sir Percy Cox, frustrated by quarrels among local rulers, single-handedly drew the borders shared by Iraq, Kuwait, and Saudi Arabia. At the Lausanne Conference of 1922–1923, Lord Curzon prevailed on Ismet Pasha of Turkey to yield all claims to Mosul, and in 1925 the League of Nations, after surveying the people of Mosul, resolved that the province would remain in Iraq. Whatever their gains for British imperial ambitions, these arrangements planted seeds for long-term conflict in the Middle East. "Britain introduced European-type notions of territorial sovereignty," the scholar Avi Shlaim notes, "to an area where tribes were much more important than the state, where tribal borders were better understood than international ones, and where the law of the desert prevailed."[15] Indeed, the borders drawn by Cox in 1922 remained a source of dispute through the early 21st century.

Photo 1-2
Six-year-old King Faisal II of Iraq, who officially occupied the throne in 1939 at age 3
and served for many years as the world's youngest ruler. SOURCE: Library of Congress, Prints &
Photographs Division, FSA-OWI Collection, LC-USW33–019084-D DLC.

Photo 1-3
Regent Abdul Ilah, the uncle to King Faisal II who ruled on behalf of the monarch until
he reached adulthood, salutes at the opening of the Iraqi parliament, in November 1942.
Prime Minister Nuri al-Said, sporting a smile and a formal black jacket, stands to the
right. SOURCE: Library of Congress, Prints & Photographs Division, FSA/OWI Collection, LC-USW33–019076-D.

Iraq failed to achieve much internal political stability under British dominance. King Faisal I died in 1933. His son, Ghazi, reigned ineffectively until
his own death in 1939, at which time Ghazi's 3-year-old son was enthroned as
King Faisal II (with his uncle, Abdul Ilah, acting as regent until Faisal II reached
adulthood). The monarchy's efforts to build a national identity and loyalty to the
throne were resisted by rural sheikhs who stood to lose power and influence. As
the national army grew in size, it fragmented among factions reflecting the diversity of the society. Other branches of government did little to fill the vacuum in
royal leadership or to challenge its pro-British tendency. Wealthy Sunnis, many
with roots in the Ottoman civil service, dominated the prime ministry, cabinet,
and elite civil service positions. Nonetheless, the civil government was beset by a
cycle of instability and coups, with 59 cabinets formed in 1919–1958 (on average,
three governments in every 2-year interval). The legislature included a senate,
whose members were appointed by the king, and a chamber, whose deputies were
elected in a process that was easily rigged by the elites. Competition between
political parties—with anti-British, anti-royalist, Shiite, Sunni, and myriad other
identities—fragmented the political order. General Nuri al-Said emerged as one of
the giants of Iraqi politics. Born in Baghdad in 1889, al-Said served briefly in the
prewar Ottoman army before joining the Arab Revolt of World War I. Staunchly
pro-British, he became prime minister in 1930 for the first of 14 terms.[16]

British officials in Iraq also faced a challenge in dealing with Kurdistan. A
militant mountain people of a distinct ethnic and linguistic identity (albeit Sunni
Muslims), the Kurds were independent tribal groups who had lived under the
loose control of Iran or the Ottomans through the dawn of the 20th century.
Although a nomadic lifestyle of tending flocks gave way in modern times to
the settlement of small villages and towns, traditional tribal political structures
remained in place. The collapse of the Ottoman authority during World War
I, together with Wilsonian rhetoric about self-determination, had encouraged
Kurdish nationalism and calls for statehood, and the Treaty of Sevres of 1920
provided for an independent Kurdistan. A state did not materialize, however,
because of resistance by Turkey, British determination to retain the oil of Mosul
province for Iraq, and lingering tribal divisions among the Kurds. The Kurdish
people were instead divided among Turkey, Iran, Syria, and Iraq, comprising
20 percent of the population of Iraq. British forces suppressed a Kurdish uprising
in the early 1920s and Iraqi Kurds chafed at the Iraqi and British governments
through the interwar years.[17]

THE ORIGINS OF U.S. INVOLVEMENT IN IRAQ, TO 1945

In contrast to Britain, the U.S. government took a passive approach to Iraq before
World War II. Whereas American consumers, missionaries, and oil companies
took interest in the region in the 19th and early 20th centuries, U.S. government
involvement remained insignificant until World War II. The dynamics of that
global conflagration—including the threat of Nazi world conquest, the exhaustion

of British power, and the expansion of American capabilities—triggered official U.S. involvement in Iraq that eventually became significant and enduring.

From the earliest days of the American republic, U.S. citizens took a vicarious interest in the Middle East—part of what they perceived as a vast Oriental world stretching from Istanbul to Tokyo. As the scholar Susan Nance shows, U.S. popular culture in the 19th century embraced exotic images of the Orient in general and the Middle East in particular. The popularity of *Arabian Nights*, a collection of Persian and Arab tales dating to Medieval times and published in various English editions in the 1800s, embedded in U.S. culture an infatuation of the Middle East as a region of mystery, intrigue, mysticism, and exotic customs. As elite Americans began traveling to the region in the late 19th century, middle class citizens monitored their adventures as readers and as members of travel clubs. Re-creations of Cairo and Damascus bazaars at the 1893 World's Fair in Chicago drew widespread attention. By the early 20th century, American consumers imported goods from the Middle East such as divans, carpets, and foods. American culture also embraced such intangibles as the Muslim motifs adopted by the Shriners and other fraternal societies; the sexual energy displayed in belly dancing, which challenged Victorian sexual mores; and, among African Americans, an image of wise Easterners as an inspiration to overcome racial discrimination at home. Such images pervaded U.S. popular culture long before the American people gained any academic knowledge about the Middle East.[18]

Evangelical Christian missionaries accounted for the earliest involvement of U.S. citizens in Mesopotamia. After pioneering churchmen reached the eastern shore of the Mediterranean in the 1810s and 1820s, veteran missionaries Eli Smith and H. G. O. Dwight were assigned in 1829 to evangelize Armenia, Persia, and Mesopotamia. During a lengthy venture through the region, Smith and Dwight established contacts with such indigenous Christian groups as the Nestorians (who traced their roots to Nestorius, a patriarch of Constantinople banished in 431 to Persia), whose influence spread east to Persia and China before the Mongols destroyed most of the church structure, and the Chaldeans (Syrians who had broken from Nestorians in the 1600s and accepted papal supremacy). Answering the call from Smith and Dwight to carry modern American Christian culture to the region, waves of missionaries established schools, churches, and printing presses in Kurdistan and upper Mesopotamia by the 1840s. By the turn of the 20th century, hundreds of U.S. missionaries had established more than 400 schools, 9 colleges, 9 hospitals, and countless churches across the region.[19]

U.S. government diplomacy in Iraq originated in the World War I era but initially proved ineffective. President Woodrow Wilson's liberal vision for the postwar era, articulated in his Fourteen Points Address of 1918, included anti-imperialism and political self-determination in such places as Iraq. Wilson appointed a commission headed by Henry Churchill King and Charles R. Crane that toured the Middle East in mid-1919. The commission recommended that the Western powers establish temporary mandates (under League of Nations authority) over Iraq and Syria and advised that the United States consider assuming a mandate. Wilson's diplomacy, however, proved quite ineffective. His liberal vision had little impact on the Anglo-French deal making in the Middle East. By the time the King–Crane Commission finished its report, Wilson was too distracted and exhausted to consider its recommendations or otherwise advance his liberal vision. Some scholars even suggest that Wilson's idealistic declarations and limited involvement via the King–Crane Commission actually aggravated the postwar turmoil by raising false hopes of U.S. liberalism among Arab peoples and by forcing the British and French to delay settlements and thereby allow tensions to fester.[20]

Behind the façade of Wilson's liberal vision for the Middle East, U.S. private petroleum firms began to consider commercial interests in the region in the 1910s. Britain had dominated oil production in the region after finding major sources in Persia in 1908. In the 1910s, Western officials began to consider Middle East oil an important commodity as their navies, followed by their other military forces, converted from coal to oil as the chief source of energy. Intense competition for such a lucrative commodity ensued among Western firms. In 1914, British and Dutch firms agreed to channel all Middle East oil development through companies that they controlled, and in 1919, British officials in Baghdad and Jerusalem interfered with American oil company geologists exploring concessions that had been granted by the Ottomans.[21]

U.S. officials vigorously protested such exclusions in the 1920s. Consistent with the U.S. open door policy of equal economic opportunity, Minister to Baghdad John W. Davis told Lord Curzon in May 1920 that territory gained by Britain "must be held and governed in such a way as to assure equal treatment in law and in fact to the commerce of all nations." U.S. officials also protested an Anglo-French agreement reached at the San Remo conference to divide Iraqi oil on a 75–25 basis. As the automobile, trucking, and highway booms of the 1920s tied the domestic consumer economy to petroleum, forward-looking American businessmen calculated that the commercial development of Middle East oil resources would prove immensely profitable (although the United States remained the world's greatest oil producer into the early 1940s). In 1928, a consortium of U.S. firms finally gained a 23.75 percent share in the Iraq Petroleum Company (IPC; with equal shares held by British, French, and Dutch firms and a 5 percent share owned by a private speculator named C. S. Gulbenkian). The IPC struck it rich with a massive oil discovery near Kirkuk in 1927 and soon developed an elaborate network of pipelines and production and shipping facilities across the region. U.S. oil corporations also gained concessions in Bahrain, Kuwait, and Saudi Arabia.[22]

Competition over Middle East oil eased in the 1930s, as seven large oil companies, known as the "majors," established dominance over the industry. The U.S. firms Standard Oil of New Jersey and Standard Oil of New York, together with their IPC partners, controlled Iraqi oil. As a surplus of oil caused by the Great Depression deflated prices in the 1930s, the majors sought to reverse the

Photo 1-4
Iraq Petroleum Company well near Kirkuk, Iraq, 1932. SOURCE: Library of Congress, Prints &
Photographs Division, LC-DIG-matpc-16248.

deflation through a series of agreements to avoid competition, protect each other's holdings against outside competition, and avoid price reductions. The U.S.
government briefly contemplated antitrust action against these firms but came
to tolerate such arrangements during World War II and the early Cold War. Yet
even when demand for oil soared, the Western partners in the IPC continued to
curtail Iraqi oil production because they stood to gain larger profits by marketing
oil from countries where they enjoyed larger shares.[23]

The U.S. government took a growing official interest in Iraq during the
1920s and 1930s, although it clearly deferred to British power in the country.
John Randolph, the U.S. Consul in Baghdad in 1923–1929, routinely addressed
the Iraqi government through the British High Commissioner. The United States
cosigned the 1930 British–Iraqi defense treaty, which recognized the "special
relations" between London and Baghdad, to secure its right to operate schools
and religious institutions in Iraq and to gain protection of U.S. property. The
United States and Iraq signed an extradition treaty in 1934 and a treaty of commerce and navigation in 1938. In 1931, American Jesuit missionaries founded
Baghdad College, which soon attracted students from the elite families of Iraq.
When Iraq's parliament passed a law in 1939–1940 imposing controls over foreign schools, U.S. diplomats protested that it violated the 1930 treaty and challenged such institutions as Baghdad College. Iraqi officials quietly explained that

they aimed the law at Iranian schools and gave assurances that U.S. institutions would be left alone.[24]

As this chapter's opening vignette about Minister Knabenshue reveals, the United States openly backed the British position in Iraq during World War II. At the outset of the conflict, Western officials feared a potential German thrust against Iraq through Turkey or the Caucasus, given that Iraqi oil powered the British Mediterranean fleet and that Iraqi territory provided a security buffer for India and a communications link to Russia. After the fall of France in May 1940, Knabenshue anticipated a German or Russian airpower assault on unguarded oil pumping stations in Kirkuk, Iraq; Tripoli, Lebanon; or Haifa, Palestine, followed by a mechanized ground assault. Such fears were accentuated by evidence that anti-British sentiment might inspire some Iraqis to facilitate German political or military conquest from within.[25]

Indeed, Iraq was ripe for internal political turmoil. The undercurrent of anti-British nationalism that originated after World War I deepened in the late 1930s over British policy in Palestine, especially after the Mufti of Jerusalem, an Arab nationalist exiled from British Palestine, relocated to Baghdad in late 1939. Numerous Iraqi military officers were attracted to the Nazis' National Socialism ideology as a vehicle for deliverance from British rule. Efforts by the crown to build a pro-British nationalism failed to head off resistance among rural sheikhs and army officers. The war in Europe distracted the British and drained their resources, creating a window of opportunity for anti-British rebellion. Nuri al-Said, who had returned as prime minister in 1938, broke relations with Germany but failed to convince the cabinet to declare war on the Nazi state or to break relations with Italy as required by the 1930 treaty. He resigned in March 1940, and Rashid Ali al-Gailani, his anti-British successor, refused to break relations with Italy even after it declared war on Britain in June 1940. Buffeted by public acclaim, al-Gailani defied a British ultimatum to comply with the 1930 treaty or resign. U.S. officials monitored reports that German agents had arrived in Iran in late 1940 to make political inroads against Britain in Iraq, that a Germany–Iraq telegraph line was established, and that anti-British and pro-Axis propaganda filled Baghdad newspapers.[26]

In this context, the United States actively promoted British interests in Baghdad. In December 1940, Secretary of State Cordell Hull warned the al-Gailani government that German conquest of the Middle East would spell the end of Iraqi independence. "Any decision or action of the Iraqi Government which might result in a less cooperative attitude in its relations with Great Britain," he observed, "could not fail to create a most painful impression in the United States." State Department officials also solicited from Turkey a statement of support for Regent Abdul Ilah. They also noted that President Franklin D. Roosevelt's radio address of December 29, vowing to bolster Britain's ability to resist Nazism, encouraged the regent to defy al-Gailani. In early 1941, Hull banned the export of arms to Iraq on the rationale that such weapons might reach the hands of German soldiers.[27]

From the Western perspective, Iraq passed through its period of maximum danger in early 1941. The most perilous moment followed the April 1 coup, when Knabenshue whisked the regent in disguise to the British air base. As Iraqi Army officers declared a "national defense government" with al-Gailani in charge, the British flew the regent to Basra, where, from the safety of a British naval cruiser, he declared a new constitutional regime and called for public support. But the people failed to rally to the regent, and the Army took control of the country. British and American officials braced for a sharp rise in German influence, the arrival of German weapons, the detention of British diplomats, or mob violence against Westerners.[28]

Several days of intense diplomacy followed the coup. Al-Gailani asked for U.S. recognition and offered the British a deal in which the regent would appoint him as prime minister and then leave the country for 4 months, with Emir Hussein (another uncle of the king) to serve as acting regent. Al-Gailani would then publicly deny any pro-German leaning and break relations with Italy. After consulting British Ambassador Kinahan Cornwallis, however, Knabenshue concluded that either al-Gailani felt vulnerable to British reprisal in light of the unlikelihood of German intervention or he was offering terms as a ruse to buy time while arranging German backing. Authorized by Hull to make crucial policy decisions, Knabenshue told Jamil Mardam Bey, a former prime minister of Syria and al-Gailani confidante, that the United States would not recognize the new regime and that "the best interests of Iraq were entirely dependent upon unequivocal cooperation with the British in [the] present world crisis." If achieving these goals meant that "individuals would have to be sacrificed," Knabenshue added, "such sacrifices should be made for the good of the state (he knew I meant [al-]Gailani himself)."[29]

Despite this firm diplomacy by U.S. and British officials, al-Gailani continued to consolidate power. On April 10–11, he arranged for the Parliament to depose the regent and appoint a new cabinet with several pro-German members. Iraqi Army units monitored movements by British diplomats, jammed British (but not German) Arabic-language radio broadcasts, and deployed combat forces near British bases. Knabenshue described al-Gailani as an "intriguer, unreliable, unscrupulous, ruthless, backed at first and now dominated by [a] group with same characteristics."[30]

Intent on restoring stability on behalf of their broader war interests, British officials decided to reverse the al-Gailani coup with military force. On April 13, 400 infantry were flown from India to the Shaiba air base near Basra, and 5 days later 2,250 soldiers arrived at Basra by sea. After Iraqi tanks besieged the British air base at Habbaniya, British units launched an attack on forces loyal to al-Gailani. After about 4 weeks of sporadic fighting, they advanced to Baghdad and deposed al-Gailani, who, along with the German and Italian ministers, fled the country. The regent returned to Baghdad on June 1 and promptly restored al-Said as prime minister. With U.S. backing, British officials also liberated Syria from the Vichy regime that had endorsed al-Gailani's coup. Allied armies

Photo 1-5
Once U.S. diplomats helped the British restore the pro-Western monarchy of Iraq during World War II, U.S.–Iraqi relations stabilized. Shown here are Darwish Haidari and Iraqi Minister to Washington Ali Jawdat, arriving at the White House for an international labor conference in May 1944. SOURCE: Library of Congress, Prints & Photographs Division, FSA-OWI Collection, LC-USW3–042451-C DLC.

occupied Damascus on June 21 and Beirut on July 10. Although they realized that these developments deepened popular anti-British sentiment, U.S. officials were relieved that wartime stability was restored. British and U.S. interests in the region "do not conflict," U.S. Under Secretary of State Edward R. Stettinius and British Foreign Minister Anthony Eden agreed in April 1944, and diplomacy "should be conducted in a spirit of cooperation based upon mutual frankness and good will."[31]

U.S. relations with the government of Iraq stabilized after the fall of al-Gailani. In late 1941, al-Said expressed confidence in U.S. liberal values and called for closer relations. In May 1942, the Roosevelt Administration declared Iraq eligible for Lend–Lease assistance. In early 1943, State Department officials facilitated a settlement of a royalties dispute between the IPC and the Iraqi government. On January 17, 1943, more significantly, Iraq declared war on the Axis powers and signed the Declaration of the United Nations. Al-Said explained to the Axis powers that their interference in internal political matters and covert efforts to promote rebellion forced his government to take this step, and he reassured his own people that Iraq's soldiers would not fight beyond its national borders and that Iraq would gain international prestige after the war by joining the United Nations. On February 2, Roosevelt expressed to al-Said his gratitude "that Iraq is now formally aligned with the United Nations in their task of ridding the world of the Axis menace to peoples everywhere." In 1944, the president added that the United States had "a vital interest" in Middle East peace and stability and he encouraged local states to promote "the faiths for which this war is being waged."[32]

Once the al-Said government declared war on the Axis, thousands of U.S. soldiers were deployed to the country to conduct noncombat operations. Those GIs experienced relatively stable conditions. An Iraqi law of March 1943 extended to them the same legal and fiscal immunities from Iraqi law that were provided to the British in the 1930 treaty and it exempted U.S. imports from taxation. To promote solid relations, the U.S. Army issued a concise field manual instructing each soldier that he could help defeat Hitler "by getting along with the Iraqis and making them your friends. And the best way to get along with any people is to understand them." Soldiers were told to expect and accept differences in culture, befriend rather than try to change the Iraqi people, avoid mosques, leave women alone, and respect local customs about alcohol, the consumption of meat, and physical contact. GIs were alerted that they might initially regret deployment to Iraq, given its heat, deprivation, and odd customs, but they were also encouraged to expect that with time and effort they would feel welcome and satisfied. "The tall man in the flowing robe you are going to see soon, with the whiskers and the long hair, is a first-class fighting man, highly skilled in guerrilla warfare," the manual instructed. "If he is your friend, he can be a staunch and valuable ally. If he should happen to be your enemy—look out!"[33]

DEEPENING AMERICAN INVOLVEMENT IN THE EARLY COLD WAR

World War II caused a number of changes in the strategic and political dynamics of the Middle East. Although the British had successfully resisted Axis encroachments on the region, they would find it difficult to maintain their imperial interests in the postwar period. Despite the wartime alliance with the Soviet Union, both the United States and Britain came to suspect Moscow's ambitions in the Middle East (and other regions) after the war and they adopted a broad policy of resisting Soviet expanionism. Vaulted by the war to a position of global preeminence, the United States embraced a fundamental willingness to become involved in political and security conflicts in the Middle East (and elsewhere) in defense of what it defined as the vital interests of the West. Although committed to anti-Soviet containment, however, the Harry S. Truman Administration (1945–1953) would struggle to gain its footing in Iraq.

Despite its weakened global position at the end of World War II, Britain initially resolved to perpetuate its imperial position in Iraq. Officials in London identified in Iraq the same vital assets—oil, military bases, communications—that had attracted their government's interest a generation before. Yet the British position in postwar Iraq faced a difficult paradox. British policies since World War I had inflamed a nationalist, anti-British movement that gained popularity, challenged the authority of the traditional elites within the country, and called for democracy and redistribution of wealth and land. Given their strategic imperatives and the anti-British character of the nationalist movement, British officials continued to rely on the old order, refraining from promoting any type of political or economic reform within the country. As a result, the anti-British feeling among the nationalists grew more acute, until the British position in Iraq—like that in other Arab states experiencing social and political change after World War II—became untenable.[34]

As the U.S. government became more involved in international affairs after World War II, it took an increasing interest in Iraq. Officials in Washington who formulated the global Cold War strategy of containment of communism naturally resolved to exclude Soviet power from the Middle East. Yet they also feared that internal problems threatened the region. Inequalities of wealth and power caused revolutionary tendencies and resentment against Western nations. Decolonization generated a wave of nationalism conducive to Soviet exploitation and intraregional conflict. The dispute over Palestine and rivalries among the Saudi monarchy, the Egyptian crown, and the Hashemite kingdoms of Iraq and Jordan added to the volatility. These factors, the State Department estimated in the early 1950s, made the region "tinder for Communist conflagrations." When Egyptian Premier Gamal Abdel Nasser emerged as an outspoken advocate of neutralism and a critic of Western imperialism, U.S. officials feared that neutralism would indirectly facilitate the spread of Soviet-backed communism in the region.[35]

In light of the Cold War, U.S. officials seemed initially predisposed to endorse the British position in Iraq. The State Department considered Iraq important given its "strategic location, its vast petroleum reserves, its control of the potentially fertile Tigris–Euphrates valley, and its control of Basra, the largest seaport on the Persian Gulf." The British presence seemed to advance Western security interests and diminish the opportunity for Soviet political inroads among Iraq's disaffected people. The continued British occupation of the air bases at Habbaniya and Shaiba, the State Department reasoned in 1952, protected "major communications lines for three continents" and provided "a base in close proximity to the Soviet border." Thus, these air bases advanced Western security interests in peacetime and would prove invaluable in the event of a hot war against the Soviet Union.[36]

Soviet inroads among Iraq's Kurdish population also concerned U.S. officials. In 1943, Kurdish rebels under Mustapha Barzani conquered Irbil and Badinan in Iraq, but British forces crushed the uprising. Barzani's forces fled to the Republic of Mahabad, a Kurdish state in northern Iran that in 1946 briefly enjoyed independence under Soviet protection. Barzani organized the Kurdistan

Democratic Party (KDP) in Mahabad, but was forced into exile in the Soviet Union after Soviet forces abandoned northern Iran to the Shah's army. In the late 1940s, Soviet agents helped Barzani field an effective Kurdish army in southern Russia, and by the 1950s, KDP operators sympathetic to Soviet communism infiltrated into northern Iraq searching for opportunities to achieve political standing. By promising to back an independent Kurdistan, the Soviets seemingly won the hearts and minds of the region's 4 million Kurds.[37]

Concerned about Soviet ambitions, U.S. officials sought to improve relations with the government of Iraq on terms consistent with Britain's imperial position. President Harry S. Truman welcomed Regent Abdul Ilah to the White House on May 28, 1945. According to Acting Secretary of State Joseph Grew, U.S. officials attending the meeting stressed their desire "to develop closer relations." Discussion ensued on civil aviation and telecommunications agreements that would establish direct ties between the two countries. The two governments signed a Lend–Lease agreement on July 31, 1945, and elevated their legations to embassies in November 1946. U.S. officials also generally promoted trade with Iraq and encouraged Iraqi applications to the World Bank for developmental loans, although these efforts bore little fruit in the short term.[38]

In late 1947, U.S. officials realized the risks inherent in endorsing Britain's reliance on the Iraqi monarchy to stabilize Iraq. Sensitive to the nationalism manifest in the al-Gailani episode of 1941 and in postwar labor unrest in Iraq, the Labour Government of Clement Attlee sought to assure British security interests in Iraq by following a more liberal approach than its Conservative predecessor had pursued. In late 1947, Foreign Minister Ernest Bevin opened negotiations with Iraq to revise the security treaty of 1930, 5 years ahead of the prescribed renegotiation date. While he hoped to retain access to the air bases at Habbaniya and Shaiba, Bevin was willing to recognize a modicum of Iraqi political equality. He also envisioned a progressive program in which British engineers would design irrigation works in the Tigris and Euphrates valleys that would make Iraq the most prosperous country in the region. U.S. officials, sensitive to the wisdom of placating Iraqi nationalism, encouraged Bevin in this approach. As directed by Under Secretary of State Robert Lovett, Ambassador to Baghdad Edmund Dorsz also lobbied the regent to ensure the maintenance of British security interests in Iraq.[39]

Unfortunately for British officials, the treaty negotiations triggered political resistance among Iraqi nationalists in early 1948. Although a new draft treaty—produced in secret negotiations in Portsmouth, England—officially recognized dual Anglo-Iraqi control of the two air bases, residents of Baghdad organized sizeable demonstrations against the deal in early January 1948 when the negotiations became publicly known. With popular passions already stirred by the conflict in Palestine and food shortages, news of the draft Portsmouth Treaty—and the fact that it was named for an English city—irritated the masses. As the Baghdad demonstrations gave way to a student strike on January 18 and general rioting on January 20, U.S. officials refrained from publicly endorsing the deal. On January 21, the regent caved in to the public pressure, rejected the draft treaty, and promised to renounce any agreement that did not fulfill Iraqi national aspirations.[40]

The dispute over Palestine generated considerable general tension in Iraq's relations with the West. A roiling conflict among Arabs and Jews for influence inside the British Mandate of Palestine in the 1920s and 1930s gave way to a major confrontation over the control of the territory after World War II, when it became clear that an exhausted British Empire would relinquish its control of the land. In 1947, the United Nations proposed a compromise solution involving a partition of Palestine into two new states. The Jewish community of Palestine— which for decades had sought to fulfill the Zionist dream of restoring a Jewish state in the ancient homeland of the Jewish people—embraced partition and declared the statehood of Israel in May 1948. But the Palestinian Arabs rejected partition and, backed by the military forces of five Arab states (including Iraq), violently resisted the State of Israel. In the Arab–Israeli War of 1948–1949, Israel repelled the invading forces, gained dominance over more than half of Palestine, and ensured the foundations of statehood. Although not completely beholden to the Zionist cause, the Truman Administration endorsed partition, promptly recognized the State of Israel, and took other steps that significantly assisted the foundation of Israel.[41]

Like virtually all Arabs, the leaders and people of Iraq resisted the emergence of Israel and regretted U.S. support of it. They feared that a Jewish state would infringe on Arab Palestinian property and would inevitably expand into surrounding territory. Anti-Zionism mounted steadily among Iraqi leaders from the late 1920s to the mid-1940s. U.S. State Department officials noted in February 1946 that Iraqis sought "to be in the vanguard of Arab opposition to the Zionists" and that U.S. support of Zionism "handicaps our efforts to develop friendly and close relations" with Baghdad. As violence mounted in Palestine in 1947–1948, the Iraqi government subjected its Jewish population, which had lived harmoniously in the country for more than 2 millennia, to restrictions on travel, communication, education, and employment. When full-scale war broke out in May 1948, an Iraqi infantry brigade and an armored battalion crossed the Allenby Bridge over the Jordan River and drove west to within 6 miles of the Mediterranean on a mission to divide Israel. But stiff Israeli resistance in early June forced an Iraqi retreat to the West Bank region. Having faulted the United States for endorsing partition and recognizing Israel, Iraqis channeled some of the humiliation and frustration over this outcome into anti-American anger. The government in Baghdad spurned U.S.-backed efforts by U.N. Mediator Ralph Bunche to negotiate an armistice with Israel. It opted instead simply to remove its forces from the Palestine battlefield without reaching any formal ceasefire or peace agreement with the new Jewish state.[42]

The Truman Administration did achieve some success in its efforts to stabilize Iraq through progressive development of its oil resources. When visiting the United States in 1945, al-Said had charged that the IPC had left Iraqi oil underdeveloped in favor of its business interests in other countries, and he asked the State Department to encourage IPC development of untapped reserves in Basra, Kirkuk, and Mosul. State Department officers, who tended to favor economic development and antipoverty reforms for humanitarian reasons and also to resist the appeal of Soviet communism, noted that ordinary Iraqis had not benefited from the operations of the IPC. Indeed, *Time* reported in 1952 that the country's infant mortality rate was 50 percent and its 5 million people lived "in diseased, ill-clothed, ill-fed poverty," although the country sat atop oil reserves of some 10.5 billion barrels.[43]

In 1947, State Department officials began encouraging the IPC to adopt progressive practices and redoubled such efforts when talk of nationalization threatened the entire oil industry. Favoring oil development "with a view to augmenting the means for economic development in Iraq and safeguarding its interests," the State Department urged the IPC to invest in the local economy and education and to adopt liberal policies toward labor. The perception among the Iraqi people that the IPC benefited the West but not their own country aggravated their anti-Western nationalism. A breakthrough occurred in 1951, after the Arabian-American Oil Company agreed to grant Saudi Arabia 50 percent of its oil revenues. When al-Said threatened to nationalize the IPC unless it made similar concessions, the company agreed to increase oil production in Iraq and to split the revenues evenly with the government in Baghdad.[44]

To the satisfaction of U.S. officials, the oil deal between Iraq and the IPC triggered a sharp rise in Iraqi oil production and in revenues accruing to the government in Baghdad. Iraqi oil output rose from 140,000 barrels per day in 1950 to 700,000 barrels per day by 1955 (and 970,000 barrels per day by 1960). In response to the profit-sharing deal of 1951, Iraq's annual oil revenue rose from $14 million in 1950 to $207 million by 1955 (and $266 million by 1960). This increase in Iraqi oil production coincided with a sustained growth in petroleum production and exploration across the Middle East during the 1950s, stimulated by mounting consumer demands in Western economies. U.S. officials were relieved to have access to such Middle East supplies so they could conserve precious Western hemisphere reserves for times of international emergency. "Oil is vital to the United States and the rest of the free world both in peace and war," U.S. officials observed in 1953. "The complex industrial economies of the western world are absolutely dependent upon a continuing abundance of this essential source of energy.... In war, petroleum is absolutely vital."[45]

Other U.S. efforts to strengthen relations with the Iraqi government hit snags, however, during the late Truman Administration. In late 1949, the United States actively discouraged conversations between Iraq and Syria about merging into a commonwealth under the Hashimite monarchy in Baghdad, on the reasoning that such a move would deepen Iraqi and Syrian intransigence toward Israel, raise the suspicions of rival Arab monarchies in Saudi Arabia and Egypt, and perhaps provoke domestic unrest. When Iraqi officials accused the United States of denying them economic aid, moreover, U.S. officials retorted that

Iraq had failed to engage in the formal work of applying for aid from the U.S. Treasury or the World Bank. A bid to renegotiate and improve the 1938 Treaty of Friendship, Commerce, and Navigation came to naught in 1950. In 1951, the Truman Administration found Iraq eligible for foreign aid under the president's so-called Point Four aid program, but cultural and political obstacles in Baghdad prevented a vigorous program from taking shape. U.S. military aid to Iraq also remained paltry because Iraq requested extensive military hardware just as the Korean War depleted U.S. equipment reserves. To nurture a better relationship, Truman lunched with Faisal II as he toured the United States in August 1952, 9 months before he reached adulthood and occupied the throne of Iraq. But U.S.–Iraq relations remained strained when Truman left office in January 1953.[46]

THE CHALLENGES OF CONTAINMENT IN THE 1950s

The mid-1950s marked the apogee of stability in U.S.–Iraq official relations during the Cold War era. The Dwight D. Eisenhower Administration (1953–1961) promoted a variety of schemes that enhanced U.S. relations with the royalist government in Baghdad and positioned Iraq to resist any prospective surge of Soviet expansionism. By mid-decade, in fact, Iraq was a charter member of a formal defense arrangement promoted by the United States to protect the region against Soviet encroachment. A revolution in Baghdad in 1958 would prove, however, that the royalist Iraqi cornerstone in the American security structure was weak and unreliable.

U.S. relations with the Iraqi government improved slightly in the early 1950s. Baghdad College, operated by American Jesuit missionaries, emerged as a prestigious school catering to elite Iraqi families. Under a technical assistance program established in April 1951, some 100 U.S. technicians were stationed in Baghdad by mid-decade, training local government officials in such areas as education, agriculture, health, and development. Al-Said expressed public appreciation for such assistance and pressed for more. Within 2 years of signing a military assistance understanding with Iraq in 1954, the United States provided more than 700 military vehicles, 86 artillery pieces, 10 British-built Centurion tanks, 30 Ferret scout cars and recoilless rifles, ammunition, and communications equipment valued at some $10 million. In response to demands from al-Said for air power to deter a Soviet assault, the Eisenhower Administration dispatched six F86-F Sabre jets and training crews in 1958. (Arriving only days before the Iraqi revolution, the trainers departed without accomplishing their mission after the revolutionary regime seized the aircraft.)[47]

U.S. official relations with Iraq briefly seemed to find solid ground in the mid-1950s, when the Eisenhower Administration erected a security system based on the states along the so-called "northern tier" of the Middle East. President Eisenhower and Secretary of State John Foster Dulles abandoned earlier efforts to base a defense pact in Egypt when that state showed no interest in cooperating. By contrast, Turkey, Iraq, and Pakistan felt "the hot breath of the Soviet Union on their necks," Dulles told the National Security Council (NSC) in spring 1953, and were "less preoccupied with strictly internal problems or with British and French imperialism." The overthrow of Iranian Premier Mohammed Mossadegh in August 1953, which was aided and abetted by the Central Intelligence Agency (CIA), made Iran another prospective partner. Because Turkey had joined the North Atlantic Treaty Organization (NATO) in 1952 and Pakistan was slated to join the Southeast Asia Treaty Organization in 1954, a northern tier pact promised to extend the cordon of anti-Soviet pacts from northern Europe to the Pacific Ocean.[48]

Certain military and strategic factors also underscored the appeal of a northern tier alliance. The concentrated British base in Egypt seemed increasingly vulnerable as Soviet nuclear strike capabilities improved in the 1950s. At the same time, development of the Atlas, Thor, and Jupiter missiles, which could deliver thermonuclear warheads but only at short ranges, made it seem imperative for the United States to have access to base sites relatively close to Soviet territory. Pentagon strategists came to favor a series of Western air and missile bases dispersed along the Soviet's southern frontier. A northern tier pact would provide such assets.[49]

U.S. officials breathed life into the northern tier concept by encouraging area states and Britain to form a defense alliance. The United States extended military aid to induce Turkey and Pakistan, on April 2, 1954, to sign an agreement pledging "to co-operate for their security and defense" and to welcome accession by any other state "actively concerned with the security and peace of this region." After months of painstaking diplomacy, Iraq and Turkey signed a more formal mutual defense pact in Baghdad on February 24, 1955. Britain adhered to the pact in April, Pakistan in September, and Iran in October. Although the United States refrained from joining formally, its support was crucial to the treaty's formulation. Ambassador to Baghdad Waldemar J. Gallman worked hard behind the scenes with al-Said to negotiate the pact with Turkey, expand it to include other powers, and resist Egyptian criticisms.[50]

From the beginning, the Baghdad Pact displayed several serious, if not immediately apparent, flaws. First, the combat forces of member states, including British units in the region, were incapable of stopping or even slowing a Soviet invasion, and the northern tier states lacked the infrastructure needed for the United States to offer a credible nuclear deterrent. Second, Egypt and Saudi Arabia criticized the arrangement for dividing the Arab community, undermining Arab League defense arrangements, and serving European colonial and Israeli interests. Denouncing al-Said as an "Anglo-American stooge," Nasser waged an intense political campaign to dissuade other Arab states from acceding to the pact. In addition, Israel opposed the treaty because it funneled weapons to Iraq and encouraged Turkey to mollify Arab states at the expense of Turkish–Israeli amity. The alliance also naturally provoked Soviet suspicions and anger. The Foreign Ministry in Moscow saw in the arrangement "the desire of certain western powers for the colonial enslavement of these countries...so as to enrich their big monopolies which are making greedy use of the natural wealth of these countries." The United States had fooled the local peoples, Moscow noted, with "ridiculous fabrications about a 'Soviet menace' to the countries of that area."[51]

The problems besetting the Baghdad Pact left Eisenhower facing a dilemma. The Pentagon endorsed the demands of the member states that the United States join the pact formally and thereby endow it with military and political integrity. Dulles and other political advisers, by contrast, cautioned that formal U.S. membership might provoke a Soviet counterstroke, attract Egyptian wrath, and prompt Israeli demands for a compensatory defense commitment (demands likely to gain favorable support in Congress). In the end, Eisenhower declined to accept formal membership in the Baghdad Pact, but he wove the United States into its structure by designating Pentagon officers to participate in the pact's military planning, directing diplomats to attend member meetings, and paying one sixth of the alliance's annual budget. By taking such steps, Eisenhower simultaneously bolstered the pact and deflected allied and Pentagon pressure to join.[52]

The U.S.–Iraqi informal security partnership was tempered by the Arab–Israeli conflict. Government officials in Baghdad continued to insist that Israel repatriate Palestinian refugees, accept international control of Jerusalem, and return territory occupied in excess of the 1947 partition plan boundaries. They also enforced the Arab boycott on trade with Israel and made hostile public declarations about Israel (even while speaking in more pacific terms in private conversations with U.S. officials). Even the pro-Western al-Said, who served intermittently as prime minister in the 1950s, confided to Ambassador Gallman that he had no problem with Jews, who had peacefully intermixed with Arabs for centuries, but considered Zionism as objectionable as Communism because it threatened Arab interests and undermined the loyalty of Iraqi Jews to his country. In an essay written for *Life* magazine in June 1957, al-Said expressed that he understood that Americans had a "bellyful of Arab intransigence about Israel" but added that Arabs also had a "bellyful of American blindness to this problem." And when *Life* delayed publishing the essay, al-Said openly suspected that it had been suppressed by Zionists within the New York publishing industry. (The article did not appear in print until August 1958, a month after al-Said's death.)[53]

The Suez Crisis of 1956–1957 aggravated the tensions stemming from the Baghdad Pact and the Arab–Israeli conflict. After Nasser nationalized the Suez Canal Company in July 1956, Britain and France prepared for military operations to force him to relinquish the prize or remove him from power. After months of stalemate, the two Western powers colluded with Israel to launch a tripartite attack on Egypt, an attack brought to a premature and inconclusive end by firm U.S. opposition. Nasser survived, his prestige across the region enhanced by his defiant resistance of the European imperialists. By contrast, the political stature of Britain—and its clients such as al-Said—lay in shambles. U.S. leaders thus feared the specter of Soviet intrusion into the region. "We have no intention of standing idly by," Eisenhower declared in December 1956, "to see the southern flank of NATO completely collapse through Communist penetration and success in the Mid East."[54]

Determined to act, the president proposed the Eisenhower Doctrine in January 1957. The doctrine pledged that the United States would distribute economic and military aid and, if necessary, use military force to contain communism in the Middle East. Congress approved the doctrine in March despite misgivings about the administration's perspective on the Middle East, the preservation of Israeli interests under the doctrine, and the surrender of congressional prerogatives to the executive branch. Special envoy James P. Richards toured the region, dispensing tens of millions of dollars in economic and military aid to friendly states, including artillery, electronics, and telecommunications and police equipment for Iraq and $12.5 million for the Baghdad Pact. "Nuri [al-Said] at once expressed warm approval" of the doctrine, Ambassador Gallman later recorded, although, ominously, local press coverage of the Richards visit was "limited and coldly factual."[55]

The cold reception accorded by the people of Iraq to the Eisenhower Doctrine provided a hint that the political order of Iraq might be vulnerable to a popular rebellion. Indeed, the elite composed of the monarchy and older, pro-Western politicians like al-Said had lost credibility among younger citizens who were enamored with revolutionary and anti-Western tendencies exhibited by Nasser and those he inspired in Syria, Lebanon, and Jordan. Vestiges of British imperialism and widespread perceptions of U.S. support for Israel tainted the monarchy's association with the Western powers. The Iraqi domestic political system provided no peaceful outlets for popular passions stirred by these pan-Arab concerns or by the corruption and stagnation of the old order. Iraqi government officials like al-Said probably realized that their grasp on power was tenuous, but they decided nonetheless to try to maintain authority against their domestic challengers by conservative rule and reliance on the Western powers.[56]

In 1957–1958, the Middle East region experienced a general tumult. Acting under the Eisenhower Doctrine in 1957, the U.S. government bolstered the monarchy in Jordan against domestic Palestinian insurgents who were sympathetic to Nasser and confronted Syrian leaders who seemed susceptible to Soviet influence. The U.S.–Syrian showdown eased only after Egypt and Syria formed the United Arab Republic (UAR) in January 1958. Twelve days later, King Faisal II of Iraq and King Hussein of Jordan agreed to merge their states into the Arab Union. Nasser-inspired Muslim nationalists in Lebanon challenged the authority of the pro-Western government of President Camille Chamoun, a Christian, with open rebellion. In May, Iraq and Jordan ratified an Arab Union constitution, convened a mixed parliament, and appointed al-Said as prime minister of the union. Al-Said busied himself with the task of invigorating the Union by enticing Kuwait, wealthy with oil revenues, to join. Worried by the unrest in Lebanon, he ordered two brigades of his army to relocate to the western sector of the country.[57]

Al-Said's order for troops to move toward Lebanon proved to be a fatal mistake because it triggered a coup against the monarchy in Iraq. Disgruntled anti-British army officers had been conspiring for several years to seize power from the country's dominant pro-British elite. Inspired by Nasser's rise to prominence in Egypt, angry at their country's membership in the Baghdad Pact, and disillusioned by the monarchical leadership, two groups representing about 200 officers merged in spring 1957 into a single coalition led loosely by General Abdul Karim Qassim and Colonel Abdal Salam Arif, vigilant for an opportunity to strike. Burgeoning Iraqi and pan-Arab nationalism, inflamed by the Arab–Israeli conflict, the rise of Nasser, and the Suez War, provided the officers the means to galvanize popular support against the monarchy.[58]

The troop movements ordered by al-Said provided General Qassim an opportunity to seize power on the night of July 13–14. Qassim ordered forces loyal to him that had been mobilized by al-Said to seize control of key points of Baghdad. Through the night, rebel forces captured and executed King Faisal II, the former regent, several royal family members, three Arab Union ministers from Jordan, and three American businessmen who were dragged from their rooms at the Baghdad Hotel, apparently in error, when rebels seized the Jordanian officials. At dawn, Qassim broadcasted that a new government had taken power, requested public support, and declared martial law. Mobs filled the streets celebrating the ouster of the old regime and chanting anti-Western slogans, and Iraqi tanks surrounded the U.S. Embassy. Al-Said eluded capture for a day before he was discovered near the U.S. Embassy, trying to flee while disguised as a woman. The Army executed him on the spot and a mob dragged his corpse through the streets of the city. "Trusting in God and with the aid of the loyal sons of the people and the national armed forces," Colonel Arif declared in a radio broadcast of Proclamation Number 1, "we have undertaken to liberate the beloved homeland from the corrupt crew that imperialism installed."[59]

The coup in Baghdad generated international turmoil across the Middle East that briefly threatened to engulf Iraq. Alarmed by the sudden deterioration of the situation in Baghdad, President Eisenhower ordered U.S. Marines to occupy Beirut on July 15 to stave off a copycat revolution there. Within days, British and U.S. forces also moved into Jordan for the same purpose. Britain proposed joint military operations against Arab radicals in Iraq and Syria, and Director of Central Intelligence Allen Dulles warned Eisenhower that the Iraqi coup, if unreversed, would imperil not only Lebanon and Jordan, but also Saudi Arabia, Turkey, and Iran. Yet Eisenhower refused to sanction "a big operation" in Iraq or Syria because it would run "far, far beyond anything which I have the power to do constitutionally." Soviet leader Nikita Khrushchev warned, moreover, that U.S. intervention in Iraq would cause "most dangerous and unforeseen consequences." Whereas the United States could manage an intervention in Lebanon, Dulles noted, "in the other countries, the thing might blow up." Eisenhower thus decided to refrain from intervention in Iraq in 1958.[60]

CONCLUSION

Eisenhower's decision to refrain from a military intervention in Iraq in 1958 also effectively removed the prospect of British intervention there. Despite the brutal overthrow of a friendly regime and security partner and pressure from the British to strike back, the president decided that sending troops to Baghdad would prove too perilous. Interventions in Lebanon and Jordan were deemed feasible and likely to achieve political benefits. Sending forces to Baghdad would be tactically difficult and politically risky within the country. Such a move would also provoke a conflict with the Soviet Union and aggravate other problems across the region. Given the weaknesses of the monarchy and the difficulties of trying to save it, Eisenhower made a sound decision.

The end of the royalist government in Baghdad marked the end of the first era of U.S. official involvement in Iraq. Preceded by U.S. Christian missionaries and oilmen who pursued varied cultural and economic interests in Iraq, U.S. government officials first took serious interest in the country when it assumed some importance in their quests to contain Nazi and then Soviet power. The government in Washington initially followed a general strategy of relying on its British partner to preserve their common interests, manifested most prominently in the action by Minister Knabenshue to help the British prevent Iraq from falling into the Nazi camp during World War II. Indeed, as some scholars argue, this policy would incur long-term costs by alienating Iraqi nationalists.[61] The American officials who made such policy cannot be faulted, however, for privileging the curtailment of Nazi power at a crucial moment in World War II over advancing the nationalistic aspirations of a relatively weak Iraqi government.

After 1945, however, the Western position in Iraq faced several new challenges. British influence in Iraq declined at the same time that Soviet expansionism seemed to imperil Western interests in the country, political tensions threatened to embroil it in regional conflict, and nationalism eroded its government's stability and pro-Western orientation. U.S. officials tried to nurture a healthy relationship with the government in Baghdad, providing it aid and arms and enlisting it as an informal security partner under the Baghdad Pact. For a brief period in the mid-1950s, it appeared that U.S. officials had concocted in the Baghdad Pact a successful scheme for enlisting Iraq as a military partner in the American quest to contain Soviet communism and preserve the alignment of the region's cultural and petroleum resources with the Western world. Such success proved to be an illusion, however, like a desert mirage.

The U.S. postwar quest to stabilize the pro-Western monarchy in Iraq foundered on the shoals of midcentury international dynamics and political conditions within Iraq. In light of their commitment to containing the Soviet Union, U.S. officials enrolled royalist Iraq in the Baghdad Pact security system but struggled to endow the pact with credibility. The rise of the Arab–Israeli conflict and of political rivalries among Arab states further complicated the U.S. quest to stabilize the region against encroachment by the Soviet Union.

At the same time, although increasingly cognizant of the political vision and appeal of Iraqi nationalists, U.S. government officials continued to embrace the pro-Western Iraqi monarchy in a calculated gamble that such a policy would best preserve Western security interests. A legacy of the British imperial era, however, the monarchy was destined for an early demise. The Iraqi revolution of 1958 clearly marked the failure of the first U.S. official mission in Iraq, a quest to align the pro-Western, British-built, royalist government of Iraq on the Western axis in the Cold War.

NOTES

1. Knabenshue to Hull, April 2, 1941, *FRUS, 1941*, 3:491–92 (quotation); Thorpe, "United States," 79–89; "Milestones," *Time*, February 9, 1942.
2. "Iraq" was an anglicized rendering of *'araqa* (literally, "well-watered"), a geographic name used by local peoples since the 6th century CE, probably in reference to the fertility of the Tigris–Euphrates region. Etymologists also theorize that the word might have originated with the premodern Sumerian city Uruk, in the south of the territory. "Iraq." *Online Etymology Dictionary*, http://dictionary.reference.com/browse/Iraq/ (accessed September 15, 2010).
3. CIA World Fact Book, "Iraq," http://www.cia.gov/library/publications/the-world-factbook/geos/iz.html/ (accessed March 17, 2008).
4. Simons, *Iraq*, 113–38.
5. Simons, *Iraq*, 139–59.
6. Hathaway, *Arab Lands*, 143–47; Tripp, *History*, 13–29; Marr, *Modern History*, 26–28.
7. Kedourie, *England and the Middle East*, 9–28; Simons, *Iraq*, 181–98; Farouk-Sluglett and Sluglett, *Iraq since 1958*, 7–8.
8. Monroe, *Britain's Moment*, 23–38 (quotation 37–38); Kedourie, *England and the Middle East*, 29–66; Trumpener, "Turkey's War," 86–88.
9. Dockrill and Goold, *Peace without Promise*, 133–40; Kedourie, *England and the Middle East*, 175–77; Monroe, *Britain's Moment*, 102–4; Simons, *Iraq*, 198–201.
10. Dockrill and Goold, *Peace without Promise*, 169–71; Kedourie, *England and the Middle East*, 175–213.
11. Batatu, *Old Social Classes*, 23; Tripp, *History*, 40–45; Simons, *Iraq*, 211–17.
12. Haldane, *Insurrection*, 298; Kedourie, *England and the Middle East*, 192–94; Monroe, *Britain's Moment*, 47, 60–61.
13. Dockrill and Goold, *Peace without Promise*, 131–32, 172–74; Lesch, *Arab–Israeli Conflict*, 62–74, Simons, *Iraq*, 202–6.
14. Marr, *Modern History*, 46–55; Dawisha, *Iraq*, 8–75; Silverfarb, *Britain's Informal Empire*, 23–33; Pedersen, "Getting Out," 975–1000.
15. Shlaim, *War and Peace*, 17 (quotation); Kostiner, "Britain and the Northern Frontier," 29–35; Dockrill and Goold, *Peace without Promise*, 238–47.
16. Batatu, *Old Social Classes*, 25–36; Marr, *Modern History*, 57–79.
17. McDowall, *Modern History*, 151–80.
18. Nance, *Arabian Nights*; Hoganson, *Consumers' Imperium*.
19. Field, *From Gibraltar to the Middle East*, 153–65, 268–7; Oren, *Power, Faith, and Fantasy*, 128–41, 285–87.

20. Dockrill and Goold, *Peace without Promise*, 144–50, 175–6; Gelvin, "Ironic Legacy," 20–24.

21. Philips to Davis, October 24, 1919, *FRUS, 1919*, 2:258–59; Hahn, *Crisis and Crossfire*, 2–3; Blair, *Control of Oil*, 31–34.

22. Rubin, "America as Junior Partner," 244 (quotation); Shaw to Sloan, March 7, 1930, *FRUS, 1930*, 3:309–11; DeNovo, *American Interests*, 167–209; Yergin, *Prize*, 298–300.

23. Kaufman, *Oil Cartel Case*, 19–33; Bunter, "Early Concessions;" Blair, *Control of Oil*, 80–85.

24. Randolph to Secretary, August 24, 1929, *FRUS, 1930*, 3:298–99; "Convention and Protocol between the United States of America, Great Britain, and Iraq," January 9, 1930, *FRUS 1930*, 3:302–6; U.S.–Iraq Treaty, June 7, 1934, *FRUS, 1934*, 2:781–87; Knabenshue to Secretary, December 3, 1938, *FRUS, 1938*, 2:769; Knabenshue to Hull, August 5, November 10, 1939, *FRUS, 1939*, 4:545–49, 553–54; Knabenshue to Hull, July 23, 1940, *FRUS, 1940*, 3:743–46.

25. Knabenshue to Secretary, May 29, 1940, November 13 and 14, 1940, *FRUS, 1940*, 3: 703–8, 710–13; Silverfarb, *Twilight of British Ascendancy*, 11–19.

26. Knabenshue to Secretary, November 27–December 2, 1940, *FRUS, 1940*, 3: 713–16; Batatu, *Old Social Classes*, 25–36; Farouk-Sluglett and Sluglett, *Iraq since 1958*, 16–23.

27. Hull to Knabenshue, December 3, 1940, *FRUS, 1940*, 3:716–17; Knabenshue to Hull, January 3, 1941, Hull to Knabenshue, March 1, 1941, *FRUS, 1941*, 3:486–87, 489.

28. Knabenshue to Hull, April 3 and 6, 1941, British Embassy to State Department, April 5 and 7, 1941, *FRUS, 1941*, 3:492–95.

29. Knabenshue to Secretary, April 7, 1941, *FRUS, 1941*, 3:497 (quotation); Knabenshue to Secretary, April 7, 1941, Hull to Knabenshue, April 7, 1946, *FRUS, 1941*, 3: 495–96.

30. Knabenshue to Hull, April 10, 1941, *FRUS, 1941*, 3:498 (quotation); Knabenshue to Hull, April 9–13, 1941, *FRUS, 1941*, 3:497–500.

31. Hull to Jacobs, May 17, 1944, *FRUS, 1944*, 5: 6–7 (quotation); Knabenshue to Secretary, April 11–30, May 31, June 1 and 5, 1941, memorandum of conversation by Hull, April 18, 1941, *FRUS, 1941*, 3:499–504, 508–9, 511–13; Weinberg, *World at Arms*, 224–232.

32. Hull to Wilson, February 2, 1943, *FRUS, 1943*, 4:639 (quotation); Roosevelt to Landis, March 6, 1944, *FRUS, 1944*, 5:1–2 (quotation); Knabenshue to Hull, November 25, 1941, *FRUS, 1941*, 3:514; Hull to Farrell, May 1, 1942, *FRUS, 1942*, 4:343; Wilson to Hull, January 13–May 7, 1943, Welles to Wilson, March 11, 1943, *FRUS, 1943*, 4:636–38, 649–55.

33. U.S. War and Navy Departments, *A Short Guide to Iraq* (quotations 4); Wilson to Hull, February 13, March 17, 1943, *FRUS, 1943*, 4:641–43.

34. Silverfarb, *Twilight of British Ascendancy*, 73–123; Kinsgton, *Britain and the Politics of Modernization*, 95–122; Halliday, "Middle East," 11–26.

35. Memorandum by Gullion, February 25, 1953, RG 59, Lot 64 D 563, box 30 (quotation); Hahn, *Caught in the Middle East*, 68–71.

36. State Department policy statement, "Iraq," November 9, 1950, *FRUS, 1950*, 5: 651–57; Bruce to Truman, August 15, 1952, PSF, Subject File, box 181, Truman Library.

37. State Department paper, "The Kurds of Iraq," May 18, 1972, http://www.state.gov/r/pa/ho/frus/nixon/e4/65607.html/ (accessed November 18, 2008); "Report on the Kurds," *Time*, September 22, 1952; "The Men of the Mountains," *Time*, May 31, 1963; McDowall, *Modern History*, 231–47.

38. Editorial note, *FRUS, 1945*, 8:586; memorandum by Colquitt, February 4, 1946, editorial note, *FRUS, 1946*, 7: 568–70; Satterthwaite to Kopper, December 1, 1948, *FRUS, 1948*, 5:207.

39. Memorandum of conversation by Henderson, September 9, 1947, State Department paper, n.d. [c. October 1947], U.S.-U.K. statement, n.d. [October 1947], *FRUS, 1947*, 5: 496–502, 522–23, 594–96; Lovett to Dorsz, November 26, 1947, Dorsz to Secretary, January 5, 1948, *FRUS, 1948*, 5:202–4.

40. Marshall to Dorsz, January 16, 1948, editorial note, *FRUS, 1948*, 5:205–6; Monroe, *Britain's Moment*, 156–57; Silverfarb, *Twilight of British Ascendancy*, 125–54.

41. Hahn, *Caught in the Middle East*, 9–62.

42. Memorandum by Colquitt, February 4, 1946, *FRUS, 1946*, 7:568–69 (quotation); Simons, *Iraq*, 237–41; Eppel, *Palestine Conflict*, 6–157; Shlaim, *Iron Wall*, 41–47.

43. "Visiting King," *Time*, August 18, 1952 (quotation); memorandum of conversation by Grew, May 29, 1945, *FRUS, 1945*, 8:49–51.

44. State Department paper, n.d. [c. October 1947], *FRUS, 1947*, 5:554 (quotation); report by the Departments of State, Defense, and Interior, January 1953, in Kaufman, *Oil Cartel Case*, 145–57 (quotation); Crocker to McGhee, January 30, 1950, *FRUS, 1950*, 5: 639–41; Crocker to Acheson, October 11, 1951, *FRUS, 1951*, 5:552–53; "50–50," *Time*, April 16, 1951.

45. Report by the Departments of State, Defense, and Interior, January 1953, in Kaufman, *Oil Cartel Case*, 145–57 (quotation); Alnasrawi, *Economy of Iraq*, 2–11; Yergin, *Prize*, 499–500.

46. Marshall to Truman, October 14, 1949, *FRUS, 1949*, 6:182–85; memorandum of conversation by McGhee, January 11, 1950, Acheson to Crocker, August 23, 1950, Crocker to Acheson, September 5, 1950, *FRUS, 1950*, 5: 636–38, 648–50; Crocker to Acheson. November 10, 1951, *FRUS, 1951*, 5:554–8; "Visiting King," *Time*, August 18, 1952.

47. Gallman, *Iraq under General Nuri*, 174–95.

48. Minutes of meeting, July 9, 1953, *FRUS, 1952–1954*, 9:394–98.

49. Hahn, *United States, Great Britain, and Egypt*, 182–83.

50. "Pact of Mutual Cooperation," February 4, 1955, http://www.yale.edu/lawweb/ avalon/mideast/baghdad.htm/ (accessed March 26, 2008) (quotation); Persson, *Great Britain, the United States, and the Security of the Middle East*; Jasse, "The Baghdad Pact," 140–56; Sanjian, "Formulation of the Baghdad Pact," 226–66; Gallman, *Iraq under General Nuri*, 21–65.

51. Stevenson to Eden, January 17, 1955, FO 371/113608, JE1057/1; statement by Foreign Ministry, April 16, 1955, http://www.fordham.edu/halsall/mod//1955Soviet-baghdad1.html/ (accessed March 26, 2008) (quotation); Podeh, *Quest for Hegemony*, 91–117.

52. Hahn, *Caught in the Middle East*, 152–54.

53. "Martyred Iraqi Premier Leaves a Last Testament," *Life*, 45:4 (July 1958):26 (quotation); State Department policy statement, "Iraq," November 9, 1950, *FRUS, 1950*, 5: 651–57; Gallman, *Iraq under General Nuri*, 167–71.

54. Eisenhower to Dulles, December 12, 1956, Whitman File: Dulles–Herter Series, box 6 (quotation); Hahn, *Caught in the Middle East*, 194–220.

55. Gallman, *Iraq under General Nuri*, 74–88 (quotations 80, 81); Hahn, *Caught in the Middle East*, 224–28; Yaqub, *Containing Arab Nationalism*, 87–121; Little, "Cold

War and Covert Action," 69–75; Ashton, *Eisenhower, Macmillan, and the Problem of Nasser,* 122–49.

56. Marr, *Modern History,* 96–147; Tripp, *History,* 108–47.
57. Gallman, *Iraq under General Nuri,* 139–47.
58. Farouk-Sluglett and Sluglett, *Iraq since 1958,* 38–50.
59. Batatu, *Old Social Classes,* 764–807 (Arif quoted 802); Gallman, *Iraq under General Nuri,* 200–213.
60. Record of conversation, July 14, 1958, PREM 11/2387 (quotation); Thompson to Dulles, July 19, 1958, Whitman File: International Series, box 36 (quotation); memorandum of conversation, July 15, 1958, Whitman File: Diary Series, box 34 (quotation); memorandum of conversation, July 14, 1958, Whitman File: Diary Series, box 34; Allen Dulles briefing notes, July 14, 1958, WHO Files, Office of Staff Secretary, International Series, box 10; Gendzier, *Notes from the Minefield,* 295–363.
61. O'Sullivan and Damluji, "Origins," 239–53.

CHAPTER 2

Cold War Challenges

The Pursuit of Stability in Revolutionary
Iraq, 1958–1979

William M. Rountree had a bad feeling about his imminent visit to Iraq. It was December 12, 1958, and the U.S. Assistant Secretary of State was in Cairo, his third stop on a goodwill tour of Arab capitals. In a cable to the State Department, Rountree reported that he had enjoyed beneficial meetings with leaders of Jordan and Lebanon and even found a "relatively good" atmosphere in Egypt. Yet intelligence reports about the political situation in Baghdad indicated that he should expect trouble there. Reporting rumors of U.S. plans for a covert operation to reverse the July 1958 revolution, one Baghdad newspaper identified Rountree as "the envoy of evil and plots." Another declared that "the Iraqi people will not permit the American envoy to enter their country."[1]

Rountree asked the State Department for permission to cancel his venture to Baghdad. "I have grave doubts [about the] wisdom [of] proceeding with [my] visit to Iraq," he cabled. His arrival might provoke a "field day in anti-Americanism" among the city's "press and Communist-inspired demonstrators," endangering U.S. property in Iraq and U.S. political interests across the region. At Washington's direction, however, officers at the U.S. Embassy in Baghdad secured "informal, personal assurances" from Iraqi Premier General Abdul Karem Qassim that Rountree would be welcomed and protected. Only then did the Assistant Secretary agree to board his Iraqi Airways flight to Baghdad on December 15. The trip nearly cost him his life.[2]

A. David Fritzlan, the *charge d'affaires* and counselor of the embassy in Baghdad, detected obvious signs of trouble as he rode in the embassy limousine to the airport to meet Rountree. Posters declaring "Rountree go home" bedecked the boulevards of the capital, and a mob chanting the same slogan jammed the road leading into the airport. Mechanics took up the cry as they circled Rountree's airplane, and angry demonstrators surged past a small Iraqi security line to affix anti-American stickers to the limousine. Once he bundled Rountree inside the vehicle, Fritzlan prudently decided to exit the airport through a side gate. "If Fritzlan had followed the route from the airport that the mob had expected,"

Photo 2-1
Career foreign service officer William M. Rountree, who, as assistant secretary of state in December 1958, experienced a fateful—and nearly fatal—visit to Baghdad. SOURCE: Courtesy Harry S. Truman Library and Museum.

Time reported, "the embassy car would certainly have been stopped, probably overturned and set afire, and the men inside could have been in gravest peril." Although Fritzlan's quick thinking avoided that fate, fringe elements of the mob nonetheless pelted the limousine with tomatoes, eggs, and mud. Halfway to the embassy, a rock shattered its windshield. As the Cadillac pulled through the embassy gates, a nearby mob continued to taunt, "Rountree go home."[3]

The next day, Rountree was able to accomplish his objective of a meeting with Qassim. After embassy officials protested the airport security lapse, Qassim sent an armed military vehicle to the Embassy to drive Rountree to the Ministry of Defense. There, Qassim suggested that the mob's actions were an expression of the Iraqi people's concern that the United States had engaged in covert operations to destabilize the new government. Rountree disputed these allegations, warned that the mob had undermined Iraq's reputation in world affairs, and declared that the U.S. government genuinely sought a stable relationship. Although refusing to apologize for the unrest, Qassim claimed also to seek good relations and promised that Rountree would face "no trouble" on his return ride to the airport. On the following day, and 24 hours ahead of schedule, Fritzlan loaded Rountree in an unmarked car and drove him to the airport, without incident.[4]

Rountree's perilous entry into Baghdad signified the difficulty that U.S. officials faced in dealing with Iraq in the 2 decades between the downfall of the monarchy in 1958 and the empowerment of Saddam Hussein in 1979. Perpetual instability afflicted the government in Baghdad during those years because a series of coups brought to power leaders seemingly incapable of exercising authority or gaining credibility. Committed to the containment of the Soviet Union on a global scale, U.S. officials naturally suspected that Soviet-backed communists continually sought to expand their influence in the oil-rich country. Iraq also played an important and complicated role in intraregional disputes, including the Arab–Israeli conflict and various political rivalries among Arab states. U.S. officials embraced a mission of containing turmoil within Iraq and within the Middle East to complement their global strategy of containing Soviet influence. This chapter will assess the strengths and weaknesses of that approach.

QASSIM AND COMMUNISM: AFTERMATH OF THE 1958 COUP

The U.S. government formulated its response to the Iraqi coup of July 1958 in light of its recent experiences in the Middle East and across the developing world. Primarily concerned with the threat of Soviet communism in the global context, Eisenhower Administration officials responded to unrest in the Third World by seeking to bolster friendly states, prolong Western influence, and deny Soviet encroachments. Whereas the 1958 Iraqi revolution fit a transregional pattern of nationalist rebellion against the vestiges of Western imperialism, it also generated political instability within Iraq that seemed to open the door to communist gains. The United States would find it difficult to adjust its policy to the revolutionary regime in Baghdad.

The Iraqis who seized power in Baghdad in July 1958 moved quickly to revolutionize their country. General Qassim declared that his purposes were to

Photo 2-2
Abdul Karem Qassim, prime minister of Iraq, 1958–1963. SOURCE: Posted on Wikimedia Commons by Jalal Naimi.

eradicate all vestiges of the monarchy, which he branded as corrupt and beholden to Western imperialists, and to establish a new regime that would unify the peoples of Iraq, serve the needs of the common people, and aspire to practice democracy. A new constitution enshrined republicanism, recognized that Arabs and Kurds would share the country, declared Islam the state religion but also recognized religious freedom, and centered executive and legislative authority in the hands of the Revolutionary Command Council. Initially, the revolution was extremely popular among the masses of Iraq's rural and urban poor as well as growing middle class, who had encountered poverty, suppression, and hopelessness under the old regime dominated by a small, privileged elite. Qassim, who had experienced an impoverished youth, promulgated a number of social welfare reforms that gratified the people. Other edicts restoring personal freedoms and allowing political parties, however, unleashed political dynamics that would soon haunt the new regime.[5]

The anti-Western flavor of the Iraqi coup made it emblematic of the pattern of revolutionary change sweeping the Third World after World War II. Imperial powers lost control of their possessions in Africa, the Middle East, and Asia. Independent nation states arose, many with an anti-Western orientation born of the anticolonial movements that had led them to independence. At the end of World War II, the Arab states appeared to be tied loosely to the West through commercial and security arrangements with Britain and cultural and business connections with the United States. Britain had a massive military base in Egypt, commanded the Arab Legion in Jordan, controlled air bases in Iraq and a naval base in Aden, dominated the Iranian oil industry and owned the largest refinery in the world at Abadan, and protected small Gulf sheikhdoms including Kuwait and nine so-called Trucial States, the largest of which were Bahrain and Qatar. Yet this Western dominance came under challenge as revolutionary movements ousted pro-Western regimes in Syria in 1949 and Egypt in 1952 and challenged the governments of Iran, Lebanon, and Jordan and as Britain lost credibility during the Suez War of 1956–1957. The Iraqi coup of 1958 very much fit the pattern of decolonization in the postwar Middle East.[6]

The Iraqi coup also augmented the influence of the Baath ("Renaissance" in Arabic) Party. The multinational political party had been established in the early 1940s by Michel Aflaq and Salahedin al-Bitar, Syrians who had met at the Sorbonne in 1929, dabbled in Marxism, returned to Syria as teachers, grown disillusioned by Stalinism, and become resistant to French colonialism. The Baath thrived during the Syrian struggle to gain independence from France in 1944 and during the Arab–Israeli War of 1948–1949. After a coup in Damascus in 1954, the Baath gradually gained political influence in the Syrian government, ultimately seizing power in 1963. Stressing pan-Arab unity, the party also branched out into Jordan and Iraq, where local politicos found it a useful mechanism to challenge British imperialism and the pro-Western monarchies.[7]

The coup in Iraq also complicated the tumultuous relationships among Arab powers. In the context of the American–Soviet Cold War and the decolonization

Map 2-1
Map of Iraq, showing provinces, major cities, and the Tigris and Euphrates Rivers.

of the Third World, Arab states engaged in a bitter rivalry for political influence across the region—what the scholar Malcolm Kerr called the "Arab Cold War." In early 1958, that rivalry had contributed to the formation of the UAR, a union between Egypt and Syria designed by Egyptian Premier Gamal Abdel Nasser and Syrian Baathists who shared a desire to prevent Syrian communists from gaining political influence. After the coup in Baghdad, Colonel Arif and Iraqi Baathists favored joining the UAR, but Qassim refused. Partnering with local Communists, who feared suppression after a UAR merger, Qassim purged Arif, suppressed the Baathists, and defied Nasser's pressure to form a common political front. Qassim privileged national aspirations over pan-Arab interests under Nasser's leadership.[8]

   Within a year of the 1958 coup, internal and transregional political dynamics caused turmoil and instability in Iraq. In March 1959, Qassim suppressed a Baathist revolt in Mosul using air power to bomb disloyal forces and relying on

Communists to arrest and execute scores of rebels. In July 1959, ethnic tensions between Turkomans and Kurds combined with political disaffection to trigger a massacre of several dozen people, mostly Turkomans, in Kirkuk. Although he had empowered the Communists to defeat the Baathists, Qassim began to suppress the Communists in 1959 after they repeatedly mobilized hundreds of thousands of demonstrators in the streets of Baghdad to demand the appointments of Communists as government ministers. Nonetheless, disgruntled Baathists, including a 23-year-old named Saddam Hussein, tried to assassinate Qassim on October 7, 1959, by raking his limousine with machine gun fire and grenades. Although wounded, Qassim survived. Although most of the plotters escaped to Syria, several dozen were arrested and six were sentenced to death (although their lives were ultimately spared). Although Qassim enjoyed a surge of public sympathy after the attempt on his life, he never reconnected with disaffected Baathists or Communists and he fell from power in a coup led by the Baath in 1963.[9]

U.S. officials approached the tumult sweeping the Middle East in the late 1950s on several levels. To protect their vital interests against revolutionary change at the regional level, they provided arms and political support to bolster conservative governments in Jordan, Lebanon, and Saudi Arabia against apparent radical intrigues; they avoided formal membership in the Baghdad Pact to avoid angering radical leaders; and they engaged in covert operations to try to unseat a radical regime in Damascus. After the turmoil grew acute in 1958, triggering the U.S. military intervention in Lebanon and Jordan (discussed in Chapter 1), President Dwight D. Eisenhower nurtured a rapprochement with Egypt in the hope of curtailing Nasser's appetite for political expansion and directing his influence toward anticommunist purposes. U.S. officials also avoided Arab–Israeli peacemaking in the late 1950s because it seemed likely to encourage Arab radicalism.[10]

Initially, the United States achieved a stable relationship with the revolutionary regime in Iraq. Upon hearing of the U.S. military intervention in Lebanon, Qassim immediately summoned Ambassador Waldemar J. Gallman to a heavily fortified army facility and extended assurances of friendship for the United States, guaranteed the security of Americans in Iraq, and consented to a mass evacuation of Americans by the U.S. military. Over the following days, Qassim reined in mob activity and restored calm to the capital.[11]

Within several weeks of the coup, U.S.–Iraqi relations achieved a modicum of stability. The revolutionary government quickly abolished the monarchy and parliament, withdrew from the federation with Jordan, and recognized China and the Soviet Union. Nonetheless, Eisenhower extended diplomatic recognition to Qassim's government in August, in large measure to encourage those political factions in Baghdad resisting Nasser's subtle entreaties to join the UAR. "The Iraqis still appeared to be undecided as to what type of relationship they wish to have with the US," Assistant Secretary of State Rountree told Egyptian Ambassador Mostapha Kamel on October 8. "We surmised that a contest was in progress between Iraqi groups favoring close relations with the UAR and those desiring to maintain Iraq's separate identity."[12]

Yet Rountree's ill-fated visit to Baghdad in December 1958 revealed how perilous U.S.–Iraqi relations remained. A month before, the NSC had resolved to "maintain friendly relations with the new Iraqi regime on a reciprocal basis." Thus, the United States acquiesced in Iraq's departure from the Baghdad Pact and yet offered to continue military and technical aid to Qassim's government.[13] After receiving an after-action briefing from Director of Central Intelligence Allen Dulles about Rountree's visit to Iraq, however, the NSC was at a loss about how best to approach the Qassim government. Suspecting that the mobs mobilized against Rountree also threatened the regime, Dulles anticipated a coup by army officers. Eisenhower suggested that the United States work with Nasser to undermine the Communists in Iraq, given that "the Kremlin is our principal enemy." The appeal of overthrowing Qassim was checked, however, by the realization that the country lacked civilian potential leaders and that the most prominent alternative among its military officers was "uncontrollable."[14]

The internal violence that wracked Iraq in 1959 complicated the U.S. challenge. U.S. officials weighed the prospects of a Nasser-orchestrated coup against Qassim versus an internal takeover by the Communists, prompting Eisenhower to agonize over a choice between "a baby-faced Dillinger or an Al Capone." Qassim's growing reliance on Communists after the Mosul uprising in March left U.S. officials fearful that the Communists were poised to grab power and that Soviet agents were infiltrating the country posing as Kurds who were repatriating from Soviet territory. The NSC advised Eisenhower to identify Communism, not Qassim, as the problem in Iraq.[15]

Yet officials in Washington remained concerned that Qassim might give way to communism. An interdepartmental task force identified three prospective courses of action to unseat Qassim, including boycotting Iraqi oil, nudging other Arab leaders to undermine him, and providing covert aid to rebels within Iraq. Several preliminary historical studies suggest that U.S. officials either knew ahead of time about the attempt on Qassim's life in October 1959 or actually armed the Baathist gunmen involved in the plot. Although these allegations are credible, according to the scholar Nathan J. Citino, they cannot be proven on the basis of available primary sources. Citino also notes that the Eisenhower Administration considered but ruled out a major covert operation against Qassim on the grounds that he would ultimately resist communist aspirations and that a major operation might backfire and galvanize nationalists in Iraq and across the region.[16]

KENNEDY AND QASSIM, 1961–63: KUWAIT, KURDS, AND COMMUNISM

Soon after taking office in January 1961, President John F. Kennedy learned first-hand the complexities of relations with Iraq. The new president proposed sending a friendly note to Qassim, but State Department officers counseled him not to. "US–Iraq relations during the past year have returned to a measure of normalcy," they advised. "A Presidential message at this juncture, coming…out of the blue, might well puzzle the Iraqis and rekindle suspicions that we have some ulterior motive."[17] Although this statement signified that Kennedy had inherited a delicate situation with Iraq, U.S.–Iraqi relations would become even more complicated during his term (1961–1963). An Anglo-Iraqi showdown over the Sheikhdom of Kuwait erupted in June 1961 and briefly threatened to escalate into hostilities that might embroil the United States. Resolution of that crisis contributed to a measure of stability, bolstered by the settlement of a potential conflict over Western oil interests in Iraq and by Kennedy's refusal to promote a Kurdish insurgency in Iraq. U.S. concerns about Qassim's ability to contain communism persisted, however, until the Iraqi leader was overthrown in 1963.

The sheikhdom of Kuwait had caused low-scale political controversy since it emerged as a semiautonomous province of the Ottoman Empire in the late 19th century. In 1899, Britain and the sheikh of Kuwait signed an accord providing British financial subsidy and protection against rival tribes in Arabia, in exchange for Britain's exclusive political influence in the emirate. In 1915, after the outbreak of World War I placed Britain and the Ottoman Empire in enemy camps, Britain unilaterally declared Kuwait an independent state under British protection. Iraqi leaders did not dispute Kuwait's legitimacy during the British mandate over their own country.[18]

After Iraq achieved its own independence in 1932, by contrast, officials in Baghdad began suggesting that Kuwait was historically part of Basra province

Photo 2-3
President John F. Kennedy (1961–1963) confronted a series of challenges involving Iraq, centered on Kuwait, the Kurds, and the appearance of communism. SOURCE: Library of Congress, Prints & Photographs Division, FSA-OWI Collection, LC-USZ62–117124 DLC; LC-USZ61–1173 DLC.

and thus should adhere to Iraq. In the late 1930s, King Ghazi laid claim to Kuwait and appealed to its subjects to reject British tutelage in favor of Arab unity. Nuri al-Said generally relinquished such claims during his stints as prime minister of Iraq in the 1940s–1950s, although he also refused British and Kuwaiti requests to pipe fresh water from the Shatt al-Arab to Kuwait. After the formation of the Arab Union between Iraq and Jordan in early 1958, however, even al-Said agitated to attach Kuwait, with its vast oil wealth, to the union. Soon after taking power in 1958, Qassim invested a loan from the Soviet Union in development of a port at Umm Qasr, near the Kuwaiti border.[19]

Tension escalated sharply in June 1961 after Britain formally recognized Kuwait's independence and withdrew its military forces from the sheikhdom. Six days after the declaration of independence, Qassim declared in a radio address that Kuwait belonged to Iraq and that he would "liberate" its inhabitants. State Department officials noted that Qassim had advanced "an old Iraqi claim, but one that has not in the past received much support from other Arab states and has had no recognition from the world at large." They suspected that Qassim acted to bolster his domestic political position by confronting a legacy of British imperialism. Secretary of State Dean G. Rusk assured Kuwait that the United States recognized its sovereignty and independence, but he refrained from public comment to avoid imperiling his relationship with Iraq or goading Qassim into even more drastic action.[20]

Photo 2-4
Secretary of State Dean G. Rusk assisted President Kennedy in handling the Iraq-Kuwait crisis of 1961. SOURCE: LBJ Library photo by Yoichi Okamoto.

In contrast to the low-key U.S. reaction, Britain responded vigorously to Qassim's declarations, and a crisis ensued. As they returned 5,000 British troops to Kuwait with orders to protect its regime, British officials nervously monitored the advance of Iraqi tanks toward the border, fearful that Iraq might invade before British power could be deployed. Qassim "is so nearly mad that military action cannot be excluded," British Foreign Secretary Alec Douglas-Home alerted Rusk on June 28. U.S. backing of Britain was "absolutely essential." On the next day, President Kennedy ordered "full political and logistical support, if required" to help Britain "forestall any Iraq[i] attempt to take over Kuwait by force." The U.S. Navy dispatched a task force consisting of two destroyers, three amphibious vessels, and some 500 Marines to steam north from the Mozambique Channel toward Bahrain.[21]

Eventually, the crisis was resolved through international diplomacy. British troops quickly gained a commanding position in Kuwait and officials in London sent word, before the U.S. fleet reached the area, that U.S. military assistance was not needed. The U.N. Security Council failed to resolve the political conflict because the Soviet Union vetoed a British resolution affirming Kuwaiti independence and because a UAR resolution demanding British withdrawal was voted down. The Arab League found a political solution in July, when it resolved to admit Kuwait as a member, to discourage Iraq from military incursion, and to replace British forces in Kuwait with Arab League forces. The Iraqi envoy "stalked out" of the meeting, U.S. officials noted, but Iraq neither invaded Kuwait nor withdrew from the League. By year's end, some 1,100 Saudi, 900 Jordanian, and 140 Sudanese troops had replaced the British forces in Kuwait.[22]

Although relieved that war was averted, U.S. officials realized that the Kuwait crisis had strained their relationship with Iraq. When Qassim eased his restrictions against domestic Communists, the State Department saw the move as a reward for the Soviet veto of the British resolution in the Security Council. Yet U.S. policy makers also resolved to resist any temptation to intervene covertly against Qassim, on the grounds that any foreign meddling in the country was fraught with risks of exposure and backlash. They called for Kuwait to secure Egyptian protection against Iraq rather than seek additional British protection. "Kuwait's independence can only be assured," NSC staff member Robert Komer wrote, "if [the] Ruler uses his fantastic oil revenues to buy support from other Arab leaders, particularly Nasser and Jordanians."[23]

By 1962, the U.S. relationship with Qassim was stabilized. The CIA noted that Qassim had proven more durable than expected, but "plotting is endemic in military circles and assassination is an ever-present possibility." Moreover, Qassim posed a passive threat to Kuwait but hesitated from action, and he strained his relationship with Moscow by cracking down again on Communists. When President Kennedy received Kuwait's new ambassador in June 1962, the Qassim regime withdrew its ambassador from Washington, downgraded its embassy in Washington to a consulate, and ordered U.S. Ambassador Jernegan to leave Iraq, but stopped short of severing relations.[24]

Resolution of a potential conflict over the IPC signified determination in both Washington and Baghdad to stabilize relations. Tension surrounding the company had lingered since the 1950s, when the Iraqi government accused the IPC of suppressing production and thereby limiting Iraq's revenues. In 1961, the Qassim government promulgated Public Law 80, which restricted the original IPC concession to those areas where oil was actually being produced. Initially, U.S. officials were concerned that Qassim's move would imperil Western business interests and enhance Soviet opportunities for gain. Yet Qassim limited his actual seizures of IPC assets to maintain production and revenue, and U.S. officials soon relaxed their fears of immediate losses to the oil industry.[25]

The Kennedy Administration's policy toward a Kurdish rebellion in northern Iraq also revealed its desire to maintain sound relations with Baghdad. Looking for political allies, Qassim had welcomed Kurdish leader Mustapha Barzani to return to Iraqi territory in 1958. But quarrels between the two leaders quickly developed on issues such as Kurdish autonomy and oil revenues, and the Kurds did not openly support Qassim when he was threatened by Baathists. Iraqi–Kurdish violence erupted in 1961 and soon spread across the northern region of the country. Barzani envoys called on U.S. officials in Baghdad and Washington, requesting arms supply and political support and offering to help defeat communism in Iraq, return Iraq to the Baghdad Pact, and provide intelligence about neighboring states. State Department officials refused these requests on the grounds that the Kurdish problem was an internal matter for Iraq, Iran, and Turkey to handle. "It has been firm U.S. policy to avoid involvement in any way with opposition to Qas[s]im," State Department officials noted in 1962, "even with Iraqis who profess basic friendliness to the U.S."[26]

By 1962, however, U.S. officials sensed that Qassim's power rested on a thin foundation. At odds with the Baathists, in rivalry with the Communists, and at war with the Kurds, Qassim "is now disliked, hated, and privately ridiculed by almost all sections of the Iraqi public," State Department officials observed, "including apparently, growing segments of the Army." In light of the Kuwait episode, U.S. officials expected Qassim to seek political support from domestic Communists or the Soviet Union, but they also noted that such a policy was fraught with risks, including challenges by empowered Communists or by anticommunist nationalists. State Department experts predicted that Qassim's days were numbered.[27]

As U.S. officials expected, the Qassim era in Iraqi politics ended suddenly on February 8, 1963, when Baathists staged a coup. After 24 hours of fighting, Qassim was arrested and executed. Baathists then arrested and killed hundreds (perhaps thousands) of Communists. King Hussein of Jordan later alleged that U.S. intelligence officers supplied the Baath with the names and addresses of those Communists, and an Iraqi Baathist leader confirmed to the scholar Hanna Batatu that the Baath had maintained contacts with American officials during the Qassim era. (Declassified U.S. government documents offer no evidence to support these suggestions.)[28]

SHORT-LIVED STABILITY: U.S.–IRAQI RELATIONS IN THE MID-1960S

The mid-1960s witnessed a brief phase of stable relations between the United States and Iraq. Monitoring the political turmoil in Baghdad that followed the 1963 coup, U.S. officials sought and found opportunities to build a detached friendship with the governing authorities. Foreign aid, political consultation, and other forms of normal diplomatic discourse ensued. The mounting Arab–Israeli tension that culminated in the Six Day War of June 1967, however, caused conflict between Baghdad and Washington. The severing of formal diplomatic relations on June 6, 1967, and the curtailment of other forms of interaction marked the end of the short era of stable relations.

The Baathist coup of 1963 opened a period of prolonged political instability in Baghdad. The Baath, numbering only some 1,000 members at the time it took power, sought to augment its power by allying with the National Guard, but the Army remained suspicious and excessive plundering by the National Guard soured public support. The Baathist movement splintered among violent factions that vied tenaciously for power. Colonel Arif, Qassim's original partner in the 1958 rebellion, seized control in November 1963 and survived a Nasser-backed coup attempt in 1965, but died in mysterious circumstances in March 1966. His brother and successor Abdul Rahman Arif survived a second Nasserite coup in June 1966, but proved unable to form a strong government. The vacuum of national power set the stage for a second Baathist coup in 1968.[29]

U.S. officials adopted a policy of detached friendliness toward the government in Baghdad. Because the February 1963 coup would limit Egyptian and Soviet influence in Iraq, Komer told Kennedy, "it is almost certainly a net gain for our side." State Department officials promptly recognized the new Baathist regime and offered to sell it technical and military equipment. "Our posture should be that of a friend whose presence is known and appreciated," State Department Advisor William H. Brubeck advised, "but is not overshadowing." U.S. officials recognized much potential trouble given Iraq's opposition to the Saudi and Jordanian monarchies, its hostility to Israel, and its ongoing conflict with the IPC, together with the possibility of Egyptian political meddling in Baghdad and Soviet instigation of Kurdish revolt. The "best policy for us," Komer told Kennedy, "is to sit tight and be prepared to deal with whoever comes out on top." U.S. officials monitored Colonel Arif's late 1963 seizure of power from a distance.[30]

In early 1964, President Lyndon B. Johnson authorized action to stabilize relations with Colonel Arif's government. Although the CIA expected Iraq "to remain highly unstable" in the near future, Rusk assured Iraqi Foreign Minister Subhi al-Hamid that "the United States maintains a keen interest in the stability and progress of Iraq and in its tranquil existence within an area of peace." U.S. officials authorized Export–Import Bank loans to Iraq, approved military equipment sales on credit, and encouraged business investments in the country.

Discussions ensued on promoting peaceful relations with Iran and Egypt, working out an amicable settlement of oil interests, and pacifying Iraqi Kurds.[31]

Indeed, U.S. and Iraqi policy on the Kurdish problem seemed to converge through the 1960s. U.S. intelligence officials suspected that the simmering insurrection among Iraqi Kurds was encouraged and abetted by the Soviets, who hoped to gain political influence in the country, and by Iran, Israel, and Britain, all of whom believed that internal turmoil would weaken the Baghdad government's capacity for making mischief abroad. Like his predecessor, President Johnson refused entreaties for help from Kurdish leader Barzani. When U.S. officials merely suggested that Iraq seek accommodation with the Kurds, however, Iraqi leaders accused them of complicity in aiding the rebels through covert operations with Iran. The State Department vehemently denied these allegations and warned Iran that any plot to undermine Colonel Arif might destabilize the region. "A high degree of autonomy or independence for the Iraqi Kurds would be disruptive of area stability and inimical to our interests in the long run," officers of the U.S. Embassy in Baghdad noted in late 1965. "Neither is the continuation of fighting in the United States interests, although the consequences do not, at least for the time being, warrant a major initiative by the United States."[32]

To the relief of U.S. officials, Iraq seemed to stabilize in 1966. Colonel Arif and Barzani, encouraged by American diplomats, agreed in effect to a ceasefire. That settlement set the stage for a U.S.–Iraqi rapprochement in late 1966. Sensing that support for communism among Iraqi leaders was superficial, State Department officials urged President Johnson to draw the Iraqi government away from Moscow through gestures of friendship. Thus Johnson commended the Arifs' Kurdish settlement as "a monument to your leadership" and called for better U.S.–Iraqi relations. Abdul Arif reciprocated with kind words and expressed interest in greater U.S. investment in his country. In January 1967, Rusk and National Security Advisor Walt W. Rostow convinced the president to receive five Iraqi generals in the Oval Office. "Iraq is at a crossroads," Rostow explained. "If its moderates—headed by Aref [Arif]—can win out, Iraq could break out of Nasser's sphere and become [a] stabilizing influence" for the entire region.[33]

The U.S.–Iraqi rapprochement was challenged by disagreements relating to Israel. Iraq had sent forces to attack Israel in 1948, and, as the only Arab belligerent not to sign an armistice with Israel in 1949, it remained technically in a state of war against the Jewish state thereafter (although geographic distance prevented actual hostilities). Through the early 1960s, U.S. officials followed a basic approach of isolating the two states from each other. Thus when Kennedy Administration officials contemplated an Arab–Israeli peace plan, they deliberately excluded Qassim, citing his "eccentricities in his attitude toward Israel," such as a report that he had forged medals to give to Iraqi soldiers upon their return from the destruction of Israel. U.S. officials also encouraged the Baathists who seized power in February 1963 to direct their energy toward political reform rather than Israel bashing. While visiting Baghdad in March 1964, Assistant Secretary of State Phillips Talbot "spent a good deal of time arguing" with Iraqi officials about U.S. policy on Israel, but he and Ambassador Robert C. Strong concluded that Colonel Arif's government "is a moderate regime and does not wish to let the Palestine issue destroy mutually advantageous relations with the US." Accordingly, Rusk assured Foreign Minister al-Hamid that Johnson "is aware of Iraqi concerns and, I can assure you, will continue to conduct the even-handed, impartial policy pursued by President Kennedy."[34]

The U.S. commitment to such even-handedness became increasingly diffi-cult as Arab–Israeli tensions flared in the middle 1960s. The foundation in 1964 of the Palestine Liberation Organization, with the expressed purpose of destroy-ing Israel, sparked violence (including Palestinian raids and Israeli reprisals) along Israel's lengthy borders. Israeli–Syrian hostilities erupted in 1964 when Israel used force to stop Syrian efforts to divert the headwaters of rivers flow-ing into Israel. Egypt and Syria, rivals for political influence, competed in their anti-Israel propaganda and provocations. U.S. arming of Israel and Soviet arm-ing of Arab states raised tensions and increased destructive capabilities across the region. State Department officials sought to ease the tensions. When Iraqi Foreign Minister Adnan M. Pachachi complained in October 1966 about U.S. arms sales to Israel and reduction of aid to Palestinian refugees, Rusk assured him that "the US would not permit Israeli territorial aggrandizement and cited US intervention during the Suez crisis."[35]

Arab–Israeli tensions finally provoked a crisis in May 1967 that led directly to the outbreak of the Six Day War on June 5. The immediate cause of the cri-sis was Egypt's decision to close the Straits of Aqaba to Israeli shipping, an act that Israel had made clear would constitute a cause of war. Nasser advanced sol-diers into the Sinai Peninsula, widely seen as a provocative move that threatened Israeli security, and Israel responded by mobilizing its military. As all powers braced for battle, U.S. officials engaged in diplomacy to reverse Egypt's deed or to neutralize it through international action. Such activity failed to work before Israel launched a preemptive strike against Egypt. Over 6 days (June 5–10), Israel engaged and thoroughly defeated the armed forces of Egypt, Jordan, and Syria, in the process occupying vast swaths of land in the Sinai, the Gaza Strip, the West Bank (including Jerusalem), and the Golan Heights. In the early stage of fight-ing, Iraqi airpower survived an Israeli preemptive strike and bombed Natanya before the Israeli air force chewed it up in aerial combat. On the ground, Iraq sent one armored and three infantry brigades into Jordan but refrained from throw-ing those forces into action. U.S. officials correctly discerned that Iraqi leaders "simply lack the ability to send meaningful amounts of troops to fight against Israel."[36]

U.S.–Iraqi relations deteriorated sharply during the war, the decline aggra-vated by U.S. diplomacy toward Iraq during the prewar crisis. Hopeful of enlisting Iraqi help in averting war, Rostow and Rusk had told Foreign Minister Pachachi on June 1 that they opposed Nasser's closing of the straits to Israeli shipping and that they would oppose any military attack in the region. Apparently aiming to deter an Arab attack, they warned Pachachi that "if hostilities occurred Israel would win and win hard" and that "we were against aggression, and against the first shot." By contrast, Pachachi pressured the U.S. officials to deter Israel by recalling the U.S. action to stop the Israeli attack on Egypt in 1956 as "something which Arab states will never forget." Rostow and Rusk also persuaded President Johnson to receive Pachachi on June 1. "In Arab eyes, we are completely committed to Israel," Rostow and Rusk advised the president. "It would be healthy, if we are to salvage any of our Arab interests from this crisis, if a responsible Arab could carry away an impression of both your resolution and your good will for Arabs who are trying to restore peace."[37]

Given this U.S. message of restraint, the Israeli preemptive strike of June 5 triggered an angry reaction against the United States in Baghdad. On June 6, Iraq severed diplomatic relations, suspended oil shipments, imposed a boycott on U.S. goods, and retracted aerial overflight rights. Rumors circulated on the street that U.S. warplanes had joined the Israeli initial assault on Egypt, triggering death threats against American diplomats and citizens. Enoch S. Duncan, the *charge d'affaires* of the embassy in Baghdad, reported that many Iraqis, suspicious that the United States had sided with the Israelis in the war despite its words of impartiality, felt betrayed. Pachachi told Strong in late June that the American failure to halt the Israeli attack as it had pledged "had shown an utter lack of concern for the Arabs.... The United States position is so close to that of Israel that there is no meaningful distinction to make."[38]

The turmoil stemming from the Six Day War persisted through the year. When Pachachi returned to Washington to press for unconditional Israeli withdrawal from the occupied territories, he found Rostow so unresponsive that "he might as well have been talking to a representative of the Israeli Gov[ernmen]t." When the United Nations took up the Middle East situation in September, Pachachi remained bitterly determined that the United States must take a lead in compelling an unconditional Israeli withdrawal, a policy eschewed by the Johnson Administration. U.S. officials also monitored a prospective resumption of Kurdish rebellion, perhaps encouraged by Israel as a means to keep Iraq preoccupied at home, and anticipated that it would trigger an anti-American reaction on the suspicion that Washington backed the rebellion.[39]

THE RISE OF SADDAM HUSSEIN AND ITS ATTENDANT CHALLENGES, 1968–1979

The 1968–1979 period marked a time of dramatic change in Iraq's internal politics and its place in the international order. Within the country, a coup in 1968 brought to power a Baathist regime that was gradually taken over by a political operator named Saddam Hussein. By 1979, Hussein was poised to seize authoritarian power and to rule Iraq with an iron fist. As it progressively fell under Hussein's influence, the Baghdad regime pursued new and independent diplomacy on such issues as control of its domestic oil industry, relations with the Soviet Union, and the Arab–Israeli conflict. Watching their relationship with Iraq deteriorate, U.S. officials closely monitored the Iraqi–Soviet relationship and crossed a major watershed in long-term policy toward Iraq's Kurdish minority. In the complicated political context of the Middle East in the 1970s, U.S. officials found it difficult to achieve stability in Iraq.

In June 1968, Abdul Arif communicated to the State Department his interest in restoring diplomatic relations severed during the Six Day War. Before he could act, however, he was ousted from power in a coup, orchestrated on July 17 by a coalition of Baathists and disaffected junior army officers led by the Baathist General Ahmad Hasan al-Bakr. U.S. officials in Baghdad observed that the coup exploited general discontent with Arif's mismanagement of the economy, his inability to resolve the Kurdish problem, and a healthy dose of anti-Zionism. Scholars would later discern that al-Bakr recruited junior officers of the Republican Guard, an elite military unit Arif had built to protect his regime, by skillfully exploiting their tribal loyalties. Upon learning of the coup, U.S. officials in Baghdad expressed relief that the Baathists rather than pro-Syrian leftists had been in charge of it and that non-Baathist army officers had played a role.[40]

Such favorable U.S. assessments of the July 1968 coup waned quickly in light of the power politics that followed. Within 2 weeks of the coup, al-Bakr began brutally consolidating control by purging the military officers who had abetted the coup and by empowering a select fraternity of political allies united by tribal and familial loyalties originating in common ancestry around the village of Tikrit. Lacking practical government experience, al-Bakr organized a Revolutionary Command Council among a small circle of loyalists and deployed a security service that ruthlessly terrorized and killed real and prospective opponents. Donning the mantle of nationalism, he portrayed his regime as an enemy of the West, Israel, and Iran, and he recognized East Germany and the Soviet Union.[41]

Saddam Hussein, a young relative of al-Bakr, soon distinguished himself as an important figure in the regime. Born on April 28, 1937, to an impoverished family in the village of al-Auja, near Tikrit, Hussein endured an abusive stepfather who encouraged him to engage in petty crime. At age 10, he moved to Baghdad, where he resided with an uncle, attended school, and eventually became swept up in the political fervor stirred by Nasser. Hussein participated in a failed coup against the monarchy in 1956 and joined the Baath in 1957. Soon after the 1958 revolution, he murdered a Communist and attempted to assassinate Qassim. Exiled to Cairo, where he briefly studied law, Hussein returned to Baghdad after the 1963 Baathist coup, slowly and methodically rose in party ranks, gained a reputation for torturing adversaries, and joined the conspiracy to seize power in 1968. Al-Bakr quickly named Hussein as second in command of the new regime, partly because of his Tikriti loyalty and partly because of his ruthlessness in eliminating rivals.[42]

Gradually, the al-Bakr regime consolidated complete authority. It employed torture, arrest, executions, and violence to silence and intimidate the wealthy, the middle class, and other potential rivals. Army officers and elite civil servants either demonstrated unwavering loyalty or were purged. The regime brutally eliminated all potential for resistance from such groups as the pro-Nasserites, Communists, Kurds, and Shiites. The government also exploited anti-Zionist fervor to win public favor. In October 1968, it announced the breakup of an Israeli espionage ring, using torture to extract confessions. In January 1969, some 200,000 Iraqis attended a festive event in Baghdad during which 14 accused spies, 11 of whom were Iraqi Jews, were hanged after leaders delivered emotional speeches deriding Zionism. In late 1970, Hussein arranged the ouster and assassination of Minister of Defense General Hardan Abdel Ghaffar because his timidity, manifest in his opposition to Iraqi intervention in the Jordanian–Palestinian hostilities of September 1970, made him unfit for office. More generally, Hussein murdered Ghaffar to deter resistance among army officers to his own mounting power.[43]

By the early 1970s, the al-Bakr regime exercised total control and Saddam Hussein claimed a pivotal role in maintaining it. A coup attempted in 1970 was crushed brutally. The final serious internal challenge to the regime was mounted in 1973 by Chief of Internal State Security Nadhim Kzar, a long-time Baathist who had a reputation for viciously torturing political prisoners and who had twice tried to assassinate Kurdish leader Mustapha Barzani. In June 1973, Kzar arrested the ministers of defense and interior and reportedly plotted to assassinate al-Bakr. But Hussein smashed the uprising, arrested Kzar and some three dozen co-conspirators, and executed them in July. Hussein then reformed the security services, taking more direct control for himself and placing other trusted allies in key positions. He also burnished his credentials by fabricating a cult of personality, claiming a law degree and a military commission as a general although he had earned neither, boasting of a family lineage extending to the Prophet Muhammed, and using postage stamps, billboards, and print media to erect a façade of heroism.[44]

Meanwhile, President Richard M. Nixon (1969–1974) crafted a policy toward the Middle East that generally disregarded Iraq. Working closely with National Security Adviser and eventual Secretary of State Henry Kissinger, the president pursued détente with the Soviet Union and Communist China in matters of global security but also continued to practice anticommunist containment in the Third World. Seeking to extricate the United States from its inherent commitments to police the Third World, the administration implemented the Nixon Doctrine, a policy of bolstering friendly powers with economic and military aid and thereby empowering them to promote Western security interests without U.S. troops. In the Middle East, the Nixon Administration heavily armed Iran and Israel and relied on them to resist Soviet encroachments in the region. Wary of Soviet influence among Arab powers, Nixon downgraded the importance of promoting Arab–Israeli peace, even eventually hindering a major peace plan promoted by his first Secretary of State William Rogers. The bipolarization of the Arab–Israeli conflict—with the United States backing Israel and the Soviet Union sustaining various Arab powers—helped trigger the Arab–Israeli War of October 1973, which started when Egypt and Syria attacked Israeli forces in an attempt to recover territory lost in 1967. Israel prevailed, but only after receiving massive, emergency arms shipments from the United States. That move triggered a substantial anti-American backlash across the Arab world, including an Arab oil embargo in 1973–1974 that debilitated Western economies.[45]

As the Baathists consolidated power in the 1970s, U.S. officials generally viewed Iraq more as a nuisance than as a threat. Not anticipating the ultimate success of Hussein's brutality, they assumed that the regime would remain hobbled by persistent instability for some time. Baathist leaders "have discredited themselves by inept leadership, factionalism, duplicity, and repression—and in the process have alienated virtually every significant political and ethnic grouping in Iraq," State Department intelligence officers wrote on February 14, 1969. "In their effort to extend their control over the Iraqi army, the Ba'this have replaced many senior officers, thereby antagonizing others, and the threat exists of a military reaction such as put an end to the 1963 Ba'thi regime." Repression of Iraqi Jews and a rising tide of anti-Americanism indicated "a frantic search for scapegoats." Recurrent reports of coup attempts in 1970–1971 fed predictions that the regime would not last long. State Department officials monitoring the downfall of Ghaffar wondered if Hussein might soon launch a coup but concluded that his "penchant for anonymity will keep him from overtly assuming power."[46]

Not surprisingly, the relationship between Baghdad and Washington remained distant. Formal diplomatic relations having been severed in 1967, the United States relied on the Belgian embassy to represent its interests, but the absence of U.S. personnel resulted in an imprecise understanding of the local situation, small-scale irritants such as the short detention of an American businessman and his wife who were arrested in 1969 for possessing a short-wave radio, and Iraqi seizure of the U.S. embassy property in 1971. The "prospects for resumption of relations with the GOI [Government of Iraq] are as remote as ever," State Department experts noted in early 1969. "The Iraqi Government is obviously hostile to the United States and the GOI has made it abundantly clear that it does not wish to resume relations." The situation remained static in 1972, when U.S. intelligence officials observed that "the Baath government sees no particular benefit in significantly improving relations with the US. American 'imperialism' . . . remains the regime's favorite whipping boy and scapegoat."[47]

U.S.–Iraqi relations were further strained when the low-level controversy over the IPC that had persisted in the 1960s flared in the early 1970s. Although financially dependent on the revenue generated by ongoing IPC production, the pre-1968 Iraqi government had founded the Iraq National Oil Company (INOC) to develop the areas claimed under Public Law 80. INOC targeted the North Rumaila oilfield, which the IPC had partially developed, but it made little progress given the political turmoil in the country, the lack of local investment capital, and the government's inexperience in managing the industry. When INOC invited Western firms to bid for contract work to develop North Rumaila, moreover, the IPC partners, as well as the Department of State, discouraged firms from cooperating. As tensions mounted in 1967, Abdul Arif told U.S. Ambassador

Strong that oil companies were among "forces at work harmful to Iraq" because they had political as well as economic ambitions.[48]

The IPC dispute climaxed after the Baath took power in 1968. The new regime announced that it would accelerate the development of INOC. In 1969, it signed a deal under which the Soviets would develop the North Rumaila field and export its products to the Soviet Union. When exports started flowing to the Soviet Union in April 1972, the IPC curtailed production and thereby limited royalties to Baghdad, cognizant of the risk that such a step might trigger Iraqi reprisals. Indeed, on June 1, 1972, Iraq nationalized the IPC, claiming title to all oil production facilities in the country. State Department officials, calculating that the Soviet oil markets were saturated, anticipated that Iraq would face substantial trouble developing its natural resource without Western involvement. Thus it encouraged the IPC firms to seek fair compensation for their lost property but to avoid any punitive measures that might undermine oil interests in other states.[49]

Iraq's seizure of its oil industry enabled the Baathist regime to consolidate its power. To curtail any counterstrikes by the IPC, the regime carefully provided adequate compensation by 1975. Nationalization also secured for the regime a foundation of popular admiration. With Soviet help, and using local labor trained in the IPC era, INOC increased Iraqi oil exports by 31 percent in 1974–1975, and the price hikes caused by the Arab oil embargo of 1973–1974 resulted in a 10-fold increase in annual oil revenues between 1972 and 1974. The Baathist regime effectively used this new wealth to win popular support through public works programs, to fortify its political position through patronage, and to fund its repressive security services. Hussein and select cronies also began to enjoy a lavish standard of living.[50]

The Soviet–Iraqi cooperation on oil development in Iraq presaged an emerging partnership between Moscow and Baghdad that also gave U.S. officials pause. In the early years of Baath rule, U.S. officials noted with some assurance evidence of Iraqi–Soviet quarrels, including Iraqi refusal to repay Soviet loans made in the 1960s, Iraqi criticism of Gamal Abdel Nasser, a Soviet client, and Baathists' suspicions that Moscow might try to unseat them. Hussein visited Moscow in August 1970, but, according to U.S. sources, the venture did little to ease the tensions. Instead, Soviet spokesmen began referring to Baathism as "national socialism," thus equating it with the defunct Nazism. The commercial gains Moscow earned by developing Iraqi oil seemingly failed to produce political influence.[51]

In the early 1970s, by contrast, Soviet–Iraqi relations found sounder footing. The Pentagon monitored the increasing frequency of Soviet naval visits to the Persian Gulf, including a January 1971 call by a task force at Umm Qasr, Iraq. In January 1972, the United States learned that the Soviets had pledged to provide Baghdad weapons valued at $250 million. Hussein enjoyed a more productive return visit to Moscow in February 1972, agreeing in principle to integrate Communists into the regime in Baghdad and to open Iraqi ports to the Soviet navy in exchange for friendship, military training, and military supplies. As the first exports from the North Rumaila oilfield flowed to the Soviet Union in April 1972, the two powers signed a 15-year Treaty of Friendship and Cooperation, pledging to cooperate in political, economic, scientific, and military matters.[52]

U.S. officials closely monitored the Soviet–Iraqi rapprochement but moderated their concern. They suspected that the Soviet motives included a desire to win political and economic influence in Iraq, in an effort to stabilize Iraqi relations with Egypt and Syria while averting an Iraqi–Iranian clash. The Baathist regime seemed anxious for political and material patronage and for prestige in the eyes of its people as well as its neighbors. Alluding to Egypt's expulsion of Soviet advisers in 1972, NSC officials advised Nixon that although the Soviets had made genuine inroads into Iraq, they "have been sacked before and they could be sacked again." The Soviet–Iraqi agreements were imperfect; Iraqi President al-Bakr remained resistant to Soviet subservience; and the regime in Baghdad remained so unstable that it could fall or change directions suddenly.[53]

As the NSC anticipated, the Iraqi–Soviet partnership did not last indefinitely. Despite pledges to integrate Communists, the Baathist regime crushed Iraqi Communists when they became restless in the late 1970s. Hussein also strongly criticized the Soviet invasion of Afghanistan in 1979. Yet even then, Hussein also refused two offers from President Jimmy Carter to restore relations on the calculation that independent neutralism would enable him to gain leadership among Arab states.[54]

While monitoring Soviet–Iraqi relations, U.S. officials also confronted anew the issue of Iraq's Kurdish minority and embraced a major change in the early 1970s. Initially, officials in Washington continued the policy of refusing appeals from Mullah Mustapha Barzani for covert aid of his rebellion against the regime in Baghdad. The CIA monitored a stream of covert aid (some $3.3 million in 1 month in early 1970) reaching the Kurds from Iran and Israel, who shared a desire to drain Iraqi strength in an internal uprising. After a Barzani emissary pled for U.S. aid on one occasion, Talcott Seelye of the State Department replied that the "United States Government does not get into this type of clandestine operation."[55]

The Kurdish situation grew more complicated after the Soviets brokered a 15-point settlement between Iraq and the Kurds on March 11, 1970. The deal provided a ceasefire in the civil war, partial autonomy for the Kurds, and a popular front government in Baghdad including representatives of the Kurds as well as Communists. State Department officials strongly doubted that the deal would last, and their expectations were soon fulfilled. Kurds complained that the Baghdad regime refused to recognize their autonomy, share oil revenues from the Kirkuk area, or relinquish an adequate share of power in the new popular front government. The Baghdad regime was annoyed when Kurdish leaders indicated approval of the Rogers peace plan after they had criticized it. In September 1971, Hussein tried, unsuccessfully, to assassinate Barzani, a move widely suspected to have been ordered or at least approved by Moscow. That experience confirmed Kurdish suspicions that the Soviet end game was the suppression of their cause. Yet Nixon and Kissinger continued to refuse Kurdish requests for covert aid, even when endorsed by the Iranian intelligence service SAVAK. CIA and State Department officials advised that U.S. covert assistance would have no positive effect on the civil war inside Iraq and would undermine the emerging U.S.–Soviet détente.[56]

Ultimately, the dynamics of the Soviet involvement in Kurdish diplomacy triggered a change in U.S. policy. In the summer of 1972, top U.S. officials overcame their traditional reluctance to aid the Kurds and approved a stream of covert economic and military aid. Although he hesitated to become involved in "one of the longest ongoing guerrilla wars in the Middle East," Hal Saunders of the NSC staff advised Kissinger, "there is a certain attraction to trying to help the Kurds maintain some independence of the Iraqi government so that they can keep the Soviets from helping the Baath party consolidate its rule and relationship with the Communists in Iraq." Covert aid to the Kurds would also avert Iraqi meddling in neighboring states and reassure friendly powers like Iran and Israel that the United States supported their interests. Kissinger and his military advisor Alexander Haig also reasoned that Egypt's recent expulsion of Soviet advisors would increase Soviet determination to achieve political influence in Iraq. On July 28, 1972, Nixon and Kissinger approved a top secret operation to supply $3 million in economic aid and $2 million in munitions to the Kurds via Iranian channels. In October, Kissinger reported to Nixon that funds and arms, including 500 Kalashnikov AK-47 assault rifles, 500 Soviet machine guns, ammunition, and other supplies totaling 182 tons, had reached Barzani "via the Iranians without a hitch.... According to CIA, all is not well with the B[a]athist regime."[57]

U.S. covert aid enabled the Kurds to resist Iraqi power through the mid-1970s. Barzani fielded a 40,000-soldier militia known as the Pesh Merga ("Facing Death"), which launched a sweeping rebellion in 1973–1974. Hussein dispatched Iraq's 90,000-man army to crush the revolt, to no avail. As casualties mounted amid a battlefield stalemate, Hussein skillfully turned to diplomacy. During a summit of the Organization of the Petroleum Exporting Countries at Algiers in March 1975, he worked out a deal with Iran in which Iraq recognized certain Iranian territorial claims along their mutual border and Iran agreed to stop aiding the Kurds. Soon after this so-called Algiers Accord was ratified in June 1975, covert aid to the Kurds was curtailed and Iraq gained the upper hand on the battlefield. Barzani was forced into exile and the Kurdish movement itself divided, as Jalal Talabani broke from Barzani's KDP and established the rival Patriotic Union of Kurdistan (PUK).[58]

Further, to consolidate its domestic authority, the al-Bakr regime pursued an assertive, albeit limited, policy toward Israel, secure in the assurance that its distance from Israel would protect it from severe consequences. Iraqi army units stationed in Jordan (some 17,000 soldiers and 100 tanks) occasionally traded cross-border artillery strikes with Israel. King Hussein resisted U.S. entreaties to expel the Iraqi forces, confident in his ability to manage any threat they posed to his monarchy. The regime in Baghdad rejected initiatives to promote Arab–Israeli peace, including the peace plan promoted by Secretary of State William Rogers in 1969 and the peace mission undertaken by Swedish diplomat Gunnar Jarring

Map 2-2

The division of the Kurdish people among Iraq, Iran, Turkey, and Syria, as depicted in this map produced by the Central Intelligence Agency in 1986, often added an international dimension to the ongoing conflict between the government of Iraq and its Kurdish minority. SOURCE: Courtesy of the University of Texas Libraries, The University of Texas at Austin.

under the auspices of the United Nations in 1970. Instead, the Baathist government goaded Palestinians to use unconventional means to undermine the Jewish state. Despite such bravado, it could afford neither to provoke Israel into open war nor to back the Palestine Liberation Organization in Jordan when the government of Jordan moved with force to suppress it in September 1970. In the Arab–Israeli War of 1973, Iraqi armored battalions raced to southern Syria to threaten the Israeli right flank as it counterattacked against Damascus, but the Israelis scored a series of tactical victories that left scores of Iraqi tanks in ruins. Angry at Egypt and Syria for starting and ending the war without consulting them, Iraqi leaders withdrew quickly and isolated themselves from postwar Arab diplomacy.[59]

Iraq grew more assertive on Arab–Israel matters when Egypt made peace with Israel through the Camp David process in 1978–1979. The government in Baghdad vehemently criticized Egypt on the grounds that its capitulation increased Israeli danger to other Arab states. Hussein took a lead in ostracizing Egypt among Arab states, probably sensing an opportunity to expand his pan-Arab leadership by filling the void created by Egypt's break with the larger Arab community. Baghdad hosted two emergency meetings of the Arab League, one following the signing of the Camp David Accords of September 1978 and the other on the heels of the formal Egyptian–Israeli peace treaty of March 1979. Iraq thus took a major role among the so-called "Rejectionist Front" states committed to the isolation of Egypt and to the ongoing fight to demolish Israel. By rallying against Egypt, Iraq and Syria healed old rivalries and found a common purpose.[60]

By 1979, Saddam Hussein was poised to capture control of the Iraqi government. He apparently felt threatened from within, as the Iranian revolution of 1979 sparked Shiite rioting in Baghdad slums that Shiite Baathists refused to suppress. An external challenge also emerged: namely, talk of a Syrian–Iraqi federation to counter Egypt's influence, with al-Bakr as president, Syrian premier Hafez al-Asad as vice president, and Hussein demoted to third in command. Thus, Hussein quickly mobilized his most loyal Tikriti allies to scuttle the unification scheme and to pressure al-Bakr to resign, ostensibly for reasons of health, on July 16, 1979. Hussein was soon declared president of the republic, commander in chief of the army, head of the government, and secretary-general of the Baath Party. Within weeks, some 500 potential or actual rivals were murdered in a bloody purge designed to ensure that no one would muster the strength to overthrow him. By the early 1980s, the Hussein regime built an elaborate fabric of security including a huge and well-funded internal security service, a network of informers, harsh penalties for the slightest affront to the state, and routine use of torture and murder against real and imagined rivals. Kurds were also brutally suppressed.[61]

CONCLUSION

The period from the fall of the Iraqi monarchy in 1958 to the accession to power of Saddam Hussein in 1979 was one of political tumult and instability in Iraq. Coups occurred in 1958, 1963, 1968, and 1979. Several other revolts were reportedly attempted or plotted. Internal conflicts among the country's political and ethnic–cultural groups stirred turmoil and violence between the formal transfers of power. Nationalists aimed to remove vestiges of foreign imperialism. An indigenous communist movement sought to achieve political influence. The Kurdish population of northern Iraq engaged in episodic resistance to the authority of Baghdad. Iraq emerged painfully from the legacy of British colonialism and indigenous monarchy that had framed the country before 1958.

During this period of turmoil, Iraq became an independent player in the international realm. Having broken the traditional bonds with the West in the 1958 coup, it pursued neutralist options and flirted with the Soviet Union and other communist states. Iraqi leaders also sought political influence within the community of Arab states and they contested bids from other Arab powers, notably Egypt, to gain a decisive upper hand. Iraq remained technically at war with Israel and occasionally issued broadsides or bombardments against the Israeli state. Management of the delicate Kurdish problem in the 1970s led the regime in Baghdad into alternating conflict and cooperation with Iran.

U.S. officials pursued interlocking goals in Iraq during the 2 decades that followed the destruction of the Iraqi monarchy in 1958. They generally sought a stable political relationship with the government in Baghdad on behalf of U.S. political and economic interests in the country and in the region. They aimed to prevent the rise of communism within the country and to deny the Soviet Union influence there. They wished to prevent Iraq from becoming a source of regional conflict or war. By contrast, the United States showed little regard for the prospects of democracy in Iraq or the advancement of its people. However unstable its internal politics, an Iraq that resisted the allure of international communism and refrained from threatening its neighbors would meet the overall U.S. objective for the country.

For several years after the 1958 coup, U.S. officials accrued some successes in achieving these goals. Despite the hostile greeting experienced by Assistant Secretary of State William Rountree in 1958, the United States and Iraq maintained diplomatic relations for several years, negotiated the termination of the Baghdad Pact, averted conflict in the showdown over Kuwait in 1961, and achieved such manifestations of good relations as U.S. foreign aid and business cooperation. Given their concerns with ties between Iraqi Kurds and the Soviet Union, U.S. officials also refrained through the 1960s from enticing Kurdish rebellion within Iraq. (U.S. covert operations to overthrow regimes in Baghdad, although widely rumored at the time and in some secondary sources, remain unproven in declassified government records.)

Starting in the late 1960s, however, U.S.–Iraqi relations experienced a surge of trouble. Iraq severed diplomatic relations in 1967 because it considered the United States complicit in Israeli military conquest and it subsequently remained deeply critical of U.S. support for Israel. Tensions rose in the early 1970s as Baghdad nationalized American petroleum interests and partnered with the Soviet Union to develop its oil capacity. Although relieved by evidence that the Soviet–Iraqi relationship remained rocky, U.S. officials were sufficiently concerned by the general direction of Iraqi policy in the early 1970s that they began covertly to equip Kurdish rebels as a means of destabilizing Iraq and curbing its capacity to cause trouble. Although the government in Baghdad neutralized the Kurdish threat through diplomacy with Iran, it criticized foreign powers that backed the Kurds and it displayed renewed anti-U.S. tendencies in its approach to Arab–Israeli issues in the late 1970s.

In 1979, Iraq crossed a major historical watershed. Hussein's seizure of power ensconced him at the head of the Iraqi government, where he would remain for a generation. Albeit by brutal means, Hussein would bring internal stability to Baghdad, ending decades of political turmoil. As a secularist and a strongman, Hussein also appeared as a bulwark against Islamic fundamentalism in Iran, where the Ayatollah Ruhollah Khomeini took power in 1979, declaring intent to export his revolutionary ideals across the region. The dawn of the Hussein era would present U.S. officials with fresh choices about the nature of their relationship with Iraq, poised to emerge as a major actor on the Middle East stage.

NOTES

1. "Top U.S. Envoy Hunted through Baghdad Streets," *Time,* December 29, 1958: 21.
2. Rountree to State Department, December 12, 1958, Gallman to State Department, n.d., *FRUS, 1958–1960,* 12:358–59.
3. "Top U.S. Envoy Hunted through Baghdad Streets," *Time,* December 29, 1958: 21.
4. Rountree to State Department, December 16, 1958, *FRUS, 1958–1960,* 12:363–65.
5. Dann, *Iraq under Qassem,* 31–62; Dawisha, *Iraq,* 171–83; Khadduri, *Republican Iraq,* 38–85.
6. Petersen, *Decline,* 11–19.
7. Batatu, *Old Social Classes,* 722–48; Farouk-Sluglett and Sluglett, *Iraq since 1958,* 87–132.
8. Kerr, *Arab Cold War*; Citino, "Oil and Arab Nationalism," 249–53.
9. Minutes of NSC meeting, April 21, 1959, *FRUS, 1958–1960,* 12:423–37; Farouk-Sluglett and Sluglett, *Iraq since 1958,* 51–76; Dawisha, *Iraq,* 172–83.
10. NSC 5820, November 4, 1958, *FRUS, 1958–1960,* 12:187–99; Hahn, *Caught in the Middle East,* 290–91.
11. Gallman, *Iraq under General Nuri,* 200–213.
12. Memorandum of conversation by Brewer, October 8, 1958, *FRUS, 1958,* 13:481–84 (quotation); Hare to Dulles, July 24, 1958, *FRUS, 1958,* 13:461–64; Gallman, *Iraq under General Nuri,* 149–51, 200–213.
13. The Qassim government formally withdrew Iraq from the Baghdad Pact alliance in March 1959. The pact's remaining members changed its name to the Central Treaty Organization (CENTO) and relocated its headquarters to Ankara, whereas the United States negotiated bilateral defense treaties with Turkey, Iran, and Pakistan. These moves did not offset the impact of Iraqi withdrawal, however, and CENTO lost much of its stature long before it was officially abolished in 1979. See Ashton, *Eisenhower, Macmillan, and the Problem of Nasser,* 192–93; Podeh, *Quest for Hegemony,* 237–41.
14. NSC 5820, November 4, 1958, *FRUS, 1958–1960,* 12:187–99; minutes of NSC meeting, December 18, 1958, *FRUS, 1958–1960,* 12:363–64.
15. Memorandum of conversation by Gleason, January 15, 1959, *FRUS, 1958–1960,* 12:375–77. See also minutes of NSC meeting, April 21, 1959, FRUS, 1958–1960, 12:423–37.
16. Citino, "Oil and Arab Nationalism," 255–60. Accounts suggesting U.S. covert involvement in anti-Qassim activities include Simons, *Iraq,* 251–59; and Jentleson, *With Friends Like These,* 31–32.
17. Stoessel to Bundy, March 7, 1961, *FRUS, 1961–62,* 17: 41–42.

18. Anscombe, *Ottoman Gulf*, 91–142; Schofield, *Kuwait and Iraq*, 50–54.

19. Elwood to Strong, June 26, 1961, *FRUS, 1961–1962*, 17:159–62; Simons, *Iraq*, 257–59; Gallman, *Iraq under General Nuri*, 147–49.

20. Elwood to Strong, June 26, 1961, *FRUS, 1961–1962*, 17:159–62 (quotation); Rusk to Consulate in Kuwait, June 27, 1961, *FRUS, 1961–1962*, 17:163–64.

21. Home to Rusk, June 28–29, 1961, *FRUS, 1961–62*, 17:168, 171; editorial note, *FRUS, 1961–62*, 17:172.

22. Strong to Talbot, July 24, 1961, *FRUS, 1961–62*, 17:197–99 (quotation); Home to Rusk, July 2, 1961, editorial notes, *FRUS, 1961–62*, 17:176–78, 179.

23. Komer to Bundy, December 29, 1961, *FRUS, 1961–62*, 17:378–80 (quotation); Talbot to Ball, December 18, 1961, *FRUS, 1961–62*, 17:364–66; Jernegan to Rusk, December 28, 1961, *FRUS, 1961–62*, 17: 374–75.

24. CIA paper, January 31, 1962, *FRUS, 1961–1962*, 17:455–56 (quotation); Jernegan to Rusk, June 2, 1962, *FRUS, 1961–62*, 17:702–4.

25. Circular by Rusk, March 2, 1963, *FRUS, 1962–1963*, 18:382–89.

26. Grant to McGhee, May 3, 1962, *FRUS, 1961–1962*, 17:654–56 (quotation); Ball to Embassy in Baghdad, June 22, 1962, *FRUS, 1961–62*, 17:746–47; Melbourne to Rusk, September 20, 1962, *FRUS, 1962–1963*, 18:116–17; Farouk-Sluglett and Sluglett, *Iraq since 1958*, 79–82.

27. Grant to McGhee, May 3, 1962, *FRUS, 1961–1962*, 17:654–56 (quotation); Brubeck to Bundy, June 20, 1962, *FRUS, 1961–1962*, 17: 740–44.

28. Batatu, *Old Social Classes*, 985–86; Farouk-Sluglett and Sluglett, *Iraq since 1958*, 82–87.

29. Farouk-Sluglett and Sluglett, *Iraq since 1958*, 87–132; Miller and Mylroie, *Saddam Hussein*, 85–90.

30. Komer to Kennedy, February 8, 1963, *FRUS, 1962–1963*, 18: 342n; Brubeck to Bundy, Febuary 13, 1963, *FRUS, 1962–1963*, 18:348–49; Komer to Bundy, March 6, 1963, *FRUS, 1962–1963*, 18:397. See also Rusk to Kennedy, February 11, 1963, *FRUS, 1962–1963*, 18:344–45; Rusk to Kennedy, February 22, 1963, *FRUS, 1962–1963*, 18:353–55; Saunders to Bundy, April 2, 1963, Brubeck to Bundy, June 19, 1963, *FRUS, 1962–1963*, 18:445–46, 595–96; circular from Rusk, November 15, 1963, *FRUS, 1961–62*, 18:786–87.

31. National Intelligence Estimate 36–64, April 8, 1964, *FRUS, 1964–1968*, 18:89–90 (quotation); Rusk to al-Hamid, May 7, 1964, *FRUS, 1964–1968*, 21:336 (quotation); Ball to Strong, December 4, 1964, ibid., 342–43.

32. Duncan to Rusk, October 30, 1965, *FRUS, 1964–1968*, 21:355–56 (quotation); Komer to Bundy, March 1, 1963, *FRUS, 1962–1963*, 18:381–82; memorandum for the record, May 16, 1963, *FRUS, 1962–1963*, 18:542–43; McKesson to Bundy, August 6, 1963, *FRUS, 1962–1963*, 18: 665–66; Rusk to Strong, June 5, 1964, *FRUS, 1964–1968*, 21:337; Rusk to Embassy in Tehran, September 3, 1964, *FRUS, 1964–1968*, 21:338–39; Strong to Rusk, October 26, 1964, *FRUS, 1964–1968*, 21:340–41; Herz to Rusk, April 12, 1965, Strong to Rusk, April 30, 1965, *FRUS, 1964–1968*, 21:346–50; Rusk to Herz, August 11, 1965, *FRUS, 1964–1968*, 21:351–52.

33. Johnson to Aref, n.d. [November 1966], *FRUS, 1964–1968*, 21:368 (quotation); Rostow to Johnson, January 21, 1967, *FRUS, 1964–1968*, 21:370–71 (quotation); Strong to Rusk, July 2, August 19, 1966, *FRUS, 1964–1968*, 21:362–64; Atherton to Hare, November 1, 1966, *FRUS, 1964–1968*, 21:366–67; Strong to Rusk, April 8, 1967, *FRUS, 1964–1968*, 21:374–76.

34. Rusk to Kennedy, July 13, 1961, *FRUS, 1961–62*, 17:187–93 (quotation); Strong to Rusk, March 24, 1964, *FRUS, 1964–1968*, 21:333–34 (quotation); Rusk to al-Hamid, May 7, 1964, *FRUS, 1964–1968*, 21:336 (quotation); circular by Rusk, March 2, 1963, *FRUS, 1962–1963*, 18:382–89.

35. Memorandum of conversation, October 5, 1966, *FRUS, 1964–1968*, 18:641–42 (quotation); Shlaim, *Iron Wall*, 228–36.

36. Rostow to Johnson with attachment, May 25, 1967, *FRUS, 1964–1968*, 19:103–5 (quotation); Hahn, *Crisis and Crossfire*, 47–55; Simons, *Iraq*, 241–43.

37. Rusk to Strong, June 2, 1967, *FRUS, 1964–1968*, 21:378–80; Rostow to Johnson, May 31, 1967, *FRUS, 1964–1968*, 21:377. State Department historians have not found any transcript of the Johnson–Pachachi meeting. See editorial note, *FRUS, 1964–1968*, 21:377n.

38. Duncan to Rusk, June 8, 1967, *FRUS, 1964–1968*, 21:381–83; Strong to Rusk, June 29, 1967, *FRUS, 1964–1968*, 21:383–84.

39. Notes on telephone conversation, June 22, 1967, *FRUS, 1964–1968*, 19:540–41 (quotation); memorandum of conversation by Battle, September 25, 1967, *FRUS, 1964–1968*, 19:848–50; Hughes to Rusk, September 1, 1967, *FRUS, 1964–1968*, 21:384–86.

40. Knight to Rusk, June 7, 1968, Foster to Rostow, 17, July 22, 1968, *FRUS, 1964–1968*, 21:386–88; Miller and Mylroie, *Saddam Hussein*, 90–98.

41. Farouk-Sluglett and Sluglett, *Iraq since 1958*, 87–132; Simons, *Iraq*, 260–67.

42. Simons, *Iraq*, 271–84; Miller and Mylroie, *Saddam Hussein*, 24–41.

43. Rogers to U.S. Embassy at United Nations, January 29, 1969, http://www.state.gov/r/pa/ho/frus/nixon/e4/65183.htm/ (accessed November 18, 2008); Buffum to Rogers, October 16, 1970, http://www.state.gov/r/pa/ho/frus/nixon/e4/65579.htm/ (accessed November 18, 2008); Miller and Mylroie, *Saddam Hussein*, 90–98; Al-Khalil, *Republic of Fear*, 47–58.

44. Al-Khalil, *Republic of Fear*, 6–16; Miller and Mylroie, *Saddam Hussein*, 24–41; Farouk-Sluglett and Sluglett, *Iraq since 1958*, 206–213; Simons, *Iraq*, 284–93.

45. Hahn, *Crisis and Crossfire*, 55–61, 69–71.

46. State Department research memorandum RNA-6, February 14, 1969, http://www.state.gov/r/pa/ho/frus/nixon/e4/65186.htm/ (accessed November 18, 2008); Buffum to State Department, October 16, 1970, http://www.history.state.gov/historicaldocuments/frus1969–76ve04/d278/ (accessed October 20, 2010) (quotation); State Department memorandum of conversation, October 15,1969, http://www.state.gov/r/pa/ho/frus/nixon/e4/69590.htm/ (accessed November 18, 2008); Rogers to Embassy in Lebanon, December 10, 1969, http://www.state.gov/r/pa/ho/frus/nixon/e4/65198.htm/ (accessed November 18, 2008); CIA information cable, August 28, 1970, http://www.state.gov/r/pa/ho/frus/nixon/e4/69596.htm/ (accessed November 18, 2008); State Department intelligence paper, July 16, 1970, http://www.state.gov/r/pa/ho/frus/nixon/e4/69593.htm/ (accessed November 18, 2008); Rogers circular cable, April 21, 1971, http://www.state.gov/r/pa/ho/frus/nixon/e4/65587.htm/ (accessed November 18, 2008).

47. Baas to Davies, March 13, 1969, http://www.state.gov/r/pa/ho/frus/nixon/e4/65190.htm/ (accessed November 18, 2008); NIE 36.2–72, December 21, 1972, http://www.state.gov/r/pa/ho/frus/nixon/e4/71796.htm/ (accessed November 18, 2008) (quotation); Leddy to Rogers, February 7, 1969, http://www.state.gov/r/pa/ho/frus/nixon/e4/65185.htm/ (accessed November 18, 2008); Eliot to Kissinger, May 25, 1971, http://www.state.gov/r/pa/ho/frus/nixon/e4/65593.htm/ (accessed November 18, 2008).

48. Strong to Rusk, April 8, 1967, *FRUS, 1964–1968*, 21:374–76 (quotation); Rusk to Strong, April 5, 1967, *FRUS, 1964–1968*, 21:373; Blair, *Control of Oil*, 85–90.

49. State Department research memorandum, RNA-10, February 21, 1969, http://www.state.gov/r/pa/ho/frus/nixon/e4/65188.htm/ (accessed November 18, 2008); CIA memorandum, June 1972, http://www.state.gov/r/pa/ho/frus/nixon/e4/69744.htm/ (accessed November 18, 2008); Cable from State Department, June 9, 1972, http://www.state.gov/r/pa/ho/frus/nixon/e4/65611.htm/ (accessed November 18, 2008); Farouk-Sluglett and Sluglett, *Iraq since 1958*, 145–48, 154–56.

50. Farouk-Sluglett and Sluglett, *Iraq since 1958*, 154–56, 172–76; Simons, *Iraq*, 268–70; Blair, *Control of Oil*, 285–86; Miller and Mylroie, *Saddam Hussein*, 100–5.

51. CIA cable, August 24, 1970, http://www.state.gov/r/pa/ho/frus/nixon/e4/69595.htm/ (accessed November 18, 2008) (quotation); Porter to Rogers, July 2, 1970, http://www.state.gov/r/pa/ho/frus/nixon/e4/65575.htm/ (accessed November 18, 2008); Beam to Rogers, August 13, 1970, http://www.state.gov/r/pa/ho/frus/nixon/e4/65577.htm/ (accessed November 18, 2008).

52. MacArthur to Rogers, January 6, 1971, http://www.state.gov/r/pa/ho/frus/nixon/e4/65580.htm/ (accessed November 18, 2000); circular cable by Rogers, January 22, 1972, http://www.state.gov/r/pa/ho/frus/nixon/e4/65600.htm/ (accessed November 18, 2008); CIA cable, March 10, 1972, http://www.state.gov/r/pa/ho/frus/nixon/e4/69728.htm/ (accessed November 18, 2008); Beam to Rogers, June 16, 1972, http://www.state.gov/r/pa/ho/frus/nixon/e4/65614.htm/ (accessed November 18, 2008).

53. Briefing paper for Nixon, "Iraq," May 18, 1972, http://www.state.gov/r/pa/ho/frus/nixon/e4/65606.htm/ (accessed November 18, 2008) (quotation); Eliot to Kissinger, April 13, 1972, http://www.state.gov/r/pa/ho/frus/nixon/e4/65604.htm/ (accessed November 18, 2008); CIA intelligence memorandum, May 12, 1972, http://www.state.gov/r/pa/ho/frus/nixon/e4/69743.htm/ (accessed November 18, 2008).

54. Miller and Mylroie, *Saddam Hussein*, 98–105.

55. State Department memorandum of conversation, June 13, 1969, http://www.state.gov/r/pa/ho/frus/nixon/e4/65195.htm/ (accessed November 18, 2008) (quotation); CIA cable, March 9, 1970, http://www.state.gov/r/pa/ho/frus/nixon/e4/69591.htm/ (accessed November 18, 2008).

56. Rogers to Embassy in Iran, March 14, 1970, http://www.state.gov/r/pa/ho/frus/nixon/e4/65201.htm/ (accessed November 18, 2008); CIA cable, August 17, 1970, http://www.state.gov/r/pa/ho/frus/nixon/e4/69594.htm/ (accessed November 18, 2008); State Department paper, "The Kurds of Iraq," May 31, 1972, http://www.state.gov/r/pa/ho/frus/nixon/e4/65607.htm/ (accessed November 18, 2008); Buffum to Rogers, November 3, 1971, http://www.state.gov/r/pa/ho/frus/nixon/e4/65596.htm/ (accessed November 18, 2008); Saunders to Kissinger, March 27, 1972, http://www.state.gov/r/pa/ho/frus/nixon/e4/69740.htm/ (accessed November 18, 2008); Helms to Kissinger, March 31, 1972, http://www.state.gov/r/pa/ho/frus/nixon/e4/69742.htm/ (accessed November 18, 2008).

57. Saunders to Haig, June 23, 1972, http://www.state.gov/r/pa/ho/frus/nixon/e4/69746.htm/ (accessed November 18, 2008) (quotation); Kissinger to Nixon, October 5, 1972, http://www.state.gov/r/pa/ho/frus/nixon/e4/71912.htm/ (accessed November 18, 2008) (quotation); Saunders to Kissinger, June 7, 1972, http://www.state.gov/r/pa/ho/frus/nixon/e4/69745.htm/ (accessed November 18, 2008); Haig to Kissinger, July 28, 1972, http://www.state.gov/documents/organization/72011.pdf/ (accessed

November 18, 2008); Kissinger memorandum, n.d., http://www.state.gov/documents/organization/72017.pdf/ (accessed November 18, 2008).

58. "Kurds in Combat," *Time*, April 29, 1974; Farouk-Sluglett and Sluglett, *Iraq since 1958*, 164–72.

59. Saunders to Johnson, December 4, 1968, Rusk to Embassy in Israel, December 5, 1968, *FRUS, 1964–1968*, 20:671–75; Symmes to Rusk, December 30, 1968, *FRUS, 1964–1968*, 20:732–33; Farouk-Sluglett and Sluglett, *Iraq since 1958*, 132–34; Batatu, *Old Social Classes*, 1095–96; Simons, *Iraq*, 241–43.

60. Lesch, *Arab–Israeli Conflict*, 264–67; Jentleson, *With Friends Like These*, 32–33; Farouk-Sluglett and Sluglett, *Iraq since 1958,* 200–5.

61. Miller and Mylroie, *Saddam Hussein*, 42–56; al-Khalil, *Republic of Fear*, 70–72; Simons, *Iraq*, 271–84.

CHAPTER 3

From Tension to Rapprochement

U.S.–Iraqi Relations in a Turbulent Decade, 1979–1989

At about 8:45 pm on May 17, 1987, Captain Glenn R. Brindel stepped onto the bridge of the USS *Stark*. Some 45 minutes earlier, he had been alerted that U.S. Airborne Warning and Control System (AWACS) aircraft had detected an Iraqi F-1 Mirage fighter flying out of Iraq on a southeasterly course, bearing generally toward his ship. When he reached the bridge at 8:45, Brindel learned that the fighter had closed the distance to some 120 nautical miles. A 22-year Navy veteran, the captain agreed with the assessments of his officers that the fighter posed no threat. No defensive or evasive maneuvers were ordered, and Brindel retired to his cabin after about 12 minutes on the bridge. His complacency would have tragic consequences.

The *Stark* was conducting a routine patrol in international waters in the central Persian Gulf. The guided missile frigate had been dispatched to the Gulf some 8 weeks earlier as a part of a growing U.S. fleet designed to prevent Iranian attacks on U.S.-flagged Kuwaiti oil tankers conveying Iraqi oil exports to Western markets. Having leaned toward favoring Iraq in its war against Iran, President Ronald Reagan had launched the naval operation both to protect vital oil supplies and to pressure a reluctant Iran to accept a ceasefire with Iraq. Naval intelligence officers had forewarned the *Stark*'s officers that although the likelihood of a deliberate attack was low, they should keep up their guard against a possible indiscriminate assault in light of the general instability and sporadic hostilities on the Gulf 7 years into the Iran–Iraq War. The *Stark*'s officers failed to heed the warning.

A few minutes before 9:00 pm, radar indicated that the Iraqi fighter turned onto an easterly course that would bring it to within 11 nautical miles of the ship. A few minutes later, Operations Specialist First Class Bobby Duncan asked for permission to send a "standard warning" to the fighter over the Military Air Distress radio frequency, but Lt. Basil E. Moncrief, the ship's tactical action officer, responded, "No, wait." Two minutes later, the fighter adjusted its direction directly at the *Stark*, a move that no one on the ship noticed. The Iraqi pilot apparently believed that the *Stark* was an Iranian oil tanker. Minutes later, he fired two Exocet missiles at the ship from ranges of 22 and 15 miles.

Seeing a bright light on the horizon, the *Stark*'s Forward Lookout reported "MISSILE INBOUND, MISSILE INBOUND." Only then did the ship's officers scramble to activate standard defensive operations—but it was too late. The first missile passed into the ship without detonating. But the second projectile, arriving 30 seconds later, exploded on impact, killing 37 U.S. sailors and extensively damaging the vessel. The *Stark*'s armaments—which included missiles, guns, a state-of-the art MK 15 Phalanx Close-In weapons system, and "Super Rapid Blooming Off-Board Chaff"—were never used either in defense of the ship or in retaliation.[1]

Ironically, the Iraqi attack on the *Stark* occurred at a moment when U.S.–Iraqi official relations were friendlier than they had been in 4 decades. In preceding years, the governments in Washington and Baghdad had kindled a rapprochement based wholly on their common antipathy to Iran in the aftermath of its revolution of 1978–1979. Fearing that Iran's Ayatollah Ruhollah Khomeini would encroach on his territory or provoke a rebellion within his country, Iraqi Premier Saddam Hussein launched an invasion of Iran designed to topple the Khomeini regime. Suspicious of both belligerents, U.S. officials initially avoided taking

Photo 3-1
The USS *Stark*, a guided missile frigate, burns and lists to port after being hit by an Exocet missile launched by an Iraqi fighter pilot, May 18, 1987. SOURCE: DoD photo by U.S. Navy.

Photo 3-2
Captain Glenn R. Brindel, commanding officer of the USS *Stark* on the night it was attacked in May 1987. The Navy demoted Brindel and forced him to retire for failure to defend his ship. SOURCE: DoD photo by unknown photographer.

sides in the conflict. As Iran gained the upper hand on the battlefield, however, the Reagan Administration came to fear that an Iranian victory would enable the Khomeini regime to project power across the Middle East, to the serious detriment of American security, political, and economic interests. Thus the Reagan Administration abandoned its neutrality and endorsed Iraq's progressively minimalist objectives of surviving Iranian counterattacks and achieving a ceasefire.

To protect such shared interests, U.S. and Iraqi leaders moved quickly to minimize the impact of the *Stark* debacle. In a stirring eulogy at a Navy memorial service, President Reagan paid tribute to the "fallen sailors" of the ship "who died so that we, a free people, might live and this great nation endure," taking care not to mention that Iraq had perpetrated their deaths. Secretary of Defense Caspar Weinberger called the attack a "single, horrible error on the part of the Iraqi pilot." Hussein apologized and offered financial reparations for the families of the dead. "I hope this unintentional incident," he wrote, "will not affect our relations and the common desire to establish peace and stability in the region."[2]

This chapter will examine the evolution of U.S.–Iraqi relations in the turbulent decade from 1979 to 1989. Driven by concern that the revolutionary regime in Iran imperiled their vital interests, U.S. officials overcame a legacy of antipathy toward Iraq and accepted a rapprochement with that state when it emerged in their view as a bulwark against Iranian expansion. Thus U.S. officials would suspend their initial neutrality in the Iran–Iraq War of 1980–1988 in favor of a tactical partnership with Iraq crafted to contain Iran by ensuring the survival of the Iraqi state, however deplorable its government appeared. The Reagan Administration settled on a goal, in short, of bolstering Iraq to ensure its survival, and not even the Iraqi attack on the USS *Stark* knocked it off course.

REVOLUTION IN IRAN AND THE ORIGINS OF THE IRAN–IRAQ WAR

The Iranian revolution of 1979 opened the path to the outbreak of the Iran–Iraq War of 1980–1988 and the eventual U.S.–Iraqi rapprochement. Khomeini's seizure of power in Tehran and his displays of deep anti-Americanism alarmed U.S. government officials who had previously eyed Iran as a pro-U.S. bastion in the region. The Iranian revolution also quickly eroded the mid-1970s understanding between Tehran and Baghdad because Saddam Hussein came to fear that Khomeini designed to overpower him. Mounting tensions in the Iraqi–Iranian relationship gave way to massive violence, as Hussein launched a full-scale invasion of Iran in September 1980 designed to bolster his international and domestic standing. Although the United States initially remained neutral in that war, its own conflicts with Iran set the stage for an eventual convergence of U.S. and Iraqi interests.

The revolution in Iran overturned a generation of American diplomacy in the Gulf region. Khomeini, an anti-American and intensely nationalistic cleric,

Photo 3-3
Saddam Hussein posing for a portrait in 1985. Soon after consolidating power in Baghdad in 1979, Hussein would lead his country on two wars of aggression against his neighbors, Iran and Kuwait. SOURCE: ITAR-TASS Photo Agency / Alamy.

ousted Shah Mohammed Reza Pahlavi, a staunch friend of the United States since the 1940s. Khomeini erected a new regime dedicated to fundamentalist Islamic principles and avowedly committed to spreading its ideology across the region and expelling Western and Jewish influence. After President Jimmy Carter admitted the deposed shah to the United States for medical treatment in 1979, Khomeini provoked the infamous Iran hostage crisis, in which a mob, with the ayatollah's blessing, stormed the U.S. Embassy in Tehran and took captive 52 officials in blatant disregard for international law. Carter's inability to win the release of the hostages through diplomacy and an ill-fated military rescue mission in April 1980 contributed to his defeat in the U.S. presidential election of 1980. Unresolved until January 1981, the hostage crisis generated deep tension in U.S.–Iranian relations.[3]

The Iranian revolution also strained the relationship between Iran and Iraq. In March 1975, the two countries had signed the Algiers Accord, overcoming a long legacy of border disputes and curtailing Iranian backing of Kurdish rebellion within Iraq (discussed in Chapter 2). They agreed to define their border as the Shatt al-Arab, to arrange mutual visits of leaders and otherwise promote good relations, and to "put an end to all infiltrations of a subversive nature wherever they may come from." Yet the rapprochement proved shallow because both governments, distracted by internal politics, did little to implement the accord.[4]

Although Saddam Hussein promptly recognized the Khomeini regime upon its founding, the Iranian revolution soon regenerated conflict between Baghdad and Tehran. As Khomeini consolidated power, he issued edicts claiming a continuity of authority from the 9th-century Shiite Caliph Ali to his own regime. The secular Sunnis who dominated the government in Baghdad saw such claims as an affront. Their annoyance turned to concern and fear as Khomeini also appealed to Iraqi Shiites to rebel against Baghdad and pronounced that he would export his theological revolution across the region, upending secular regimes like the Baath as well as pro-West monarchies along the Gulf. Hussein and Khomeini "were by their very nature prepared to engage in ideological warfare," the scholar Majid Khadduri notes. Khomeini's call for Iraqi Shiites to rebel against Hussein, William Cleveland and Martin Bunton observe, "was not only a political threat to the existence of the regime, it was also an ideological threat that pitted the universalist principles of Islam against the Ba'th's secular nationalism."[5]

In 1980, the tension provoked hostilities. Beginning in February, territorial disputes along the Iran–Iraq border regularly flared into violence. On April 1, members of the Da'wa Party—Iraqi Shiites who had battled the Baath for more than a decade and who were believed initially to have the support of Khomeini—attempted to assassinate Deputy Prime Minister Tariq Aziz. As tension mounted, Hussein abruptly terminated the Algiers Accord on September 17. Five days later, he ordered the Iraqi Army to launch a massive invasion of Iran.[6]

A combination of internal and external factors triggered Iraq's invasion of Iran. First, according to some scholars, the very nature of Baath rule predisposed the country toward violence. Saddam Hussein had consolidated power by ruthlessly suppressing Shiites, Kurds, and other potential dissident groups, but his political supremacy was conditioned by an abiding fear of rebellion. In this context, Khomeini's rhetoric about fomenting theocratic revolution in other states made Hussein suspicious of Iranian intrigue with rebellious Iraqi Shiites. In the view of the scholar Samir al-Khalil, Hussein's decision to attack Iran was an external manifestation of the same ruthless political value system he had practiced in coming to power in Iraq and it reflected his consistent egotistical drive to achieve vainglory and power.[7]

Second, Hussein calculated that war would advance his strategic and diplomatic objectives. A quick military assault promised to undermine the strength of his country's historic rival and to bolster his reputation among secular Arab and Western leaders who shared his fear about the Iranian revolution. The invasion also promised to result in a favorable adjustment of the border, perhaps including annexation of the oil-rich province of Khuzistan.[8]

Hussein's decision for war was based on miscalculations. He probably exaggerated the danger of a political alliance between Iran and Iraqi Shiites. He misread the turmoil in the Iranian armed forces as a serious weakness that he could exploit with aggressive action. He was lulled into overconfidence by the predictions of Iranian expatriates, congregating in Baghdad since Khomeini's revolution, that an invasion would disintegrate the Iranian officer corps. Hussein erred in expecting that his attack would stymie the Islamic revolution, affirm him as a leading Arab statesman and dominant power broker in the Gulf, and earn the gratitude of other Arab states. He also overlooked significant tactical disadvantages. Iran had a three-to-one advantage in population resources and thus more capacity to fight along the lengthy, 800-mile border. Baghdad sat a mere 125 miles from the Iranian frontier; by comparison, Tehran sat behind a mountain range some 400 miles from enemy territory. Iraq would prove unable to develop naval power in wartime, whereas Iran would develop open communication through its long coastlines on the Gulf and the Indian Ocean.[9]

Preoccupied by the Iranian revolution and the hostage crisis, the Carter Administration initially remained distant from Iraq. President Carter had a vague understanding of Iraq as an oil-rich, anti-Israel power that had opened the Middle East to Soviet influence and hindered the Arab–Israeli peace process. He was deeply troubled that Hussein had called for the assassination of Egyptian Premier Anwar Sadat as punishment for his making peace with Israel under U.S. leadership. As top U.S. officials debated how to replace Iran as a security partner, they eyed Saudi Arabia and other Gulf monarchies, not Iraq. On January 23, 1980, a month after the Soviet invasion of Afghanistan raised fears of a Soviet move into Iran, the president issued the Carter Doctrine, a declaration that he would use military force to stop "an attempt by any outside force to gain control of the Persian Gulf region." Saddam Hussein responded on February 8 with the Pan-Arab Charter—also called the Hussein Doctrine—a statement calling for Arab defense of the Gulf and forewarning against any foreign intrusions.[10]

There is no evidence to support the Iranian contention that the Carter Administration encouraged Hussein to invade Iran. As tensions increased during early 1980, Iran openly accused the United States of instigating an Iraqi assault, a charge that Carter strongly denied. "We had no previous knowledge of nor influence over this move," Carter wrote in his memoirs about a reported Iraqi threat to invade Iran in April 1980, "but Iran was blaming us for it nevertheless." As the scholar Bruce Jentleson notes, it seems unlikely that Carter—having staked his domestic political reputation to his ability to resolve the Iran hostage crisis— would have supported Iraqi aggression that complicated his mission to liberate the hostages either in the military rescue mission of April 1980 or in the diplomatic initiatives launched later in the year. Indeed, in mid-September, U.S. officials negotiated terms of a hostage release deal with Sadegh Tabatabai, an Iranian emissary who agreed to present the terms favorably to Khomeini. But the Iraqi invasion of September 22 delayed Tabatabai's return to Tehran and thereafter distracted the Khomeini regime from considering the terms. The U.S. president also expressed fears that the invasion would imperil the lives of the hostages or envelop other Gulf states. Carter first contemplated sending military aid to Iraq only in December, after he had lost the presidential election of 1980.[11]

LOCAL AND REGIONAL IMPACT OF THE IRAN–IRAQ WAR

The Iran–Iraq War of 1980–1988 caused repercussions across the Middle East. It inflicted massive loss of human life and other dislocations within both belligerent states and calcified their political regimes. It reoriented intra-Arab politics because ties between Iran and Syria eroded the traditional anti-Israel front among the Arab powers. It created circumstances for a renewal of long-dormant armed confrontation between Israel and Iraq. The war also complicated the status of Iraq's Kurdish minority. Such political dynamics aggravated the challenge facing U.S. officials responsible for making policy in the region.

The hostilities between Iran and Iraq quickly grew to epic proportions and subjected both countries to enormous losses. Initially, Iraqi forces invaded Iran along a broad battle front, captured a bridgehead at Khorramshahr, and occupied 10,000 square miles of Iranian territory. Iran stymied that offensive in 1981, however, and in 1982 it counterattacked, regaining Khorramshahr and pressing the battle front into Iraq. His fortunes reversed, Hussein suggested a truce and restoration of the status quo antebellum, but Khomeini insisted that Iraq must depose Hussein and pay reparations as conditions for peace. In 1984, Hussein widened the war by attacking Iranian oil tankers in hopes of cutting off Iran's oil revenues, whereas Iran retaliated by attacking tankers registered in Kuwait and Saudi Arabia, Iraq's material supporters. This "war of the tankers" was followed in 1985 by a "war of the cities," in which both sides bombed or fired missiles against civilian population centers. Throughout the melee, a series of major offensives by ground troops generated massive casualties but proved ineffective at breaking the stalemate. By 1988, the two powers collectively suffered more than 1 million casualties.[12]

The war caused significant hardship for the Iraqi people. It generated substantial casualties, drained away young men to military service, cost some $500 billion, and disrupted civic, economic, and family life. Additional misery resulted from Hussein's decision to expel 300,000 Shiites to Iran and his brutal subjection of Shiite Da'wa Party leaders to arrest, torture, and execution. Public dismay was manifest in at least four assassination attempts against Hussein in 1982–1987, which triggered even more brutal acts of repression by the state.[13]

Despite these setbacks for the people of Iraq, Hussein emerged from the war with his domestic political position enhanced. His regime developed an arms industry, broadened the industrial plant, and fostered capacity for weapons of mass destruction (WMD). The armed forces swelled from 200,000 to 1 million soldiers and the number of tanks increased from 1,900 to 6,300. While repressing the Kurds, Shiites, and other potential resistance groups, moreover, the Baath used rhetoric, symbols, and mythmaking to develop pan-Iraqi and pro-Hussein nationalism as a means of resisting Iranian conquest. Hussein also knitted a web of political alliances that assured the loyalty of his top officials. The "regime was at least as politically strong coming out of the war as it was going in," the scholar W. Thom Workman notes, "a considerable feat considering the war's steep economic, military, and human tolls."[14]

The Iran–Iraq War also changed Iraq's relations with other Arab powers. Solidarity with Syria, based on common opposition to Egypt's peacemaking with Israel, withered as Saddam Hussein and Syrian Premier Hafez al-Asad increasingly eyed one another as political rivals. Increasingly dependent on Iranian funding, al-Asad refused to endorse Iraq's cause in the war and he closed his borders to Iraqi oil exports. By contrast, Iraq's relationships with Jordan, Egypt, and the Gulf monarchies improved on the basis of a shared recognition of danger in Iranian expansionism. These states provided Iraq access to supply lines, critical for both the import of military equipment and the export of oil. Whereas Iraq was denied membership in the Gulf Cooperation Council (a pact founded in May 1981 among Saudi Arabia, Kuwait, Bahrain, Oman, Qatar, and the United Arab Emirates to facilitate cooperation on security matters), Saudi Arabia promoted oil price cuts based on the Organization of the Petroleum-Exporting Countries that hurt Iran financially and Kuwait supplied tankers that conveyed Iraqi oil to world markets. Such support from Arab states was an important factor in Iraq's continuing ability to fight.[15]

Iraq's relations with Israel were also shaped by the Iran–Iraq War. An acute conflict resulted from Israel's action in 1981 to demolish Iraq's fledgling nuclear program. Iraq had launched the program in 1959 and soon gained Soviet aid in building a small research reactor. With technical help and materials supply from France and Italy, Iraq expanded the research program in the late 1970s and started construction of a reactor at Osirak, near Baghdad. French firms built reactor cores for Osirak in 1979, but they were destroyed, before shipment, in a warehouse explosion attributed to Mossad agents. France delivered a second set of cores and in mid-1981 prepared to deliver "hot" uranium that would enable Osirak to become active on July 1.[16]

The Israeli government of Menachem Begin decided that it could not tolerate the activation of the Osirak reactor. As early as 1980, Begin had warned U.S. and French leaders that Iraqis would use the reactor to develop nuclear weapons that might be used aggressively on Israeli cities. He contemplated launching a preemptive, surprise air raid on the reactor. His concerns deepened in April 1981, when President Ronald Reagan announced a sale of the AWACS aerial surveillance aircraft to Saudi Arabia, inasmuch as such planes in Arab hands would negate Israel's ability to strike the reactor by surprise. Finally, word of the impending French shipment of "hot" uranium convinced Begin to act. On June 7, 1981, the Israeli Air Force (using U.S.-supplied aircraft and, probably, U.S.-produced bombs) demolished Osirak's critical above-ground facilities such as the control room and reactor containment vessel, effectively halting the Iraqi nuclear program.[17]

U.S. officials reacted to the Osirak raid with mixed minds. Secretary of State Alexander Haig privately sympathized with the Israeli action, whereas Secretary of Defense Caspar Weinberger favored tough sanctions on Israel because it had used American equipment without permission. President Reagan was initially torn between these two positions, writing in his diary on June 9, "I can understand his [Begin's] fear but feel he took the wrong option." Yet the president eventually decided to go easy on Israel. Although forced by law to ask Congress to investigate whether Israel violated the terms of arms supply deals, he resolved privately to issue a waiver if Congress found Israel at fault. He also resisted pressure from Cabinet members to punish Israel and limited U.S. action to a note of criticism and a slight delay in arms shipments. Reagan's "deep natural sympathy for Israel," Haig noted, carried the day. Reagan and Haig also tried to soften the blow on Iraq by declaring publicly that they had not known about or approved the raid ahead of time and offering American assistance in rescuing or caring for victims of the attack. Reagan also soon released the AWACS to Saudi Arabia, which increased the difficulty facing Israel in conducting additional raids.[18]

Tensions between Iraq and Israel diminished during the 1980s. Animosities stemming from the attack on Osirak were initially aggravated by evidence that Iraq fomented terrorism against Israel, including the attempted assassination of Israeli Ambassador to London Shlomo Argov in June 1982 (which probably triggered the Israeli invasion of Lebanon of that month). Iraq would have hoped that a renewal of Arab–Israeli conflict would bolster Arab solidarity, which would provide advantage in its war against Iran. The development of Iraqi–Syrian tensions, however, prevented the emergence of a radical anti-Israel coalition, and the regime in Baghdad softened its rhetoric about Israel. In 1984, Tariq Aziz declared that Iraq was not "a direct party to the conflict" with Israel.[19]

The Iran–Iraq War also imperiled Iraq's Kurdish minority. The Kurds had suffered Iraqi repression in the late 1970s, after Iran reduced covert aid to them consonant with the Algiers Accord of 1975 (see Chapter 2). After the outbreak of the Iran–Iraq War, Saddam Hussein briefly divided the Kurds by backing Jalal Talabani's PUK in its rivalry with the KDP, led by Massoud Barzani since the death of his father, Mustapha Barzani, in 1979. Before long, however, the Kurdish factions united in common cause against Hussein's regime and even abetted the Iranian military offensive into Iraq in 1982. Hussein reacted with a fury, imprisoning or massacring Kurds and demolishing their villages on a massive scale. In the al-Anfal Campaign of 1986–1989, which peaked in 1988 as the Iran–Iraq War waned, Iraqi security forces demolished some 4,000 Kurdish villages. Hussein's cousin Ali Hasan as-Majid (known as "Chemical Ali") ordered the use of poison gas to kill some 20,000 Kurds and drive more than 150,000 into exile. The Iraqi regime also permitted Turkey to commit cross-border raids on Kurdish targets. On behalf of their desire to bolster Iraq, U.S. officials generally ignored the evidence of Iraqi abuses against the Kurds, thus sacrificing human rights ideals on the altar of power politics. In March 1988, State Department officials received Talabani in Washington, but Hussein's angry reaction prompted Secretary of State George P. Shultz to ban further contacts with the Kurdish leader.[20]

U.S.–IRAQI WARTIME RAPPROCHEMENT

As the Iran–Iraq War dragged on, the United States became gradually enmeshed as a backer of Saddam Hussein's Iraq. Although the two powers had not had formal diplomatic relations since 1967, Reagan Administration officials began to contemplate the advantages of cooperation with Iraq as early as 1981, and top officials of both governments met face to face in 1983 to affirm a common purpose in containing Iran. Alarmed at the prospect of an Iranian military victory, President Reagan authorized a series of policies to bolster Iraq with weapons, intelligence information, and financial resources. U.S. officials remained uneasy about Hussein's political despotism and his use of chemical weapons (CW) against his military enemies, but such concerns did not hinder the emerging partnership between Washington and Baghdad.

Taking office in January 1981, a moment when the Iraqi invasion appeared successful, the Reagan Administration initially reiterated the neutrality espoused by the Carter team. "The U.S. position has been to avoid taking sides," Secretary of State Haig wrote in a circular cable to U.S. embassies in February 1981, "in an effort to prevent widening the conflict, bring an end to the fighting, and restore stability to the area." Haig recalled in his memoirs that he advocated a policy of "strict neutrality.... We wanted neither side to win." This position was at variance with U.S. public opinion as captured by the Gallup poll in late 1980. Among the one-third of Americans who expressed opinions about the war, some 80 percent favored an Iraqi victory.[21]

Yet U.S. policy gradually leaned toward favoring Iraq. The ice was broken in the spring of 1981, when Iran registered deep displeasure over the commercial sale of five Boeing jets to Iraq and the announcement of a U.S. embargo on arms sales to Iran. Deputy Assistant Secretary of State Morris Draper called on Iraqi Foreign Minister Sa'dun Hammadi in Baghdad for a full airing of their foreign policies. "The atmospherics were good," Draper concluded after two long conversations with Hammadi; "the welcome was genuine, and the stage was set for a significantly expanded dialogue on global as well as regional and bilateral issues." The next month, William Eagleton, the head of the U.S. interests section in Baghdad, had a friendly audience with Tariq Aziz, a confidante of Saddam Hussein and the highest-level Iraqi official to meet a U.S. envoy since diplomatic relations had been severed in 1967.[22]

Several factors led American officials to tilt toward Iraq. The threat of Iran's power grew in 1982 as it advanced its army into Iraq, continued plotting to export its revolution into neighboring states, and backed extremists in Lebanon who kidnapped U.S. citizens. At the same time, Iraq grew distant from its traditional Soviet patronage. In the late 1970s, Baghdad had suppressed the Iraqi Communist Party and condemned the Soviet invasion of Afghanistan, and Moscow had reacted by withholding weapons supplies, curtailing financial aid, and criticizing the Iraqi invasion of Iran. In the eyes of U.S. officials who calculated security interests, in short, Iran grew seemingly more dangerous and Iraq became slightly more benign. Hussein's deplorable record of violent repression and political ruthlessness did not deter U.S. officials from shifting in his favor.[23]

By 1983, State Department experts Nicholas A. Veliotes and Jonathan Howe recommended a modest tilt toward Iraq that would prevent an Iraqi collapse but honor the broad parameters of the neutrality policy. They reasoned that adherence to the original neutrality policy had become too risky. In the absence of any U.S. backing, Hussein, in desperation, might broaden the war by attacking Iran's oil infrastructure, to the detriment of international economics. Worse, Iran might win the war and spread its political influence in Iraq. These experts also recognized that a full partnership with Hussein carried risks of incurring Iranian wrath, alarming Israel and its domestic supporters, and providing Iraq leverage to extract future U.S. concessions.[24]

Consistent with this thinking, U.S. officials engaged Iraqi leaders in a series of conversations designed to stabilize relations. At a meeting in Paris on May 10, 1983, Secretary of State Shultz had a frank but friendly discussion with Foreign Minister Aziz on a number of regional security issues. On December 19–20, U.S. Special Mideast Envoy Donald Rumsfeld visited Baghdad to call on Aziz and Saddam Hussein. The Iraqi leaders indicated a desire to collaborate in curbing Iranian and Syrian influence and to restore formal diplomatic relations, whereas Rumsfeld welcomed interaction with Arab powers in pursuit of regional stability and security, reaffirmed the U.S. arms embargo against Iran, and offered to promote Iraqi oil exports. Rumsfeld's meetings "marked [a] positive milestone in [the] development of US–Iraqi relations," U.S. officials noted, "and will prove to be of wider benefit to [the] US posture in the region."[25]

The tilt toward Iraq was manifest in a series of changes in U.S. official policy. In early 1982, the Reagan Administration removed Iraq from a list of states sponsoring terrorism, and in 1983, it granted Iraq $400 million in agricultural purchase credits (by 1987, some $2 billion would be provided). In 1984, the Export–Import Bank opened a $684 million credit line to Iraq despite initial reservations about Baghdad's ability to repay loans. The Reagan administration authorized sales of ambulances, electronics, and trucks despite the risk that such items might be diverted from avowed civil to military purposes, and it encouraged France and Italy to arm Iraq. In 1984, Reagan authorized the sharing of intelligence, including U.S. satellite photos and communications intercepts that helped Iraq survive a series of Iranian attacks. On April 5, 1984, he also signed National Security Decision Directive 139, ordering the Defense Department, CIA, and State Department to bolster American security in the Gulf against the threat of an Iranian surge, coordinate the defense of Saudi Arabia, Bahrain, and Oman, shore up intelligence collection in the region, strengthen measures to stymie Iranian-backed terrorism, and develop "a plan of action designed to avert an Iraqi collapse."[26]

Tensions remained in the U.S.–Iraqi relationship, most notably over Iraqi use of CW against Iran. U.S. officials discerned that Iraq suspended its use of CW after they expressed disapproval in late 1983. When Iran launched a major offensive in early 1984, however, the Hussein regime resumed the use of CW after warning publicly that it would use "insecticide" against "every harmful insect" that invaded the country. U.S. officials firmly censured this Iraqi action on March 5, 1984, and banned exports of weapons-grade chemicals to Iraq, with the State Department blocking a U.S. company's impending shipment of 22,000 pounds of phosphorous fluoride. U.S. officials tried to soften the censure by assuring Baghdad that they remained interested in improving relations and, when Iran raised the issue of CW at the United Nations, they favored a Security Council resolution discouraging both of the belligerents from using CW. Nonetheless, when Rumsfeld returned to Baghdad in late March, he noted that the relationship with Iraq had cooled noticeably because of the censure.[27]

Tensions over CW and other issues did not prevent the United States and Iraq from restoring formal diplomatic relations in November 1984. U.S. officials remained concerned by Hussein's harsh rhetoric about the United States and Israel, by his ruthless suppression of his Kurdish people, by his diversion of Western imports with dual-use capability to military purposes, and by his refusal to relinquish his right to build nuclear weapons. Despite these handicaps, the momentum toward a more favorable policy persisted. Shortly after his reelection as president, Reagan approved the restoration of diplomatic relations with Baghdad. Foreign Minister Aziz called on Secretary of State Shultz in Washington to celebrate the deed and to ask the United States to educate its friends and allies on the danger of Iranian power.[28]

Soon after U.S.–Iraqi relations were restored, they were briefly threatened by public disclosures of secret U.S. arms supplies to Iran. Since taking office, Reagan had organized an international embargo on arms supply to Iran. "The

United States gives terrorists no rewards and no guarantees," he explained. "We make no concessions. We make no deals." Nonetheless, members of the Reagan Administration surreptitiously provided Iran with weapons (including hundreds of antitank and antiaircraft missiles) in 1985–1986, in the hope of improving the badly strained U.S. relationship with Iran and winning the release of several Americans held hostage by radical Islamic groups in Lebanon. When the media reported the arms sales (and the diversion of the proceeds to the Contra rebels in Nicaragua, in violation of U.S. law), public criticism mounted against the president. Given that U.S. officials had long denied to Iraqis the rumors of a secret channel of arms to Tehran, disclosure of the Iran arms sales stressed the U.S.–Iraqi relationship. To reassure Iraq as well as Saudi Arabia and Kuwait, who were naturally mistrustful of the United States when the covert arms sales were exposed, the State Department expedited arms export licenses and financial loans to Iraq. Nonetheless, the damage caused by Reagan's covert arms supply to Iran was considerable.[29]

ESCALATION AND END OF THE IRAN–IRAQ WAR, 1985–1988

As the Iran–Iraq War ground on into the late 1980s, the Reagan Administration became more deeply enmeshed in its international diplomacy and tilted more pronouncedly toward Iraq. The persistence of the war and its expansion to include tankers carrying Iraqi oil to Western markets convinced the Reagan Administration to back Iraq more assertively. By 1987, Reagan ordered the U.S. Navy to bolster its presence in the Gulf as a means of neutralizing Iranian naval power, and a series of small-scale U.S.–Iranian naval battles ensued. Not even knowledge of Iraqi use of illegal WMD deterred the Reagan Administration from such a pro-Iraqi stance. Reagan also became more deeply involved in diplomacy, collaborating with other powers through the United Nations to promote a framework for a ceasefire and then using forceful diplomacy to convince a reluctant Iran to embrace a ceasefire.

Reagan was deeply concerned by the eruption of the "war of the tankers," in which the two belligerent powers attacked ships bearing oil exports from the other side, because it imperiled oil supplies deemed vital to the United States. "Because of the real and psychological impact of a curtailment in the flow of oil from the Persian Gulf on the international economic system," Reagan decided in 1983, "we must assure our readiness to deal promptly with actions aimed at disrupting that traffic." He ordered U.S. national security agencies to consult with other powers about joint security patrols to protect the oil infrastructure in the Gulf, specifically to defeat Iranian threats to close the Straits of Hormuz. Recognizing that Iraq bore as much responsibility as Iran for provoking the war of the tankers, Reagan later noted that "we were determined to keep the sea lanes open." Ultimately, when Iranian naval power attacked U.S. ships in the Gulf, "we had to respond in kind."[30]

As Reagan moved toward favoring Iraq, he overcame his disdain for Iraq's role in the tanker war. The shift in the president's policy was evident in his decision to reflag Kuwaiti oil tankers at a time when Iran seemed poised to achieve a military victory. In late 1986, Iranian forces occupying the Faw Peninsula geared up for a major offensive against Iraq and began small-scale attacks on Kuwaiti territory and ships. Kuwait asked U.N. Security Council members for protection of its tanker fleet, and the Soviet Union offered to protect five of the ships. Although U.S. officials had initially balked at the Kuwaiti request, news of the Soviet offer convinced them to reflag 11 Kuwaiti tankers. Under a deal struck in March 1987, the Kuwaiti ships were chartered under the Stars and Stripes and gained the protection of the U.S. Navy. "U.S.-flag ships have received U.S. protection since the beginning of the U.S. Navy," Secretary of Defense Weinberger testified to a Senate committee, "and will continue to have this protection as long as they fly the U.S. flag." By this move, the Reagan Administration protected oil supplies, enhanced the principle of freedom of the seas, contained Soviet influence, and challenged Iran's military interests.[31]

The tilt toward Iraq proved strong enough to survive the Iraqi attack on the USS *Stark* in May 1987. As discussed in the opening section of this chapter, the Reagan Administration quickly accepted Iraq's apology and explanation of pilot error. The United States and Iraq set up joint commissions to investigate the incident and to establish safeguards against any recurrence. Ironically, as Cameron Hume points out, this follow-up activity actually promoted cooperation between Washington and Baghdad. Thus, the *Stark* tragedy drew the two powers closer at the working level.[32]

In their favoritism toward Iraq, U.S. officials even went so far as to accept the Iraqi use of WMD. According to the scholar Bruce Jentleson, U.N. officials documented four instances in 1984–1987 of Iraq using mustard gas against Iranian forces. In contrast to their firm censure of Iraq's use of CW against Iranians in March 1984, U.S. official criticisms of later uses were less pointed. Although the State Department had interdicted toxic chemicals bound for Iraq in 1984, by 1987, the Commerce Department allowed Iraq to purchase U.S. technology that enhanced its ballistic missile, explosives, and WMD capabilities. Jentleson notes that when the "war of the cities" erupted in early 1988, Iraq displayed a new ability to strike Tehran with Al-Husayn missiles, locally developed weapons whose range of 650 kilometers was double the range of the Soviet-made Scud B projectiles that had formed its earlier arsenal.[33]

Nor did the Reagan Administration flinch at news that Iraq used poison gas in the al-Anfal campaign against Kurds in 1988. The U.S. Senate passed a bill to impose economic sanctions on Iraq because it had violated the Geneva Protocol Banning the Use of Chemical Weapons in War (1925) and had used U.S.-supplied helicopters in violation of aid agreements allowing civilian use only. Although Shultz had protested to Baghdad its use of poison gas, the Reagan Administration resisted the Senate bill on the grounds that sanctions would imperil sound relations with Baghdad. According to Jentleson, the oil industry, having watched

Photo 3-4
Saddam Hussein greets jubilant Iraqi citizens in Samara on August 9, 1988, at a celebration of the end of the Iran-Iraq War. Within 2 years, Hussein would trigger another war by invading Kuwait. SOURCE: AP Photo.

U.S. purchases of Iraqi oil climb from nil in 1981 to $1.6 billion by 1988, resisted sanctions. The farm lobby and such business advocates as the U.S. Chamber of Commerce and the U.S.–Iraq Business Forum acted similarly. Pressure from such groups and from the administration stalled the Senate sanctions bill in the House of Representatives. The bill died, Senator Claiborne Pell (D-RI) explained, because "special interests got into the act."[34]

The beginning of the end of the Iran–Iraq War lay in the changing dynamics of superpower relations in the mid-1980s. Deadlocked by East–West rivalries before 1985, the U.N. Security Council became more proactively involved in promoting an Iran–Iraq armistice as Cold War tensions declined in the latter half of the decade. Under the leadership of Secretary General Perez de Cuellar, the ambassadors of the five permanent members of the Security Council began meeting privately to discuss cooperative schemes to end the fighting, motivated by revulsion at the war's mounting casualties, its resulting instability, and its escalation to missile warfare. In July 1987, the Security Council adopted by a 15–0 vote Resolution 598, calling for a ceasefire and implying the threat of sanctions for noncompliance. Reeling on the battlefield, Iraq accepted the resolution. But Iran refused unless Iraq was identified as the aggressor and assessed penalties for reparations. Iran instead prepared to launch another massive offensive.[35]

Building on the foundation of U.N. action, the Reagan Administration applied firmness on Iran to promote an end to the war. Having reflagged Kuwaiti oil tankers, for example, Reagan ordered the U.S. Navy to escort them through the Persian Gulf. Iran contested the U.S.-flag tankers with speedboat assaults and naval mines. Before long, the U.S. Navy was at war with the navy of Iran. Major clashes ensued in July–October 1987 and April–July 1988, as U.S. forces struck at Iranian minelayers, speedboats, oil platforms, and frigates. Tragedy capped the violence: on July 3, 1988, following a clash with Iranian naval vessels, the USS *Vincennes*—whose captain was well aware of the *Stark*'s fate—accidentally downed an Iranian civilian airbus flying overhead, killing 290 passengers and crew.[36]

In the end, the two-track policy of U.N. diplomacy and U.S. firmness seemed to work in ending the war. Apparently concluding that the airbus disaster indicated a military escalation by the United States, Iran accepted the 1987 U.N. ceasefire resolution on July 18, 1988. The financial and human costs of the war had exceeded Khomeini's tolerance, and Iranian public morale had waned as Iraq regained the military initiative, retaken the Faw Peninsula, fired missiles at Iranian cities, and used poison gas on Iranian soldiers. The decision to make peace was "in the best interests of the revolution," Khomeini declared to his people, although it "is more lethal to me than poison." A ceasefire took effect on August 20, ending the Iran–Iraq War.[37]

CONCLUSION

The Iran–Iraq War dominated the Middle East in the 1980s. It caused massive human fatalities and physical destruction in both of the belligerent states. It reoriented intra-Arab dynamics and threatened to plunge the entire region into war. It exacerbated Iraq's ethnic divisions, complicated the Arab–Israeli situation, and seemingly provided new opportunities for Soviet expansionism. U.S. officials gradually concluded that they must become politically involved and even militarily engaged to guide the war to an outcome that served their interests in the region. At no time in its history had the government in Washington undertaken a riskier mission involving Iraq.

President Reagan gradually led the United States down a path of increasing involvement in the war. His administration abandoned its initial neutrality in the conflict and tilted toward Iraq, providing the political and tangible support needed by Baghdad to avoid military defeat. Officials in Washington suspended their traditional concerns over the use of WMD and turned a blind eye to Iraq's use of CW. The Reagan Administration eventually provided naval support to protect reflagged Kuwaiti tankers that transported the oil upon which Iraq's capability to fight depended. Reagan politically and militarily squeezed Iran until it succumbed to the pressure and agreed to sign the 1988 ceasefire as Iraq desperately desired. The Reagan Administration fulfilled its mission of containing Iranian influence by ensuring the survival of the Iraqi regime.

From the U.S. perspective, the Iran–Iraq ceasefire promised to restore a semblance of stability to the Gulf region for the first time in more than a decade.

Peace on the battlefields would end the bloodletting between the two belligerents, restore lucrative commerce, and significantly reduce the likelihood of additional destabilizing events like the attack on the USS *Stark* in 1987 and the downing of the Iranian airbus in 1988. By the time of the ceasefire, moreover, U.S.–Soviet relations had improved dramatically, removing the traditional U.S. concern that Soviet communism would sweep across the region. Ten years after the Iranian revolution, U.S. leaders also became increasingly confident that the expansion of Islamic fundamentalism by Ayatollah Khomeini's revolutionary regime could be contained.

By the time of the ceasefire, the Reagan Administration had clearly taken a liking to the Saddam Hussein regime. Some State Department officials urged caution against excessive dependence on the Iraqi dictator. Zalmay Khalilzad of the Policy Planning Staff advised a more even-handed approach to Iran and Iraq to maintain a balance between the two powers. Richard Schifter, who had been named Assistant Secretary of State for Human Rights in 1985, expressed new concerns about Hussein's record of human rights abuses. But Secretary of State Shultz accepted the prevailing view among administration officials that Hussein had the potential to stabilize Iraq and that after the Iran–Iraq War he might lead his country, and the Middle East, into an era of peace and moderation. That thought and the waning of the Cold War raised hopes that the Gulf region would grow stable and prosperous in the 1990s.[38]

As the next chapter will show, however, the Reagan Administration's strategy of partnering with Hussein's regime to achieve U.S. goals carried enormous risks not recognized in the 1980s. So agitated were American officials about the prospect of Iranian expansionism that they essentially built a security framework on the unstable foundation of Saddam Hussein. Thus Reagan Administration officials supplied Iraq with the political, military, and material aid it needed to stymie Iranian expansionism, but they refrained from addressing Iraq's dreadful record of human rights abuses, its aggressive tendencies, and its political despotism. Nor did they take any steps to curtail the Western thirst for Iraqi oil. Within 2 years of the end of the Iran–Iraq War, these legacies of Reagan's policy would complicate the mission of his Oval Office successors.

NOTES

1. Department of Defense, "Formal Investigation into the Circumstances Surrounding the Attack on the USS Stark (FFG 31) on 17 May 1987," June 12, 1987, http://www.dod.gov/pubs/foi/reading_room/65rev.pdf/ (accessed June 12, 2010). The Navy considered courts-martial against Captain Brindel and Lt. Moncrief for failure to defend their ship, but ultimately demoted Brindel to commander and allowed him to retire and allowed Moncrief to resign. Brindel later blamed the tragedy on malfunctions in the ship's electronic systems rather than crew error, and he accused the Navy of a cover-up in its official investigation. "Stark's Skipper Blames Faulty Radar," *Los Angeles Times*, November 15, 1987, http://articles.latimes.com/1987-11-15/news/mn-21064_1_radar-equipment/ (accessed June 12, 2010).

2. Ronald Reagan, "Remarks at a Memorial Service," May 22, 1987, *Public Papers of President Ronald W. Reagan*, http://www.reagan.utexas.edu/archives/speeches/1987/052287a.htm/ (accessed June 12, 2010); "Why Did this Happen?," *Time*, June 1, 1987, http://www.time.com/time/magazine/article/0,9171,964508-1,00.html/ (accessed June 12, 2010).

3. Hahn, *Crisis and Crossfire*, 69–76.

4. Algiers Accord, March 6, 1975, http://www.mideastweb.org/algiersaccord.htm/ (accessed December 6, 2008) (quotation); Khadduri, *Gulf War*, 57–63.

5. Khadduri, *Gulf War*, 65–68, 79–86, 104–5 (quotation 104); Cleveland and Bunton, *History*, 416.

6. Khadduri, *Gulf War*, 79–86; Miller and Mylroie, *Saddam Hussein*, 107–8; Farouk-Sluglett and Sluglett, *Iraq since 1958*, 255–57.

7. Workman, *Social History*, 59–81, 93–9; Al-Khalil, *Republic of Fear*, 262–76; Tripp, *History of Iraq*, 220–28; Marr, *Modern History of Iraq*, 292. Samir Al-Khalil was a pseudonym for an Iraqi exile and scholar named Kanan Makiya.

8. Abdullah, *Short History of Iraq*, 185–90; Tripp, *History of Iraq*, 230–33; Workman, *Social History*, 99–110.

9. Farouk-Sluglett and Sluglett, *Iraq since 1958*, 255–57; Miller and Mylroie, *Saddam Hussein*, 108–10.

10. Hahn, *United States–Middle East Relations*, 37 (quotation); Carter, *Keeping Faith*, 205, 265, 286, 297; Brzezinski, *Power and Principle*, 451–54; Vance, *Hard Choices*, 347; Miller and Mylroie, *Saddam Hussein*, 107–8.

11. Carter, *Keeping Faith*, 506 (quotation), 558–60; Jentleson, *With Friends Like These*, 34–35.

12. Hiro, *The Longest War*, 7–212; Farouk-Sluglett and Sluglett, *Iraq since 1958*, 255–62; Tripp, *History of Iraq*, 235–37.

13. Miller and Mylroie, *Saddam Hussein*, 112–19; Farouk-Sluglett and Sluglett, *Iraq since 1958*, 255–57, 270–75; Marr, *Modern History of Iraq*, 300–9.

14. Farouk-Sluglett and Sluglett, *Iraq since 1958*, 270–79; Workman, *Social Origins*, 145–63 (quotation 163); Tripp, *History of Iraq*, 238–42.

15. Kaufman, *Arab Middle East*, 133, 143; Abdullah, *Short History of Iraq*, 185–90; Farouk-Sluglett and Sluglett, *Iraq since 1958*, 255–62, 266–69; Khadduri, *Gulf War*, 123–37, 138–48.

16. CIA paper, June 1983, http://www.gwu.edu/~nsarchiv/NSAEBB/NSAEBB82/iraq19.pdf/ (accessed March 31, 2008).

17. CIA paper, June 1983, http://www.gwu.edu/~nsarchiv/NSAEBB/NSAEBB82/iraq19.pdf (accessed March 31, 2008); Haig, *Caveat*, 182–83; Simons, *Iraq*, 319–21.

18. Reagan, *An American Life*, 412–16 (quotation 413); Haig, *Caveat*, 182–84 (quotation 184).

19. Farouk-Sluglett and Sluglett, *Iraq since 1958*, 255–62 (quotation 262); Jentleson, *With Friends Like These*, 42–47; Vance, *Hard Choices*, 347.

20. Jentleson, *With Friends Like These*, 73–77; Abdullah, *Short History of Iraq*, 185–90; Farouk-Sluglett and Sluglett, *Iraq since 1958*, 268–70; Marr, *Modern History of Iraq*, 306–7; "Massoud Barzani," http://news.bbc.co.uk/2/hi/middle_east/2480149.stm (accessed October 16, 2005).

21. Circular cable by Haig, February 16, 1981, http://www.gwu.edu/~nsarchiv/NSAEBB/NSAEBB82/iraq03.pdf/ (accessed March 31, 2008) (quotation); Haig, *Inner Circles*, 552 (quotation); *Gallup Poll*, Nov. 7–10, 1980.

22. Eagleton to Department of State. April 12, 1981, http://www.gwu.edu/~nsarchiv/NSAEBB/NSAEBB82/iraq06.pdf/ (accessed March 31, 2008) (quotation); Eagleton to Department of State. April 4, 1981, http://www.gwu.edu/~nsarchiv/NSAEBB/NSAEBB82/iraq04.pdf/ (accessed March 31, 2008); Eagleton to Department of State, May 28, 1981, http://www.gwu.edu/~nsarchiv/NSAEBB/NSAEBB82/iraq10.pdf/ (accessed March 31, 2008).

23. Jentleson, *With Friends Like These*, 35–39.

24. Veliotes and Howe to Eagleburger, October 7, 1983, http://www.gwu.edu/~nsarchiv/NSAEBB/NSAEBB82/iraq22.pdf/ (accessed March 31, 2008).

25. Embassy in London to Shultz, December 21, 1983, http://www.gwu.edu/~nsarchiv/NSAEBB/NSAEBB82/iraq31.pdf/ (accessed March 31, 2008) (quotation); Shultz to Department of State, May 11, 1983, http://www.gwu.edu/~nsarchiv/NSAEBB/NSAEBB82/iraq17.pdf/ (accessed March 31, 2008); Shultz to Eagleton, May 23, 1983, http://www.gwu.edu/~nsarchiv/NSAEBB/NSAEBB82/iraq18.pdf/ (accessed March 31, 2008); embassy in Rome to Shultz, December 20, 1983, http://www.gwu.edu/~nsarchiv/NSAEBB/NSAEBB82/iraq30.pdf/ (accessed March 31, 2008).

26. National Security Decision Directive 139, April 5, 1984, http://www.gwu.edu/~nsarchiv/NSAEBB/NSAEBB82/iraq53.pdf/ (accessed March 31, 2008) (quotation); Department of State circular cable, February 27, 1982, http://www.gwu.edu/~nsarchiv/NSAEBB/NSAEBB82/iraq13.pdf/ (accessed March 31, 2008); Eagleburger to Draper, December 22, 1983, http://www.gwu.edu/~nsarchiv/NSAEBB/NSAEBB82/iraq33.pdf/ (accessed March 31, 2008); Shultz to Consulate in Jerusalem, January 14, 1984, http://www.gwu.edu/~nsarchiv/NSAEBB/NSAEBB82/iraq38.pdf/ (accessed March 31, 2008); Jentleson, *With Friends Like These*, 33–34, 42–47, 55–56; Simons, *Iraq*, 318–23.

27. Eagleton to Shultz, February 22, 1984, http://www.gwu.edu/~nsarchiv/NSAEBB/NSAEBB82/iraq41.pdf/ (accessed March 31, 2008) (quotation); Howe to Eagleburger, November 21, 1983, http://www.gwu.edu/~nsarchiv/NSAEBB/NSAEBB82/iraq25.pdf/ (accessed March 31, 2008); Shultz to Eagleton, March 4, 1984, http://www.gwu.edu/~nsarchiv/NSAEBB/NSAEBB82/iraq33.pdf/ (accessed March 31, 2008); Eagleton to Shultz, March 7, 1984, http://www.gwu.edu/~nsarchiv/NSAEBB/NSAEBB82/iraq45.pdf/ (accessed March 31, 2008); Shultz to Embassy in Khartoum, March 24, 1984, http://www.gwu.edu/~nsarchiv/NSAEBB/NSAEBB82/iraq48.pdf/ (accessed March 31, 2008); Overmyer to Placke et al., March 30, 1984, http://www.gwu.edu/~nsarchiv/NSAEBB/NSAEBB82/iraq51.pdf/ (accessed March 31, 2008); State Department paper, November 16, 1984, http://www.gwu.edu/~nsarchiv/NSAEBB/NSAEBB82/iraq59.pdf/ (accessed March 31, 2008).

28. Shultz to Embassy in Baghdad, November 29, 1984, http://www.gwu.edu/~nsarchiv/NSAEBB/NSAEBB82/iraq60.pdf/ (accessed March 31, 2008); Jentleson, *With Friends Like These*, 42–47, 55–56.

29. Jentleson, *With Friends Like These*, 31–60 (quotation 58); Haig to Eagleton, June 3, 1981, http://www.gwu.edu/~nsarchiv/NSAEBB/NSAEBB82/iraq11.pdf/ (accessed March 31, 2008); Reagan, *An American Life*, 504–7; Shultz, *Turmoil and Triumph*, 783–859 (quotation 807).

30. National Security Decision Directive 114, November 26, 1983, http://www.gwu.edu/~nsarchiv/NSAEBB/NSAEBB82/iraq26.pdf/ (accessed March 31, 2008); Reagan, *An American Life*, 684, 704.

31. Caron, "Choice and Duty," 153–57 (quotation 156); Jentleson, *With Friends Like These*, 61–62.

32. Hume, *United Nations*, 104–5; Jentleson, *With Friends Like These*, 60–62.
33. Jentleson, *With Friends Like These*, 62–67, 75–76.
34. Jentleson, *With Friends Like These*, 68–69, 77–86 (quotation 86).
35. Malone, *International Struggle over Iraq*, 22–47; Hume, *United Nations*, 88–102, 114–48.
36. Hiro, *Longest War*, 223–40.
37. Bakhash, *Reign of the Ayatollahs*, 270–74 (quotation 274); Hiro, *Longest War*, 241–50.
38. Jentleson, *With Friends Like These*, 86–92.

CHAPTER 4

Reversing Iraqi Conquest
The Gulf War of 1990–1991

April C. Glaspie claimed a small piece of American history in 1989 when she was appointed U.S. Ambassador to Iraq, the first women to hold such a post in any Arab state. A 23-year veteran of the Foreign Service, Glaspie was an expert on the Arab world with field experience in Kuwait, Syria, and Egypt. She took charge of the embassy in Baghdad just after the end of the Iran–Iraq War, as the United States and the countries along the Gulf were adjusting to the restoration of calm in the region and the decline of Cold War tensions. Presumably, Glaspie aspired to be remembered foremost as the foreign service officer who broke through a professional gender barrier. But any such hopes were dashed because of an unusual conversation she had with Iraqi Premier Saddam Hussein on July 25, 1990, days before Iraq launched an invasion of Kuwait.[1]

Initially, Ambassador Glaspie proved to be an effective envoy of the George H. W. Bush Administration as it strove to find a solid footing for U.S.–Iraqi relations. She accurately conveyed to the regime in Baghdad that President Bush and Secretary of State James Baker sought to engage Iraq and direct it toward progressive and peaceful pursuits. She faithfully articulated the administration's approach, which remained consistent although regional tensions mounted in early 1990 amid veiled threats of military action by Iraq against its neighbors.

On July 25, Hussein abruptly summoned Glaspie to a meeting that same day in his office. The invitation was somewhat startling, because Hussein was known to avoid speaking directly with foreign diplomats and because its immediacy left Glaspie little time to prepare. Sitting in Hussein's office hours later, Glaspie listened to Hussein detail his grievances against his Arab neighbors and bluster about taking corrective measures. How she responded to the Iraqi premier soon became a significant controversy that overshadowed Glaspie's achievement of poking a hole in the glass ceiling at the State Department.

In light of the outbreak of war between Iraq and Kuwait days after Glapsie's meeting with Hussein, controversy about the meeting ensued because of conflicting accounts of the ambassador's remarks to the Iraqi leader. According to an Iraqi transcript released a short time after the meeting, Glaspie repeatedly reassured Hussein of her government's friendly intentions and indicated that the United States had no position on specific border disputes. "I have a direct instruction from the President to seek better relations with Iraq," she reportedly said. "We have no opinion on the Arab–Arab conflicts, like your border disagreement with Kuwait." Secretary Baker, she added, believed that the Iraq–Kuwait border issue "is not associated with America." In light of mounting tensions with Kuwait, Glaspie asked Hussein to explain his intentions, adding that "I received an instruction to ask you, in the spirit of friendship—not in the spirit of confrontation—regarding your intentions." Because Iraq invaded Kuwait 8 days after this conversation, many Americans eventually concluded that Glaspie's posture of accommodation, as recorded in the Iraqi transcript, encouraged Iraqi aggression by signaling that the United States would not intervene.[2]

Recalled for consultations in Washington on July 30, 1990, Glaspie was unable to return to Baghdad because of the outbreak of war, and she soon became a scapegoat for the administration's failure to anticipate or head off the invasion. Reassigned to other duties, she gained an opportunity to defend her performance when the Senate Foreign Relations Committee summoned her to testify in the spring of 1991. Glaspie boldly asserted that the Iraqi transcript had been "maliciously" edited "to the point of inaccuracy." She also claimed that she had forthrightly warned Hussein not to initiate hostilities. The only mistake by administration officials that she acknowledged was the failure to "realize that he [Hussein] was stupid—that he did not believe our clear and repeated warnings that we would support our vital interests." Glaspie's testimony restored her reputation among many American people.[3]

The controversy over Glaspie's message to Hussein continued to unfold in the early 2000s, however, when the State Department declassified a report that Glaspie had cabled to Washington hours after the July 25, 1990 meeting. When Hussein suggested that the CIA disliked him, the Ambassador replied that "the President had instructed her to broaden and deepen our relations with Iraq." Glaspie also stressed "first President Bush's desire for friendship and, second, his strong desire, shared we assume with Iraq, for peace and stability in the Mid East." Only then did Glaspie ponder, "Is it not reasonable for us to ask, in the spirit of friendship, not confrontation, the simple question: what are your intentions?" Far from denying interest in the Iraq–Kuwait border, Glaspie welcomed news that Iraq was seeking peaceful resolution of the conflict and "made clear that we can never excuse settlement of disputes by other than peaceful means." This document seemed to clarify that Glaspie had responsibly conveyed the Bush administration's policy of using friendly means to direct Iraqi behavior toward progressive and peaceful outcomes.[4]

The miscommunication and misinterpretation between Glaspie and Hussein, whether willful or unintended, revealed much about U.S.–Iraqi relations during the critical moment that followed the Iran–Iraq War. U.S. officials hoped that the end of that conflict would mark the start of an era of peace and stability in the Gulf region. The decline of U.S.–Soviet conflict on a global scale in the late 1980s stirred optimism that regional strife might be mitigated. Having supported Hussein in his fight with the Islamic Republic of Iran, U.S. officials planned to maintain sound relations with his regime and count on it to serve U.S. interests.

Within 2 years of the end of the Iran–Iraq War, however, U.S. and Iraqi objectives sharply diverged, as Iraq crept toward another war of aggression, this one with Kuwait. What was said between Hussein and Glaspie on July 25, 1990 clearly failed to heal the growing breach. The Iraqi invasion of Kuwait on August 2, 1990 liquidated the U.S. hope for peace and stability through partnership with Hussein. Instead, the United States embraced a new mission that led to the largest deployment of U.S. troops to the Middle East in U.S. history and to a short but intense war against Iraq.

ORIGINS OF THE GULF WAR

The end of the Iran–Iraq War and the coincidental decline of Cold War tensions placed the U.S.–Iraqi relationship at a major crossroads. For his part, Saddam Hussein quickly moved to stabilize his authority in Baghdad and across the region and soon entertained the notion of precipitating yet another war of conquest. Bush administration officials, having inherited a legacy of growing cooperation with Iraq to contain Iran, initially sought to perpetuate a cooperative relationship. As evidence of Iraqi belligerence mounted, however, U.S. officials confronted a painful dilemma between seeking good relations and using firm constraints as the most effective means to stimulate proper Iraqi behavior.

The Iraqi invasion of Kuwait originated in the political dynamics confronting Iraq in the aftermath of the Iran–Iraq War. Although the Iraqi people were elated by the end of the war, Saddam Hussein confronted serious internal challenges. The economy faced staggering problems. During the war, oil production had fallen by two thirds and a surplus of $45 billion in foreign capital had become a debt of some $100 billion. Popular morale had been strained by war and social dislocations, attorneys and journalists pressed for more freedoms, and military veterans expressed their discontent with the political order. The relative decline of Soviet power left Hussein worried that Moscow's patronage would diminish, and the popular revolts against the Soviet-backed dictatorships of Eastern Europe in 1989 stoked rumors of a military coup or people's uprising against his regime. Ultimately, Hussein would address these domestic troubles by tightening his reins on power, embracing tribalism and Islam, keeping his military on a war footing, and distracting his people by pursuing an assertive foreign policy.[5]

Regional political dynamics also encouraged Iraqi aggressiveness. Portraying himself as the dominant Arab statesman and heir to Gamal Abdel Nasser's legacy, Hussein escalated his rhetoric against Israel and, indirectly, the United States. Upset by Syrian backing of Iran during the recent war, he retaliated by backing anti-Syrian groups in Lebanon and by drawing the Palestine Liberation Organization and Jordan from Damascus's orbit into Baghdad's. Hussein also demanded financial assistance (loan forgiveness and new credits) from Saudi Arabia and Kuwait as a reward for having fought the Iranian menace for nearly a decade. Before long, Hussein revived the traditional Iraqi claim that Kuwait historically had been part of Iraq, and he eventually offered to make concessions on the Shatt al-Arab controversy to Iran if the latter acquiesced in his annexation of Kuwait. "Having saved Iran's intended victims" in the Arab world, one scholar observes, "Saddam set out to make them his own."[6]

Distracted by the momentous events marking the end of the Cold War, the United States only belatedly discerned the regional dynamics that vaulted Iraq toward aggression against Kuwait. President Bush, who took office in January 1989 in the wake of the Iran–Iraq ceasefire, was inclined to bolster the U.S. relationship with Iraq, which he had viewed during much of his vice presidency (1981–1989) as a counterweight to Iranian expansionism. To be sure, Bush worried about Saddam Hussein's record of brutality and aggressiveness, his use of CW against domestic and foreign foes, and his maintenance of a disproportionately large army. As the scholar Bruce W. Jentleson notes, a military hardware exhibition in Baghdad in April 1989 revealed that Hussein had developed advanced weaponry including the so-called Super Gun that could launch 1,000-pound bombs, with conventional or unconventional payloads, more than 600 miles. In June–September 1989, U.S. intelligence officials discovered that Hussein had built a global network of front companies to secure key military weapons components on a steady and reliable basis. The Atlanta branch of the Italian government-owned Banca Nazionale del Lavoro floated $4 billion in unauthorized loans to bankroll Iraqi arms purchases. By 1990, U.S. officials also concluded that Iraq had recently stockpiled Soviet-made Scud missiles.[7]

Despite these signs of danger, President Bush calculated that an improvement in U.S.–Iraqi relations would pay sufficient dividends. Cooperation would prove more effective than confrontation, he reasoned, in discouraging Iraq from developing its WMD. Secretary of State Baker hoped that a friendly Iraq would promote Arab–Israeli peace and feared that an unfriendly Iraq would foment conflict. "We wanted to explore the proposition," he later recorded, "that closer political and economic ties with Iraq might persuade it at the very least to be less of a stumbling block." Stable political relations also promised to enhance economic opportunities in Iraq's oil industry and protect the interests of American farmers: by 1989, Iraq purchased U.S. agricultural products valued at some $1 billion per year. Signals that Russia and France sought better relations with Baghdad created incentives to explore commercial opportunities in Iraq. Baker reasoned that the United States could test the viability of a cooperative policy and, if it failed, adopt a more confrontational pose.[8]

The Bush Administration's pursuit of better relations with Baghdad immediately experienced obstacles. On October 2, 1989, Bush signed National Security

Directive 26, indicating that his administration would seek "normal relations" with Iraq and offer "economic and political incentives" for Hussein to moderate his policy. Four days later, Secretary of State Baker asked Foreign Minister Tariq Aziz for Iraq's help in starting Arab–Israeli negotiations. Aziz, however, refused to endorse an Egyptian plan to advance the Arab–Israeli peace process, accused the CIA of plotting to overthrow Hussein, and complained of a proposal to reduce agricultural subsidies from $1 billion to $400 million per year because of Iraqi involvement in the Banca Nazionale del Lavoro scandal. Intent on nurturing the relationship, Baker gave assurances, eventually verified by Bush, that no covert operations against Hussein were underway and he restored the $1 billion in subsidies and approved an additional $200 million in Export–Import Bank credits. Baker later noted that that moment was "the high-water mark of our efforts to moderate Iraqi behavior."[9]

Indeed, the U.S.–Iraqi relationship remained rocky despite Baker's efforts. Hussein refused to endorse the Arab–Israeli peace process launched by the Bush Administration and he encouraged the Palestinian uprising (*intifada*) against Israel that had erupted in 1987. In December 1989, Iraq tested two long-range missiles capable of striking Israel from protected launching sites. U.S. and British authorities seized steel tubes—of a type needed to build nuclear weapons—on the verge of shipment to Iraq. Reportedly, Iraqi agents tried to assassinate a dissident living in the United States. In March 1990, Iraq executed Farzad Bazoft, an Iranian-born, British-based freelance journalist who had published stories on Iraq's nuclear weapons program, on the grounds that he had spied for Israel, and in the process rejecting clemency appeals from Western governments. Days later, Gerald Bull, a naturalized U.S. citizen who had been involved in Iraq's weapons development program, was shot to death by unidentified assailants in Brussels. Although tensions rose, Baker downplayed the evidence of Iraqi WMD development and pressed ahead with the policy of accommodation manifest in National Security Directive 26. He directed Ambassador Glaspie to affirm to Iraqi leaders the U.S. quest for good relations. After Iraq's Deputy Foreign Minister protested a Voice of America radio broadcast of February 15 that encouraged the spread of democracy into Iraq, Baker apologized to Iraq and reproached the Voice of America for airing the editorial.[10]

Yet tensions continued to rise, culminating in an angry speech by Hussein on April 2, 1990. Defending his decision to execute Bazoft and probably recalling Israel's 1981 air raid against the Iraqi nuclear reactor at Osirak, Hussein vowed that "by God, we will cut the spy who comes to Iraq into four pieces" and that "we will make fire eat up half of Israel" if it attacked Iraq. The White House called Hussein's words "deplorable and irresponsible" and temporarily suspended various financial aid programs to Iraq. The State Department warned Iraq that it "will be on a collision course with the U.S. if it continues to engage in actions that threaten the stability of the region, undermine global arms control efforts and flout U.S. laws." In response, Hussein retreated slightly, clarifying that his threat against Israel was a deterrent against Israeli aggression and not a warning of a preemptive Iraqi strike.[11]

Tensions spiked again in May after Israeli authorities foiled a terrorist attack near Tel Aviv. U.S. intelligence officials attributed the attack to Abu Abbas of the Palestine Liberation Front, which had operated in Baghdad since the mid-1980s. The State Department warned that it might return Iraq to its list of state sponsors of terrorism, which would trigger economic and trade restrictions. Prudently, Iraq disavowed strong ties to some Palestinian groups to avoid a break with the United States.[12]

The rising tensions of April–May confronted the Bush Administration with a classic foreign policy dilemma. On the one hand, some State Department officials believed that Iraq had crossed the boundaries of appropriate state behavior and deserved the firm hand of containment. Yet others, notably NSC staff, reasoned that Iraq could best be managed by diplomacy aimed at improving or modifying its extremist tendencies rather than sanctions that might trigger even more deplorable behavior. Certain members of Congress, including six senators who visited Hussein in Iraq, also advocated continuation of the rapprochement policy. On April 25, Ambassador Glaspie noted that Hussein had improved his record on human rights and observed that "Iraq is not spoiling to open a second front." Secretary of State Baker sided with those advocating continued efforts to deal constructively with Hussein and persuaded President Bush to avoid a break in relations.[13]

The dilemma intensified in the summer of 1990, when Hussein essentially provoked a fight with his Arab neighbors. Having nursed a grudge about the wealth that Kuwait had accumulated while Iraq had spent its own treasures fighting Iran in the 1980s, Hussein accused the Gulf monarchies of conspiring with the United States to deflate oil prices, which made it impossible for Iraq to retire its war debts, and he charged that Kuwait had stolen Iraqi oil worth some $2.5 billion via wells drilled near the border. On July 17, Hussein threatened to do "something effective" to redress his grievances, and 2 days later he advanced two divisions of Republican Guards to Kuwait's border. Even as Arab statesmen negotiated with him, Hussein moved 100,000 Iraqi troops and hundreds of tanks to his southern border in late July.[14]

Uncertain of Hussein's intentions, the United States took steps to deter military action. Bush ordered the U.S. Navy to deploy additional ships into the Gulf and to conduct drills with the navy of the United Arab Emirates. With limited effect (as explained in the opening pages of this chapter), Baker directed Ambassador Glaspie repeatedly to warn Hussein that the United States would oppose the use of force to settle intra-Arab disputes. Yet Bush also showed some reservation about vigorous action. Saudi officials encouraged him to allow the Arab states to resolve the situation. Glaspie cautioned that excessive U.S. criticism might spur Hussein to take drastic action even if it proved self-destructive. On July 28, Bush sent Hussein a message expressing pleasure that Iraqi and Kuwaiti officials scheduled a meeting in Jiddah on July 31 to discuss differences. "We believe these difficulties are best resolved by peaceful means," the note intoned, "and not by threats involving military force or conflict."[15]

Contrary to U.S. hopes, however, Iraq invaded Kuwait on August 2 and easily overpowered its tiny army. A combination of factors motivated Saddam Hussein's bold move. Alluding to British action to establish Kuwait in 1922, Hussein publicly justified the attack as a correction of an anomaly of Western imperialism set up by "the colonialists, to ensure their petroleum interests." The Iraqi leader also gambled that an aggressive foreign policy would consolidate his domestic political position and earn him the aura of a strong Arab statesman. He probably also sought to repair Iraq's ailing economy by capturing Kuwait's oil wealth and to redress his grievances with Kuwait's war profiteering and assertive financial dealings. Hussein also might have calculated that recent U.S. tolerance of his weapons development, use of CW, and promotion of terrorism presaged an innate unwillingness to confront him, and he assumed that the legacy of the Vietnam War would prevent the U.S. government from contesting an invasion of Kuwait with force. He gambled that he could consolidate military gains in Kuwait through diplomacy, counting on Soviet support to neutralize any U.S. pressure to withdraw and on Israeli hostility to galvanize pan-Arab support for his country.[16]

Iraq's attack on Kuwait naturally triggered evaluation of the wisdom of the Bush Administration's policy. James Baker later acknowledged that the president's July 28 message to Hussein was obviously insufficient to deter the aggression. Yet he defended the overall approach, noting that neither Congress nor the American people would have supported a firm move against Iraq prior to the actual invasion and observing that no other power, including Israel, Egypt, and Saudi Arabia, anticipated that Hussein would actually invade. Among scholars, Bruce Jentleson criticizes Bush for trying to bring Iraq into the "family of nations" until the very moment of the invasion of Kuwait. Amatzia Baram concludes, by contrast, that "the United States, though not doing all it reasonably could to deter Saddam from invading Kuwait...did enough to alert the Iraqi regime to the fact that in the medium and long terms the two countries were on an unavoidable collision course."[17]

Clearly, the Bush Administration failed in its effort to channel Iraqi behavior toward peaceful pursuits. Lacking an effective intelligence apparatus within Iraq that might have revealed Hussein's true intentions, officials in Washington were forced to gamble that friendly gestures would win Hussein's cooperation with their vision of regional peace and stability. Lacking a political or legal mandate for more vigorous action, Bush administration leaders relied on diplomatic statements to motivate Hussein. As the Iraqi leader began to show signs of his latent aggressiveness toward Kuwait, the government in Washington was slow to shift its policy from accommodation to deterrence. Thus Ambassador Glaspie—accurately representing the tenuous policy of her superiors in Washington—delivered an ambiguous message to Hussein on July 25, 1990, setting the stage for the outbreak of war.

U.S. RESISTANCE TO THE INVASION OF KUWAIT

The Iraqi invasion of Kuwait clearly spelled the failure of the Bush Administration's initial approach of accommodation with Iraq. It rendered untenable the concept of modifying Hussein's behavior through interaction, thus resolving the policy dilemma that had faced U.S. officials since 1989. By stark contrast, it immediately led to a determination that the United States must exercise a firm hand of containment against Hussein's regime. The Iraqi leader's stubborn insistence on keeping the spoils of his military advance and President Bush's equally stubborn refusal to accede to such an outcome placed the United States and Iraq on a collision course that would result in the first war between their two countries.

The conquest of Kuwait alarmed U.S. officials on four levels. First, U.S. officials feared that Hussein's gambit might prove to mark the beginning rather than the end of his expansionist ambitions. Leaders in Washington trembled at the possibility that Iraq's huge army might quickly seize the oilfields of northern Saudi Arabia or perhaps occupy that entire kingdom and dismantle its monarchy, especially after three reported incidents in which Iraqi troops breached the Saudi border on August 3–6. If Hussein should conquer that kingdom, NSC officials calculated, he would control 70 percent of Gulf oil reserves, and if he also overran the United Arab Emirates, he would control 90–95 percent. "It would be very

Photo 4-1
President George W. Bush discusses Iraq's conquest of Kuwait with the emir of Kuwait, Jabir al-Ahmad al Jabir al-Sabahin, at the White House, September 28, 1990. SOURCE: George Bush Presidential Library and Museum.

easy for him to control the world's oil," White House Chief of Staff John Sununu warned the NSC. "This would be heady for Saddam." Had Hussein entertained such grand goals, Bush later commented, "he would have had a free run" against the badly outnumbered Saudi military. Hussein thereby could have gained control of extensive oil resources as well as the military bases that the United States eventually used against him.[18]

Second, U.S. leaders predicted that even if he refrained from additional frontal aggression, Hussein would gain extraordinary economic and political power if he were permitted to consolidate his victory in Kuwait. Even without physical control of the oil resources of other Arab states, they feared, Hussein would exert political control over the Organization of the Petroleum-Exporting Countries' decisions regarding prices and production, thereby achieving the means to accumulate wealth and to price gouge Western consumers. Higher oil revenues would equip him to expand his military firepower and perhaps even develop nuclear weapons. Political supremacy among Arab statesmen would enable him to intensify political attacks or provoke a military assault on Israel. Bush Administration leaders shuddered at the prospect of Hussein emerging as the master of his neighborhood. In words that summarized the views of top administration officials, National Security Adviser Brent Scowcroft declared to the NSC on August 3 that "to accommodate Iraq should not be a policy option."[19]

Third, U.S. officials calculated that an unprovoked attack by one power on another implicitly threatened to destabilize the international order. British Prime Minister Margaret Thatcher, who encountered Bush at a previously scheduled conference in Colorado only hours after the invasion, encouraged the president to resist Hussein's action by citing the conventional wisdom that acceptance of Nazi aggression in the years preceding World War II magnified the costs of that conflict. "Aggressors must never be appeased," she argued. "We learned that to our cost in the 1930s." The next day, Deputy Secretary of State Lawrence Eagleburger asserted during a meeting of the NSC in Washington that "this is the first test of the postwar system" since the Cold War had eased. "If he [Hussein] succeeds, others may try the same thing. It would be a bad lesson."[20]

Fourth, Hussein's behavior seemed to validate a new security doctrine devised by the Pentagon in early 1990 in response to the decline of Soviet power. Known as the "New Strategy" or "Regional Defense Strategy," the doctrine posited that newly emerging regional powers—dubbed "rogue states" or "outlaw states"—would pose threats to U.S. security after the demise of Soviet strength. Rogue states were identified by dominant regional status, possession of large militaries and WMD, and expansionist goals. Saddam Hussein's invasion of Kuwait confirmed in U.S. minds both the validity of the Regional Defense Strategy and the need to confront Iraq under it.[21]

In light of such security concerns, the leaders of the administration soon embraced the notion that U.S. military forces would probably prove necessary to end the Iraqi occupation of Kuwait. Initially, the NSC resolved to use diplomatic pressures and economic sanctions to achieve an Iraqi retreat, although they were

pessimistic that Hussein would relent to diplomacy or that the international community would enforce meaningful sanctions. Officials such as Eagleburger and
Secretary of Defense Richard Cheney thus quickly resolved that the Pentagon
should prepare for action. Citing Hussein's megalomania and the Iraqi army's
recent combat experience, Chairman of the Joint Chiefs of Staff General Colin
Powell cautioned that offensive operations against the Iraqi military "would be
the N[ational] F[ootball] L[eague], not a scrimmage. It would mean a major confrontation." President Bush, however, expressed skepticism at such caution, noting that Iraq's military had performed unimpressively in its war against Iran.
Bush's contemplation of military operations placed him out of sync with public
opinion. According to a Gallup poll, some three quarters of the American people
favored economic sanctions as the means to deal with Iraq and only 23 percent
favored the initiation of combat operations.[22]

Determined first to contain the dangers posed by Hussein, President Bush
acted immediately to ensure the security of Saudi Arabia. Within days of the
attack on Kuwait, he ordered warships at Diego Garcia to head to the Gulf
and rushed two squadrons of F-15 fighters and a brigade of the Eighty-Second
Airborne Division to Saudi Arabia. Under the so-called Desert Shield plan, some
100,000 U.S. soldiers and airmen reached the kingdom by the end of August.
According to the Gallup poll, these steps gained the approval of 77 percent of the
American people and President Bush's approval rating soared from 52 percent

Photo 4-2
President Bush discussing the Iraqi occupation of Kuwait with King Fahd of Saudi Arabia
during a visit to the kingdom, November 21, 1990. source: George Bush Presidential Library and
Museum.

on August 4 to 80 percent on August 12. The immediate threat to the Saudi state subsided when Hussein relocated several elite units from the frontier to reserve positions in southern Iraq, although both Iraq and the United States continued to build up forces in the border area.[23]

With regard to Kuwait, by contrast, Iraq's plan to consolidate its occupation and U.S. resolve to contest that occupation placed the two powers on a collision course. To build support among Arab states, Hussein offered, on August 12, to withdraw from Kuwait—on terms consistent with "the historic rights of Iraq to its territory and the choice of the people of Kuwait"—if Israel withdrew from the Occupied Territories and Syria departed from Lebanon. Hussein also demanded U.S. withdrawal from Saudi Arabia and cancellation of economic sanctions on Iraq. "If the United States and its allies and lackeys fail to respond positively to our initiative," Hussein threatened, "we shall oppose their evil inclination with force, assisted by the worthy sons of the Arab nations and the great Iraqi people, and we shall triumph with the help of God, causing the forces of evil, who will be routed and forced to leave the region defeated, vanquished, damned, and humiliated, to regret their acts." In an apparent effort to exploit the legacy of Vietnam, Hussein published an open letter to President Bush warning that if the United States used force against Iraq, thousands of GIs "will go home shrouded in sad coffins." To deter Western military action, Iraq also detained 2,000 Americans and 4,000 Britons caught in Kuwait.[24]

Yet the United States resolved to contest Iraq's conquest of Kuwait and carefully assembled an international coalition of supporters. President Bush demanded "the immediate, unconditional, and complete withdrawal of all Iraqi forces from Kuwait," imposed economic sanctions on Iraq, and encouraged other states to follow suit. At the U.N. Security Council, U.S. diplomats pushed through Resolution 660, which condemned the Iraqi aggression, demanded Iraqi withdrawal, and encouraged settlement of intra-Arab disputes through negotiations. Bush telephoned other leaders around the world to promote the idea of collective action to reverse the aggression. He declared publicly on August 5 that "this will not stand, this aggression against Kuwait." Various officials in Washington declared that Bush had drawn a "line in the sand" along the Saudi border that Hussein should not dare to cross. By late August, the U.N. Security Council added Resolution 664, denouncing the detentions of American and British nationals in Kuwait, and Resolution 665, authorizing the use of military means to enforce economic sanctions. But Hussein defied such admonitions, asserting that Kuwait no longer existed and telling his own people to prepare for the "mother of all battles."[25]

In September, Bush intensified his drive to align other powers to U.S. policy. He convinced most Arab states, including Syria, to endorse the U.S. perspective, and he persuaded the Israelis to appreciate that a U.S.–Arab coalition arrayed against Iraq served their interests. Hussein's hope of gaining Soviet backing was deflated when Bush met Soviet Premier Mikhail Gorbachev in Helsinki on September 9 to close ranks. Gorbachev rejected a plea from Iraqi Foreign Minister Aziz to link Kuwait to other problems in the region and instead signed a joint statement with Bush that, while affirming a desire for a peaceful outcome of the Kuwait issue, clarified that "we are determined to see this aggression end, and if the current steps fail to end it, we are prepared to consider additional ones consistent with the U.N. Charter. We must demonstrate beyond any doubt that aggression cannot and will not pay." Two days after meeting Gorbachev, Bush declared to a joint session of Congress that "our objectives in the Persian Gulf are clear, our goals defined and familiar: Iraq must withdraw from Kuwait completely, immediately, and without condition.... This is not, as Saddam Hussein would have it, the United States against Iraq. It is Iraq against the world."[26]

As President Bush implemented this policy of firmness toward Iraq, public confidence in his policy diminished. Public approval of the president's handling of the Middle East crisis, according to Gallup polls, steadily declined from 80 percent on August 12 to 54 percent on November 18. Although nearly two thirds of Americans continued to approve the stationing of U.S. soldiers in Saudi Arabia, barely one quarter expressed favor for U.S. offensive operations to

Photo 4-3
President Bush and Mrs. Barbara Bush with General H. Norman Schwarzkopf Jr. during a visit with U.S. troops deployed to Saudi Arabia, November 22, 1990. Within 6 weeks, Bush would order U.S. forces to begin aerial attacks against Iraqi forces, followed by a ground invasion that liberated Kuwait from Iraqi control. SOURCE: George Bush Presidential Library and Museum.

liberate Kuwait. As the domestic economy experienced instability, moreover, the Republican president came under criticism during campaigning for the congressional elections on November 6. When the votes were counted, the Democratic Party gained one seat in the Senate and seven in the House of Representatives, increasing its majorities to 56–44 and 267–167, respectively.[27]

Undeterred by such public reluctance, President Bush shifted his Iraq policy from diplomacy to war preparations soon after the congressional elections. Given that Hussein would not yield under the international pressure that the United States was bringing to bear, the president concluded that he could not rely indefinitely on diplomacy given the possibilities that his coalition among Arab powers might fracture in light of Israeli–Palestinian violence or that Soviet leaders, having watched their European empire tumble, might show an inclination to protect their traditional client in Baghdad. Immediately after the midterm elections, Bush announced that he would relocate 200,000 U.S. soldiers from Germany to Saudi Arabia, a move that would enable offensive action. On November 29, the United States also pushed through the U.N. Security Council Resolution 678, which ordered Iraq to withdraw from Kuwait by January 15, 1991, and authorized member states, if Iraq remained defiant, "to use all necessary means...to restore international peace and security in the area." Bush convinced leaders of 28 other countries to contribute troops to such an operation and still other powers to bankroll it. Interestingly, public opinion rallied in support of Bush's military deployments. Support for the launching of an attack on Iraq if the stalemate remained in January 1991 increased from 37 percent in mid-November to 53 percent by early December, according to the Gallup poll, and the president's overall approval rating ticked up from 58 percent to 61 percent by early December.[28]

In early 1991, the Bush Administration provided Hussein one additional opportunity to relinquish Kuwait. When Baker met Aziz in Geneva on January 9, however, neither statesman would budge on his government's policy. "There was now no question in my mind," Baker later wrote, "we were going to war." Hussein offered to arrange an additional meeting on January 12, but Bush rejected the offer as an insincere stalling ploy. "I've got it boiled down very clearly to good vs. evil," he remarked; "I think what's at stake here is the new world order." Instead of another meeting with Iraq, Bush secured from Congress a resolution (passed by margins of 250–183 in the House and 52–47 in the Senate) authorizing the president to use force to liberate Kuwait. Gallup polls confirmed that from December to early January, support among the American public for dealing with Iraq through sanctions declined from 47 percent to 36 percent, whereas support for a military offensive rose from 46 percent to 57 percent.[29]

THE LIBERATION OF KUWAIT

Bush quickly acted on the international and domestic legal sanction he had secured to wage war to liberate Kuwait. In partnership with allied powers, he launched a two-phase military operation, beginning with a sustained air bombardment

Photo 4-4
A stern-faced President Bush prepares to address the American people regarding the
start of Operation Desert Storm, January 16, 1991. SOURCE: George Bush Presidential Library and
Museum.

of targets in Iraq and occupied Kuwait and following with a massive ground
offensive. Iraqi resistance proved futile, and political challenges attending to the
war were readily resolved by the U.S. government. In 6 weeks of operations from
mid-January to late February 1991, the United States and its partners inflicted a
devastating military defeat on Iraq.

Bush ordered the start of offensive military action on January 17, 1991. Under
Operation Desert Storm, U.S. and allied aircraft launched a walloping aerial blitz,
first, against command, control, and communications facilities and antiaircraft
defenses in Iraq and Iraqi-occupied Kuwait and, eventually, against Iraqi ground
troops in Kuwait. Influenced by their experiences in Vietnam, the officers who
planned the assault avoided the concept of graduated escalation and attacked
on an extensive scale. On the first day alone, the Allies flew some 2,400 combat
missions, gaining complete control of the skies, inflicting immense damage, and
suffering relatively few losses. They also exploited their overwhelming technical superiority in airpower against a large ground army with antiquated equipment positioned in a desert environment with few hiding places. Moreover, the
U.S. Air Force took a very broad interpretation of its mission, attacking not only
military targets but also state power assets, the loss of which would reduce Iraq's
long-term regional influence and Hussein's hold on power. Although U.S. war

planners realized that ground operations would be necessary to liberate Kuwait, they calculated that the air assault would minimize the duration and the U.S. casualty rate of a ground campaign. These operations garnered the approval of more than 80 percent of the American people, according to Gallup polls, a level of support that would remain steady through the end of hostilities.[30]

Iraq's military proved incapable of offering significant resistance to the onslaught. Its army faced substantial institutional weaknesses. A cultural gap divided the Sunni-dominated officer corps and the Shiite-dominated enlisted ranks. To ward off potential revolts, Hussein's state security apparatus had long interfered with the army's command structure and its operational units, which had eroded the competence of the officer corps and morale and cohesion across all ranks. Nor was there much coordination between air and ground units. Not having realized that the U.S. military had become a professional force since the 1970s, moreover, Hussein falsely expected the American military to sputter under the problems of fragmentation and demoralization that had burdened it in the Vietnam era. He resisted the air attack by launching Scud missiles against Allied positions in Saudi Arabia, Bahrain, and Qatar, as well as against Israel; although most missed their targets, one Scud hit a U.S. base in Saudi Arabia, killing 27 GIs. Hussein also tried to stymie the assault by occupying the Saudi border town of Khafji in late January, but U.S. Marines supported by airpower quickly repulsed that move. Apparently, the threat of U.S. nuclear retaliation convinced Hussein not to use his WMD against U.S. or allied forces.[31]

The Scud missile attacks on Israel briefly threatened to change the course of war. Iraq fired the missiles, beginning on January 18 and continuing for several days, in hope of provoking an Israeli response that would splinter the U.S. partnership with other Arab states. Indeed, the attacks enraged Israeli leaders. Citing Israel's security doctrine of launching reprisals for assaults on its people, Prime Minister Yitzhak Shamir indicated his intent to retaliate against Scud launching sites in western Iraq. Secretary of Defense Richard Cheney advised Bush to unleash Israel, but Chairman of the Joint Chiefs of Staff General Colin Powell reasoned that "if we were going to preserve the Arab end of the coalition, we had to keep the Israelis out of this fight." Scowcroft prevailed on the president to restrain Israel by "deconfliction," meaning withholding identification codes that Israeli pilots would need to traverse the war zone safely. To ease the pressure, Bush also dispatched Patriot missile batteries to Israel to defend against Scuds, diverted U.S. soldiers and aircraft to western Iraq to root out Scud sites, dispatched Deputy Secretary of State Lawrence Eagleburger to Jerusalem "to hold the Israeli hand," and signaled Iraq that any use of WMD would invite a massive retaliation in kind. "There is a limit to Israeli restraint," Eagleburger cabled at one tense moment, "and we are close to it." But the leash held, and Hussein's ploy to fracture the alliance failed.[32]

Soviet Premier Mikhail Gorbachev also posed a wartime diplomatic challenge to Bush by adopting the role of peace broker. Apparently upset by U.S. air attacks on Baghdad and perhaps seeking to burnish his faltering reputation as a world leader, Gorbachev in late January proposed a deal including a ceasefire, an Iraqi withdrawal from Kuwait, and negotiations on the issue of Palestine. Bothered by the prospect of Hussein keeping his army intact, Bush immediately rejected these terms as inconsistent with the U.N. resolutions demanding unconditional withdrawal. Then Gorbachev, on February 15, convinced Hussein to accept U.N. Resolution 660, but the Iraqi leader added certain conditions pertaining to a ceasefire, an American withdrawal, revocation of other U.N. resolutions, and Israeli policy. Bush promptly rejected these terms as well, calling Hussein's offer "a cruel hoax" that raised but then spoiled the hopes of his own people for peace. In light of the steady erosion of Soviet power and decline of Cold War tensions, Bush felt confident disregarding Soviet wishes.[33]

As the air war and the Soviet-inspired diplomacy unfolded, Bush came to the conclusion that he must launch a ground war to finish the task at hand. Many of Bush's top advisers, including Pentagon officers, had identified several perils in a ground war, including substantial casualties, the prospect of facing Iraqi CW, and political fallout from attacking an Arab state. But Bush reasoned that if he allowed Hussein to save his army then Iraq would remain a menace to its neighbors far into the future, longer than the United States could afford to contain it. "We had to act now," Scowcroft later wrote, "while we were mobilized and in place." Hussein's brazen aggression and diplomatic audacity, together with reports of Iraqi atrocities against Kuwaitis and environmental depredation caused by Iraq's massive release of oil into the Gulf, further convinced Bush that

Photo 4-5
U.S. Marines from Company D, 2nd Tank Battalion, drive their M-60A1 tank with M-9 dozer kit through a sand berm while practicing for Operation Desert Storm on January 25, 1991.
SOURCE: DoD photo by Staff Sgt. M. D. Masters.

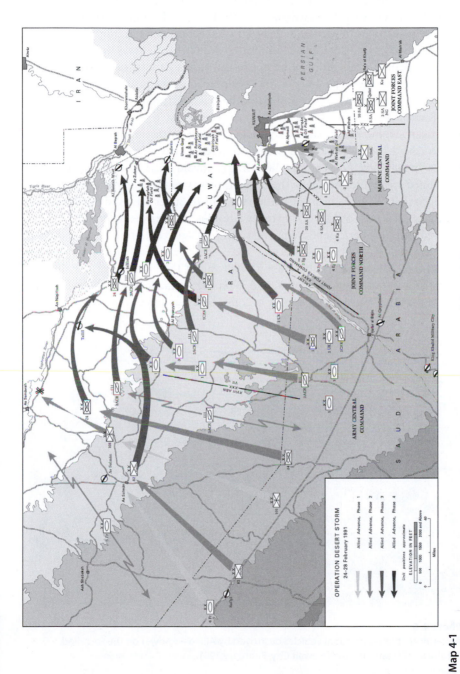

Map 4-1

A Pentagon map depicting ground offensives against Iraq and Iraq-occupied Kuwait in Operation Desert Storm, February 24–28, 1991. SOURCE: U.S. Army Center of Military History.

Hussein deserved little mercy. On February 21, Hussein offered to withdraw from Kuwait if the United States ceased its aerial attacks. But Bush responded the next day by issuing an ultimatum that Iraq must leave Kuwait within 24 hours.[34]

The February 22 ultimatum triggered the final phase of the war. Hussein failed to comply with U.S. demands, so Bush ordered a major ground assault against Iraqi troops in Kuwait on February 23 (February 24 in Iraq). Flanked by Arab forces, U.S. Marines invaded Kuwait, while the U.S. Army and the ground forces of Britain and France raced north and then east into southern Iraq in a flanking maneuver. The Iraqi army collapsed quickly in death, retreat, and surrender; the Allied powers destroyed the bulk of Iraqi armor and artillery; and Kuwait was liberated in a combat phase that lasted exactly 100 hours. As American airpower decimated Iraqi units heading north from Kuwait City—on the so-called "highway of death"—Bush ordered a provisional cessation of hostilities on February 27 (February 28 in Iraq) to avoid criticism in the media that he abetted a slaughter, although the Iraqi army was neither completely destroyed nor encircled. With the help of its allies, the United States achieved the liberation of Kuwait at a cost of 148 U.S. combat fatalities. At war's end, President Bush enjoyed a stratospheric public approval rating of 89 percent, the highest such rate ever detected in a Gallup poll.[35]

The rapid success in liberating Kuwait raised the prospect of pressing on with the war, occupying Baghdad, and deposing Hussein. Some observers suggested that Hussein posed a danger as long as he remained in power, given his

Photo 4-6
Aerial view of retreating Iraqi vehicles destroyed by Allied air power on the so-called "Highway of Death" north of Kuwait City, February 1991. SOURCE: *Gulf War Air Power Survey.* Volume II, Part I: *Operations.*

Photo 4-7
Kuwaiti civilians and coalition soldiers wave Kuwaiti and Saudi flags to celebrate the evacuation of Kuwait by Iraqi forces. SOURCE: DoD photo by CW02 Bailey.

aggressiveness, CW, nuclear research, missiles, and army. But Bush decided not to advance, later explaining,

> I firmly believed that we should not march into Baghdad. Our stated mission, as codified in UN resolutions, was a simple one—end the aggression, knock Iraq's forces out of Kuwait, and restore Kuwait's leaders. To occupy Iraq would instantly shatter our coalition, turning the whole Arab world against us, and make a broken tyrant into a latter-day Arab hero. It would have taken us way beyond the imprimatur of international law bestowed by the resolutions of the Security Council, assigning young soldiers to a fruitless hunt for a securely entrenched dictator and condemning them to fight in what would be an unwinnable urban guerrilla war. It could only plunge that part of the world into even greater instability and destroy the credibility we were working so hard to reestablish.

The president's "absolutely correct judgment," Baker added, was "enthusiastically endorsed by the military, our coalition partners, the Congress, and American public opinion." "It is naïve...to think," Colin Powell later explained, "that if Hussein had fallen, he would necessarily have been replaced by a Jeffersonian in some sort of desert democracy where people read *The Federalist Papers* along with the Koran. Quite possibly, we would have wound up with a Saddam by another name." Bush calculated that the best long-term plan was to stay out of Iraq, preserve the anti-Hussein coalition, promote Arab–Israeli peace, and contain a chastened Iraq through sanctions and U.N. diplomacy.[36]

AFTERMATH OF THE LIBERATION OF KUWAIT

The rapid success of the operations to liberate Kuwait and punish the Iraqi military triggered euphoria in the United States. Yet subsequent events soon caused many to reconsider the wisdom of Bush's decision to terminate offensive operations. Within months of the ceasefire, Hussein was able to restore the prowess of his elite Republican Guard units to a greater extent than U.S. officials had predicted. Worse, Hussein mercilessly crushed uprisings among the Kurds of northern Iraq and the Shiites of the south, in the process reinvigorating his stature among Iraq's minority (but politically dominant) Sunni community. Because certain statements and policies of the Bush administration seemed to associate the United States with the rebellions, pressure mounted on the U.S. president to intervene militarily in Iraq on behalf of the rebels. But Bush resisted such a move.

The cessation of hostilities soon gave way to a number of problems on the ground. In a meeting with Iraqi officers at Safwan Airbase on March 3, 1991, General H. Norman Schwarzkopf Jr. imposed terms for a permanent ceasefire, including establishing a demilitarized zone, halting missile attacks, revealing minefields, and releasing prisoners. He also gave assurances that the United States had no intention of permanently occupying Iraq. When an Iraqi officer, citing the poor quality of his country's roads, asked for permission to fly helicopters over Iraqi territory, Schwarzkopf conceded, provided they did not threaten U.S. forces. The general's spontaneous concession on the helicopters issue would prove to be a major blunder with tragic consequences.[37]

It appears that President Bush also committed a second major postwar blunder that caused grim fallout. Apparently hoping to trigger a coup against Hussein from within Iraq's Sunni majority, Bush in mid-February urged Iraqis "to take matters into their own hands, to force Saddam Hussein, the dictator, to step aside." Bush and Secretary of State Baker also issued subtle statements designed to prompt a rebellion among Iraqi army officers who felt frustrated by the debacle they had experienced during the war. "While we had been careful not to embrace it as a war aim or a political aim," Baker later recorded, "our

Map 4-2

This map depicts areas of Iraq predominantly inhabited by Kurds and Shias and briefly under open rebellion by those groups against Saddam Hussein's Sunni-dominated government in Baghdad.

administration had made it publicly clear for some time that we would shed no tears if Saddam were overthrown."[38]

This U.S. gambit backfired badly, however, as rebellions erupted among the Shiite and Kurdish communities rather than the Sunni elite or army officers. The Shiite people of southern Iraq murdered prominent Baathists and seized authority in several southern cities and towns. The Kurds of northern Iraq took control of most of Kurdistan. Although the Shiite rebellion was probably a spontaneous outburst against Sunni domination, aggravated by wartime dislocations, and although the Kurdish revolt reflected an aged struggle in northern Iraq, the timing of Bush's call to the Iraqi people created a firm impression in public thinking that the United States had stimulated the uprisings.[39]

Tragically, the Hussein government methodically crushed the Shiite and Kurdish rebellions. Exploiting the spontaneous concession by General Schwarzkopf, Iraqi security forces used helicopters to deliver firepower on the rebels. The results were brutal: some 350,000 Shiites and Kurds were killed and millions were displaced by the fighting. Hussein's successes against the rebel groups helped him consolidate his position among his Sunni political base and thereby removed the prospects of an internal coup. To the extent that Bush had prompted the uprisings and that Schwarzkopf had enabled the Hussein regime to suppress them, the Bush administration, albeit unintentionally, had abetted a nasty situation in which multitudes of anti-Hussein Iraqis perished while Hussein consolidated his hold on power.[40]

The situation in Iraq confronted President Bush with a quandary. Critics suggested that he had provoked the uprisings and then heartlessly stood back while the Iraqi government suppressed them. Some public pressure mounted in favor of U.S. military intervention in the situation both for moral reasons (to rescue those who seemingly had rebelled under U.S. prodding) and for security reasons (to check the resurgent power of Hussein). Bush, however, promptly dismissed such ideas. Although moved by the tragedy of the rebellions, he reasoned, U.S. involvement would entail "incalculable human and political costs." Empowering the Kurds would anger Turkey, assisting the Shiites would embolden Iran and anger Saudi Arabia, dividing Iraq into three states would upset the delicate balance of power in the Gulf region, and taking any action would cost American lives. The United States also lacked legal sanction to intervene in an Iraqi internal conflict. According to a Gallup poll of April 1991, only 29 percent of the American people favored resumption of ground operations to rescue the Shiite and Kurdish rebels and a majority opposed such action.[41]

CONCLUSION

The Gulf War of 1990–1991 proved to be a bittersweet experience for President Bush. Having mobilized an international military and political coalition with consummate diplomatic skill, he achieved a rapid and overwhelming military victory against an adversary who commanded a sizeable military force arrayed in a defensive position. Under Bush's direction, the United States and its partners ensured the defense of Saudi Arabia, liberated Kuwait, and inflicted widespread destruction on the Iraqi military at relatively low costs. Bush failed to achieve, however, his implied goal of sharply curtailing Hussein's domestic political stature if not ousting him from power. Beset by a variety of domestic problems, moreover, Bush also lost his own bid for reelection as president in 1992.

Bush's overall record toward Iraq was imperfect but generally positive. The administration's initial approach of trying to channel Iraq into a cooperative relationship through friendly gestures ended abruptly and unsuccessfully when Hussein attacked Kuwait in August 1990. Granted, few other viable options existed for managing Hussein's regime in the aftermath of the Iran–Iraq War, and a policy of firmness might have enjoyed little success. That said, the U.S. government's hope of winning over Hussein through accommodation—a policy that required ignoring his abysmal human rights and foreign policy records— proved futile.

Bush deserves acclaim, by contrast, for his carefully measured response to the invasion of Kuwait. He skillfully assembled an international coalition of nations to resist the conquest, secured the confidence of the initially reluctant American people and Congress, and led a military operation that achieved its goal of liberating Kuwait at relatively minimal cost to the victorious alliance. General Schwarzkopf's spontaneous blunder at the Safwan conference and President Bush's call for a coup without adequate consideration of the possible unintended consequences constituted two blemishes at the tail end of what had been a storied wartime performance by the administration in Washington and the American and allied militaries.

Bush's decisions to refrain from invading Iraq after liberating Kuwait and from intervening in the Iraqi postwar insurrections remained controversial after the war. Many elite editorial writers affirmed Bush's restraint in the immediate aftermath of war. "Continuing the war would have been seen by the world, with reason, as a pointless snuffing out of lives," *Time* editorialized. "Critics may argue that the same Iraqi soldiers who were spared went on to slaughter anti-Saddam rebels. But on balance the decision to stop the bloodshed the moment victory was assured was right—and very American." But public opinion proved more fickle: whereas 55 percent of Americans consulted by the Gallup poll in March 1991 considered the war a victory, only 36 percent expressed that assessment 1 month later and a mere 25 percent remained favorable in August 1992.[42]

Over the subsequent years, critics and defenders of Bush's decisions voiced their interpretations in light of the twists and turns in the U.S.–Iraqi relationship under Bush's successors in the Oval Office and in reference to the latter-day policies toward Iraq that they advocated or opposed. Some observers affirmed the prudence of Bush's reliance on international cooperation to contain Iraq even as Hussein remained in power. Others came to believe, in light of evidence of a re-emergent Iraqi menace, that Bush had fumbled a golden opportunity to remove Hussein from power while he had a major military force on a forward march and within reach of Baghdad. A final verdict on the wisdom of Bush's decision to leave Hussein in power ultimately would be tied to assessments of the subsequent decisions of President George W. Bush (son of George H. W. Bush) to remove Hussein through a military invasion in 2003. In the immediate term, however, the elder President Bush's decision to halt operations with the liberation of Kuwait was clearly reasonable and sound given the international context in early 1991.

Hussein's display of power in crushing the Shiite and Kurdish rebellions in 1991 made clear that he remained a power to be reckoned with despite the military defeat inflicted upon him during Operation Desert Storm. Other signs soon followed that Iraq would need attention for some time to come. Although reluctant to become involved in Iraqi internal politics, U.S. officials soon realized that they would not be able to disengage from Iraq or from its neighborhood.

NOTES

1. Department of State, "Women in Diplomacy," November 2007, http://www.state. gov/s/d/rm/rls/perfrpt/2007/html/98610.htm/ (accessed June 16, 2010).
2. The Iraqi transcript was acquired by ABC News, which translated it from Arabic into English and shared it with *New York Times*, which published it on September 23, 1990. The document also appears in Sifry and Cerf, *Gulf War Reader*, 122–33. See also Bruce W. Nelan et al., "Who Lost Kuwait?", *Time*, October 1, 1990, http://www.time. com/time/magazine/article/0,9171,971291,00.html/ (accessed June 16, 2010).
3. Christopher Ogden, "In from the Cold," *Time*, April 1, 1991, http://www.time. com/time/magazine/article/0,9171,972631,00.html/ (accessed June 16, 2010) (quotation); Jentleson, *With Friends Like These*, 169–76.
4. Glaspie to State Department, July 25, 1990, http://www.margaretthatcher.org/docum ent/0DFD0DDB2BA34EF59F2570CE7EEE03C8.pdf/ (accessed June 16, 2010). As late as 2008, Glaspie continued to maintain that she had warned Hussein to "keep your hands off this country." "Ex-Envoy Details Hussein Meeting," *The Washington Post*, April 3, 2008, http://www.washingtonpost.com/wp-dyn/content/article/2008/04/02/ AR2008040203485_pf.html/ (accesssed March 17, 2008).
5. Miller and Mylroie, *Saddam Hussein*, 126–38; Tripp, *History of Iraq*, 248–53; Dawisha, *Political History*, 225–26; Baram, "Iraqi Invasion," 7–8.
6. Rubin, "United States and Iraq," 259 (quotation); Baram, "Iraqi Invasion," 5–15; Lesch, *Arab–Israeli Conflict*, 320–21; Freedman, *Choice of Enemies*, 213–14; Tripp, *History of Iraq*, 248–53.
7. Jentleson, *With Friends Like These*, 105–27; Carus, *Ballistic Missiles*, 12–16.
8. Baker, *Politics of Diplomacy*, 261–67 (quotation 263); Bush and Scowcroft, *World Transformed*, 305–7; Jentleson, *With Friends Like These*, 95–105.
9. Baker, *Politics of Diplomacy*, 264–67 (quotation 267); Baram, "U.S. Input," 332.
10. Baker, *Politics of Diplomacy*, 267–71; Jentleson, *With Friends Like These*, 139–54; Miller and Mylroie, *Saddam Hussein*, 13–14.
11. Speech by Hussein, April 2, 1990, FBIS-NES-90–064, Daily Report, April 3, 1990, 32–36 (quotation); Baker, *Politics of Diplomacy*, 267–71; Jentleson, *With Friends Like These*, 154–6 (quotations 155, 156–57); Bush and Scowcroft, *World Transformed*, 307–8.
12. Jentleson, *With Friends Like These*, 164–66.

13. Baker, *Politics of Diplomacy*, 267–71; Jentleson, *With Friends Like These*, 157–62 (quotation 161).

14. Baker, *Politics of Diplomacy*, 271–74 (quotation 271); Khadduri and Ghareeb, *War in the Gulf*, 79–88; Jentleson, *With Friends Like These*, 168.

15. Baker, *Politics of Diplomacy*, 271–73 (quotation 272); Bush and Scowcroft, *World Transformed*, 309–13; Freedman and Karsh, *Gulf Conflict*, 42–61.

16. Glenn Frankel, "How Lines in the Sand in 1922 Sketched the Invasion of 1990," *Washington Post National Weekly Edition*, September 10–16, 1990, 16 (quotation); Freedman, *Choice of Enemies*, 216–17; Baram, "U.S. Input," 341–47; Baram, "Iraqi Invasion," 25–28; Rubin, "United States and Iraq," 261–63; Palmer, *Guardians of the Gulf*, 163–74.

17. Baker, *Politics of Diplomacy*, 271–74 (quotation 272); Jentleson, *With Friends Like These*, 139–45; Baram, "U.S. Input," 327.

18. Minutes of NSC meeting, August 3, 1990, http://www.margaretthatcher.org/document/110701/ (accessed November 11, 2010). Bush and Scowcroft, *World Transformed*, 335; Francona, *Ally to Adversary*, 55–67.

19. Minutes of NSC meeting, August 3, 1990, http://www.margaretthatcher.org/document/110701 (accessed November 11, 2010).

20. Thatcher, *Downing Street Years*, 817; minutes of NSC meeting, August 3, 1990, http://www.margaretthatcher.org/document/110701/ (accessed November 11, 2010).

21. Klare, *Rogue States*, 33–34, 38–41; Hahn, "Grand Strategy," 200–212.

22. Minutes of NSC meeting, August 3, 1990, http://www.margaretthatcher.org/document/110701/ (accessed November 11, 2010); *Gallup Poll Monthly*, August 1990.

23. Bush and Scowcroft, *World Transformed*, 313–24; *Gallup Poll Monthly*, August 1990.

24. Hume, *United Nations, Iran, and Iraq*, 193–95 (quotations 193, 194); Abdullah, *Short History of Iraq*, 193.

25. Greene, *Presidency of George Bush*, 116–17, 124–25 (quotations 117, 125); Bush and Scowcroft, *World Transformed*, 324–48 (quotation 333); Bruce W. Nelan, "Planes against Brawn," *Time*, August 20, 1990 (quotation); U.N. Security Council Resolution 660, August 2, 1990, U.N. Security Council Resolution 664, August 18, 1990, U.N. Security Council Resolution 665, August 25, 1990, http://www.un.org/Docs/scres/1990/scres90.htm/ (accessed March 31, 2008).

26. Hume, *United Nations, Iran, and Iraq*, 200 (quotation); Lesch, *Arab–Israeli Conflict*, 319–23; Baram, "Iraqi Invasion," 26–28; Bush speech to Congress, September 11, 1990, http://millercenter.org/scripps/archive/speeches/detail/3425/ (accessed March 21, 2009).

27. *Gallup Poll Monthly*, November 1990; Morris, "1990."

28. Baker, *Politics of Diplomacy*, 325–28 (quotation 327); Powell, *My American Journey*, 475–89; *Gallup Poll Monthly*, December 1990.

29. Baker, *Politics of Diplomacy*, 355–65 (quotation 363); Kaufman, *Arab Middle East*, 161 (quotation); Bush and Scowcroft, *World Transformed*, 377–83, 442–49; *Gallup Poll Monthly*, January 1991.

30. Bush and Scowcroft, *World Transformed*, 461; Baker, *Politics of Diplomacy*, 382–95; Atkinson, *Crusade*, 244–53; Freedman, *Choice of Enemies*, 235–39; *Gallup Poll Monthly*, February 1991.

31. Freedman and Karsh, *Gulf Conflict*, 299–330; Heller, "Iraq's Army," 38–46; Freedman, *Choice of Enemies*, 245.

32. Powell, *My American Journey*, 511–12 (quotation 511); Bush and Scowcroft, *World Transformed*, 451–57 (quotation 453); Baker, *Politics of Diplomacy*, 385–90 (quotation 388); Freedman and Karsh, *Gulf Conflict*, 331–41.

33. Bush and Scowcroft, *World Transformed*, 460–61, 468–77 (quotation 472); Baker, *Politics of Diplomacy*, 396–410.

34. Bush and Scowcroft, *World Transformed*, 477–79 (quotation 478); Palmer, *Guardians of the Gulf*, 224–27; Francona, *Ally to Adversary*, 91–96, 132–34.

35. Bush and Scowcroft, *World Transformed*, 478–87; Freedman and Karsh, *Gulf Conflict*, 386–409; Atkinson, *Crusade*, 469–87; *Gallup Poll Monthly*, March 1991.

36. Bush and Scowcroft, *World Transformed*, 464; Baker, *Politics of Diplomacy*, 435–38; quotations 436, 435); Powell, *My American Journey*, 524–28 (quotation 525).

37. Francona, *Ally to Adversary*, 147–57; Atkinson, *Crusade*, 5–10.

38. Atkinson, *Crusade*, 488; Baker, *Politics of Diplomacy*, 438–41.

39. Bengio, "Iraq's Shia and Kurdish Communities," 53–63; "Who Are the Kurds?" *Time*, April 15, 1991.

40. Farouk-Sluglett and Sluglett, *Iraq since 1958*, 288–90; Kaufman, *Arab Middle East*, 167–68; Freedman, *Choice of Enemies*, 252.

41. Bush and Scowcroft, *World Transformed*, 488–92 (quotation 489); Baker, *Politics of Diplomacy*, 438–42; *Gallup Poll Monthly*, April 1991.

42. "Schwarzkopf's 100 Hours: Too Few?," *Time*, April 8, 1991; *Gallup Poll Monthly*, August 1992.

CHAPTER 5

The Enduring Menace of Saddam Hussein

U.S. Containment of Iraq in the 1990s

A U.S. Air Force pilot, known by the nickname "Loose," was conducting a routine patrol over northern Iraq in late 1999 when three Iraqi missiles were fired at his F-15E Strike Eagle fighter. The 25-year-old pilot outran the missiles and then retaliated for the attack by dropping two 500-pound bombs on Iraqi targets. The battle represented the sporadic warfare that had developed between the United States and Iraq in the airspace over northern and southern Iraq during the decade after the Gulf War ended in early 1991. "People can say this is a low-intensity conflict," Loose told a *Time* reporter, "but I can tell you that having somebody shoot at me definitely makes me feel like I'm at war. And I guarantee that the people I dropped bombs on feel they are at war."[1]

Loose's mission was a small part of a massive aerial operation known as Operation Northern Watch. Originating in 1991, the enterprise involved U.S., British, and French warplanes based at the U.S. airfield at Incirlik, Turkey, flying over Iraqi territory north of the 36th parallel for the purpose of protecting the Kurdish people of northern Iraq from the Iraqi military. By the time Operation Northern Watch was terminated in March 2003, more than 200,000 sorties had been flown from Incirlik and hundreds of Iraqi command and communications posts and antiaircraft batteries had been destroyed. U.S. and British warplanes based on carriers and in Saudi Arabia also conducted Operation Southern Watch, a similar strategic program designed to protect the Iraqi Shiites living south of the 31st (eventually 33rd) parallel. Some 153,000 sorties were flown in the south from 1992 to 2003. Although Iraqi Premier Saddam Hussein reportedly offered a $14,000 bounty to any Iraqi soldier who downed an enemy aircraft, not a single Western airplane was lost to Iraqi gunfire in more than 11 years of operations.[2]

Operations Northern Watch and Southern Watch were vital parts of a multifaceted U.S. strategy for dealing with the defeated but still viable regime of Saddam Hussein after the Gulf War of 1990–1991. The presidential administrations of George H. W. Bush, who won the Gulf War, and William J. Clinton, who defeated Bush in the 1992 election, consecutively sought to neutralize Iraq

Photo 5-1
A U.S. Air Force F-15C Eagle, like the one flown by "Loose," on a routine patrol over northern Iraq on December 30, 1998. SOURCE: DoD photo by Staff Sgt. Vince Parker, U.S. Air Force.

by formulating a diverse containment policy. In addition to aerial patrols and combat strikes, they used financial sanctions, political pressures, and intrusive arms inspections to contain the Hussein regime. While confronting other major foreign policy challenges such as transitioning to post-Cold War relations with Russia and promoting the Arab–Israeli peace process, both presidents essentially hoped to keep Hussein in check until his capacity and inclination for trouble-making eroded. This chapter will illustrate how their mission enjoyed short-term success but also failed to resolve the Iraq puzzle definitively.

THE POSTWAR POLICY OF THE
BUSH ADMINISTRATION

The Bush Administration carefully assessed its options in Iraq in the months following the Gulf War. President Bush remained thoroughly opposed to a prospective march to Baghdad to overthrow Hussein because such a move would fragment the international political coalition that had won the war, galvanize political support for Hussein within Iraq, generate criticism at home, and subject U.S. soldiers to significant risks. The Bush Administration also hoped to avoid any fragmentation of Iraq among its Sunni, Shiite, and Kurdish populations. Kurdish separatism would bother Turkey, a U.S. ally, given political sensitivities around that country's own Kurdish minority. The Shiite majority of Iraq seemed prone to ideological if not political alliance with the unfriendly theocratic regime in Iran. Once Hussein brutally suppressed the Shiite and Kurdish rebellions of 1991, the Bush Administration accepted the need to deal directly with his re-emergent regime.

The Bush Administration's policy toward Iraq was formulated in the context of its adjustments to U.S. grand strategy in the aftermath of the Cold War. While updating a standard strategic plan known as the Defense Planning Guidance document in 1992–1993, Pentagon officials postulated that in the post-Cold War era the United States should seek to maintain preponderant military power, nuclear and technological superiority, and the ability to project military strength into various regions of the world. The United States should build international coalitions to "preclude hostile nondemocratic powers from dominating regions critical to our interests and otherwise work to build an international environment conducive to our values," and it also should prepare to deal with threats unilaterally if necessary.[3]

Pentagon strategists named Iraq as a potential, future threat to the regional defense strategy. In the Middle East, they noted, "we should seek to foster regional stability, deter aggression against our friends and interests in the region, protect U.S. nationals and property, and safeguard our access to international air and seaways and to the region's important sources of oil . . . . Some near-term dangers are alleviated with the defeat of Iraqi forces, but we must recognize that regional dynamics can change and a rejuvenated Iraq or a rearmed Iran could move in this decade to dominate the Gulf and its resources. We must remain prepared to act decisively in the Middle East/Persian Gulf region as we did in Operations Desert Shield and Desert Storm if our vital interests there are threatened anew." Pentagon officials also hoped to promote Arab–Israeli peace and to protect friendly regimes from "terrorism, insurgency, and subversion."[4]

Given the failure of the effort to provoke a suitable internal rebellion and in line with the regional defense strategy, the Bush Administration concocted a long-term policy to contain the Saddam Hussein regime. The goal, Secretary of State Baker later wrote, was to "put Saddam Hussein in [a] cage." U.S. leaders also calculated that an intensive effort to promote Arab–Israeli peace, manifest in the Madrid Conference organized by the United States in October 1991, would stabilize the Middle East and thus reduce Hussein's opportunities to make mischief. They also hoped that the collapse of the Soviet Union and the abatement of Cold War tensions would open a new era of international stability and leave Iraq without a patron among the great powers.[5]

The U.S. containment of Iraq rested on three foundations. First, the Bush Administration promoted an international understanding that the financial sanctions enforced against Iraq under the authority of U.N. Security Council Resolution 661 of August 1990 would remain in effect until Hussein complied with all U.N. resolutions. Second and related, the United States demanded that Iraq adhere to all terms of U.N. Security Council Resolution 687, which insisted that Iraq eliminate its WMD, recognize Kuwait, release prisoners of war, and accept financial responsibility for damages caused by its invasion of Kuwait. The Bush Administration promoted the principle that Iraq must submit to inspections by the International Atomic Energy Agency and the newly created U.N. Special Commission (UNSCOM) to verify destruction of Iraq's WMD capabilities and its ballistic missiles with ranges of more than 150 kilometers. "This was not arms control," Charles Duelfer, who served in 1992–1998 as deputy executive chairman of UNSCOM, later observed. "This was coercive disarmament, like the Treaty of Versailles imposed on Germany after World War I." Gallup polls conducted in the summer of 1991 revealed majority support among U.S. citizens for rigorous financial sanctions on Iraq and for the renewal of military operations against Iraq if Hussein defied the disarmament provisions of U.N. resolutions.[6]

Third, the Bush Administration adopted a policy of providing a sanctuary to the Kurds, some 1.5 million of whom had become refugees to Iran and Turkey by early 1991. On a personal visit to the Turkey–Iraq border in April 1991, Secretary of State Baker observed tens of thousands of Kurdish refugees clustering in abysmal conditions along the mountainous frontier. Moved by their suffering and their testimony about Iraqi atrocities, Baker immediately arranged Operation Provide Comfort, a massive humanitarian aid program by U.S., British, and French military forces to provide more than 12,000 tons of relief supplies to some 1 million Kurds. Baker later recalled that his heart-wrenching tour "also

Photo 5-2
Under Operation Provide Comfort, a UH-60 Black Hawk helicopter delivers supplies to Kurdish refugees living in tents near Zakhu in northern Iraq in April 1991. SOURCE: DoD photo by LCDR Skip Burdon.

galvanized me into pressing for a new policy, announced by the President on April 16, of establishing safe havens for Kurds in northern Iraq—refugee camps secured by U.S. forces and administered by the United Nations." With its humanitarian purpose, Operation Provide Comfort enjoyed widespread, tacit support from U.N. member states.[7]

Operation Provide Comfort formed the foundation of an enduring U.S. commitment to protect Kurds from Iraqi government assaults. After an Iraqi helicopter attack on Kurds in April 1991, the United States, Britain, and France declared that some 19,000 square miles of Iraq—all territory north of the 36th parallel—was off limits to Iraqi aircraft and that the Western allies would enforce this so-called "no-fly zone" policy with warplanes based at Incirlik, Turkey. The Western powers declared that their authority to act was invested in U.N. Security Council Resolution 688, which prohibited Iraq from harming its own people. That legal claim was endorsed by Boutros Boutros-Ghali, U.N. Secretary-General in 1992–1997, although it was gradually questioned by such countries as Russia and even France, which withdrew from the operation in 1997 on the grounds that the mission had lost its humanitarian purpose. Eventually dubbed Operation Northern Watch, the air initiative continued until the eve of the U.S. invasion of Iraq in 2003.[8]

The Bush Administration also eventually established a southern no-fly zone to contain Hussein's power and protect Iraqi Shiites. To avoid fracturing the country or enhancing Iranian interests, Bush had initially refrained from contesting Baghdad's suppression of the Shiite uprising. In August 1992, however, he declared that U.S. aircraft would enforce a second no-fly zone, south of the 31st parallel, to ensure that Iraqi air power neither harmed Shiite communities nor threatened the territorial security of Kuwait. National Security Advisor Brent Scowcroft asserted that the operation was designed "to protect minority groups, . . . not to cause or encourage the split-up of Iraq." Kuwait openly endorsed the initiative and Saudi Arabia and Bahrain quietly supported it, although Morocco, Egypt, and Syria criticized the operation on the grounds that it would encourage Shiite extremists and separatists.[9]

Not surprisingly, Saddam Hussein resisted the containment devices that the United States arrayed against him. In September 1992, Western warplanes first intercepted Iraqi aircraft in both no-fly zones. By December, Iraqi and Western warplanes engaged in a cat-and-mouse game—called "cheat and retreat" by U.S. military officers in the area—in which Iraqi aircraft flew quickly in and out of the zones to defy the restrictions and test Western resolve while minimizing risk. An American F-16 downed one such Iraqi airplane on December 27. Iraq positioned surface-to-air missiles in the southern no-fly zone, although it later withdrew them under a multilateral ultimatum threatening military action. In addition, Iraq raided northern Kuwait to capture Silkworm missiles left over from the Gulf War and under U.N. guard. Hussein's political motives were to win the political support of his own people and to keep his military busy fighting foreign adversaries rather than plotting against him.[10]

Map 5-1
This Air Force map shows the "no-fly" zones of Iraq, which covered territory north of 36 degrees north latitude and south of 33 degrees north latitude. Allied aircraft routinely patrolled those zones to protect their Kurdish and Shiite residents—as well as such neighboring countries as Kuwait—from abuse by the Iraqi government. SOURCE: U.S. Air Force Graphic.

Photo 5-3
General Henry Hugh Shelton, chairman of the Joint Chiefs of Staff, dines with soldiers while visiting Ali Al Salem Air Base in northern Kuwait, during Operation Southern Watch, in 1998. SOURCE: DoD photo by TSGT James D. Mossman, U.S. Air Force.

Concerned by the mounting Iraqi resistance, President Bush ordered a major retaliatory strike against Iraq during the final week of his term. On January 13–17, 1993, more than 100 U.S., British, and French warplanes pounded Iraqi command bunkers and missile sites and downed Iraqi aircraft in both no-fly zones, and 40 U.S. Cruise missiles demolished a 20-building facility near Baghdad that was believed to house Iraq's nuclear research program. Eighty percent of the U.S. public registered approval of the action. The Western forces cooperated closely in the operation, but criticism emerged worldwide, with the Chinese government and various Arab and European commentators noting that the United Nations had never approved the Western actions in the no-fly zones.[11]

It is possible that Bush's military strikes reflected his frustration with having lost his bid for reelection in November 1992. James Baker later expressed regret that the Hussein regime had outlasted the U.S. administration "that defeated him in a textbook case of diplomatic and military skill." Baker conceded that U.S. leaders underestimated Hussein's knack for survival. "In occasionally reflecting on this perverse twist of history," Baker noted, "I'm reminded of something Tariq Aziz said to me in Geneva: 'We will be here long after you're gone.' It was one of the few things he said that proved to be true."[12]

THE CLINTON APPROACH

Inaugurated in January 1993, President Bill Clinton formulated an approach to Iraq that generally affirmed the broad contours of Bush's postwar policy. He hoped, in short, to practice a policy of containing Iraq in the hope of stabilizing the situation if not achieving a diminution of tension so that his administration could concentrate on pressing foreign policy challenges involving NATO, Russia, China, and India. Thus the president formulated an elaborate containment policy featuring military, economic, and arms control techniques. As the decade passed, however, Clinton found that his multipronged approach encountered a multitude of challenges that tested its viability.

Initially, Clinton extended the containment policy founded by the Bush administration. The president calculated and his U.N. Ambassador and eventual Secretary of State Madeleine Albright later recorded that "the combination of sanctions, inspections, military pressure, and possible air strikes had placed him [Hussein] in a box." Thus the new administration embraced an overall approach of "dual containment" of Iraq and Iran. A subsidiary of the approach was to downplay the significance of Saddam Hussein to the overall security objectives of the United States. "I am not obsessed with the man . . . ," Clinton told a reporter. "If he wants different relations with the United States and the United Nations, all he has to do is change his behavior."[13]

Officials and scholars debated the wisdom of Clinton's approach to Iraq. Martin Indyk, who served Clinton as ambassador to Israel and assistant secretary of state, justified dual containment as the best means to assure the security of friendly powers in the Gulf region and to isolate the Arab–Israeli peace process from Gulf conflicts. Clinton's resolve not to "deal with the devil" in Baghdad provided an opportunity for a change of power to occur. By contrast, some scholars faulted Clinton's fundamental approach. "Dual containment [of Iraq and Iran] was in itself a poorly conceived strategy," according to the scholars William Cleveland and Martin Bunton, that "revealed a bankrupt US policy that substituted force for diplomacy . . . . Arab public opinion saw little more than an imperious superpower unilaterally deploying its vast military arsenal against an Arab country."[14]

Clinton's policy of containing Iraq came to rest on four pillars. First, Operations Northern Watch and Southern Watch grew more extensive as the 1990s passed. On several occasions, Iraqi antiaircraft units either fired upon Allied aircraft or locked on their radars. Intermittently, Allied aircraft bombed and strafed Iraqi artillery and radar stations. July–August 1993 and June 1998 witnessed concentrated U.S. assaults on Iraqi antiaircraft missiles and radars in the no-fly zones. In 1991–1999, some 280,000 sorties were launched by Allied air power in the two zones, with zero losses of aircraft, and the cost of the operations to the U.S. government rose to $1 billion per year.[15]

Second, Clinton occasionally ordered punitive airstrikes on Iraqi targets when Hussein's behavior seemed threatening. In early 1993, Kuwaiti intelligence broke up an Iraqi conspiracy to assassinate former president Bush as he toured the liberated emirate. Charging that the plot on Bush was "an attack against our country and all Americans," Clinton ordered a strike with 23 cruise missiles on

Photo 5-4
U.S. Navy EA-6B Prowler aircraft on a mission near Incirlik Air Base, Turkey, in April 2002, in support of Operation Northern Watch. SOURCE: Photograph by TSGT Cecil D. Daw Jr., USAF.

Iraqi intelligence facilities in Baghdad (delaying the action until a Saturday evening, to minimize civilian casualties). Two thirds of U.S. citizens, according to a Gallup poll, approved the assault. In October 1994, when Hussein threatened Kuwait by sending 10,000 Republican Guards toward the border, Clinton declared that "we will not allow Saddam Hussein to defy the will of the United States and the international community." The U.S. president deployed 36,000 U.S. troops and 100 aircraft to Kuwait, backed by an aircraft carrier battle group, and placed 155,000 soldiers on alert. On October 15, the U.N. Security Council endorsed these moves by passing Resolution 949, which demanded that Iraq withdraw all military forces from southern Iraq and refrain from again moving forces into that region. "Saddam got the message," Secretary of State Warren Christopher declared, "stopped dead in his tracks, and pulled back." In September 1996, Clinton ordered the bombings of Iraqi army units that approached the Kurdish town of Irbil, forcing them to retreat. He also retaliated asymmetrically by broadening the southern no-fly zone to the 33rd parallel, ordering cruise missile strikes on Iraqi military assets in the newly expanded zone, and increasing the number of U.S. troops in Kuwait from 1,200 to 3,500.[16]

Third, Clinton maintained Bush-era trade sanctions on Iraq as a means to limit its financial as well as military capacities until it complied with U.N. disarmament resolutions. Passed on August 6, 1990, days after Iraq invaded Kuwait, Security Council Resolution 661 had imposed stringent financial sanctions on Iraq, allowing only imports of medical goods and small quantities of food. Resolution 687 (April 1991) offered to lift sanctions if Iraq eliminated WMD, recognized Kuwait, and accepted financial responsibility for war damages. Although Iraq would recognize Kuwait in 1994, it remained defiant on the other terms. Previously strained by the Iran–Iraq War and the Gulf War, the Iraqi economy languished under the sanctions regime, experiencing sputtering industrial production, high inflation, stagnant business dynamics, parts shortages, and emigration of talented workers. In 1992–1999, the Iraqi gross domestic product grew from $29 billion to $31 billion, a paltry 7 percent. Deterioration of the health care system and such crucial components of the infrastructure as water and sewage treatment plants sparked a rise in disease, malnutrition, and child mortality. U.N. experts estimated that the sanctions resulted in the deaths of some 500,000 children aged five or younger.[17]

Despite these catastrophic human losses, Hussein refused to comply with the U.N. resolutions and resisted the sanctions by political means. He deftly blamed the suffering of Iraqi people and their immense loss of life on the Western powers that maintained the sanctions against his country, gaining political support at home and sympathy among other peoples in the region and even in the West. U.S. government officials counterargued that Hussein must bear the moral guilt for the suffering because of his refusal to comply with U.N. resolutions designed to safeguard the region from his aggressiveness. Hussein was probably encouraged to remain defiant, moreover, by the gradual wavering on sanctions by such powers as Russia, France, and China, which grew eager to recover or capture commercial interests in Baghdad. He was also buoyed by lax enforcement and corruption among U.N. officials that enabled him to mitigate the effects of sanctions by importing certain commodities through illicit trade routes.[18]

To redress the moral malodor surrounding sanctions, Western powers offered an Oil-for-Food program as a major loophole in the sanctions regime. As early as 1991, the United Nations had offered to allow Iraq to sell limited quantities of oil if the proceeds were used to meet the humanitarian needs of its people, but Iraq declined the offer. In April 1995, the Security Council passed Resolution 986, proposing anew the Oil-for-Food deal. This time, Hussein accepted the offer in a written agreement signed in May 1996. The first Iraqi oil exports were sold by

Map 5-2

Iraq's rich oil resources and Saddam Hussein's astute efforts to perpetuate sales of his Iraqi oil to other states created a major obstacle to U.S. efforts to enforce economic sanctions against Iraq in the 1990s. This map, produced by the Central Intelligence Agency, depicts Iraq's major oilfields and delivery infrastructure. SOURCE: Courtesy of the University of Texas Libraries, The University of Texas at Austin.

the end of that year, and the first shipments of food reached Iraq in March 1997. Managed by the United Nations, the Oil-for-Food program transferred some $28 billion in imports to Iraq by the time the program was terminated in 2003. Oil-for-Food significantly improved the quality of life for the Iraqi people.[19]

The Oil-for-Food program left U.S. officials in a quandary. Given the program's humanitarian purposes and popularity among U.N. members, the United States acquiesced in it. But parallel U.S. efforts to tighten the sanctions on imports of military items to Iraq as a condition of Oil-for-Food did not gain ground. Worse, the improvement of living conditions in Iraq shored up Hussein's political image at home, and Hussein channeled popular resentment at the remaining sanctions to those foreign powers that enforced them. Corruption in the administration of the Oil-for-Food program, including deals among Iraqi officials and U.N. administrators, frustrated U.S. officials and further weakened the solidarity behind the original sanctions initiatives. By the early 2000s, at least one scholar of the United Nations believes, mounting frustrations with the U.N. program kindled resolve in the United States to make policy in Iraq unilaterally.[20]

The fourth pillar in the Clinton Administration's containment of Iraq was a U.N.-backed system of inspections designed to ensure Iraqi disarmament. Action was based on Security Council Resolution 687 of April 1991, which provided, in addition to the ceasefire ending the Gulf War, the elimination of Iraq's WMD and its ballistic missiles with a range exceeding 150 kilometers. The resolution empowered the International Atomic Energy Agency to enforce these terms with regard to nuclear devices and it created UNSCOM to act likewise with regard to biological, chemical, and other weapons. U.N. inspectors were given authority to enter and travel freely through Iraq, to investigate suspicious facilities, and to order the destruction of weapons systems and related production facilities. As early as June 1991, UNSCOM inspectors supervised the destruction of sophisticated uranium-enrichment equipment that was at the heart of Iraq's nuclear weapons program.[21]

For several years, the inspections seemed to achieve certain disarmament goals. Inspectors clarified the extent of Hussein's WMD arsenals and verified the demolition of large stockpiles of them. In November 1993, Foreign Minister Aziz announced that Iraq would accept terms of U.N. Security Council Resolution 715, which demanded that Iraq allow UNSCOM and the International Atomic Energy Agency to establish a permanent monitoring system in Iraq. The inspection process enjoyed a windfall in 1995, when two of Hussein's sons-in-law named Hussein Kamal and Saddam Kamal defected to Jordan and divulged details of Iraq's WMD capabilities. That information enabled UNSCOM to dismantle Iraq's biological weapons facility at Al Hakam in 1996. By the mid-1990s, Albright claimed, U.N. inspectors had eliminated more Iraqi WMD capability than Iraq had lost in the Gulf War. UNSCOM inspector Charles Duelfer later claimed that for a cost of less than $5 million, UNSCOM found and dismantled "28,000 munitions, 480,000 liters of agents, 1.8 million liters of liquid chemical precursors, and a million kilograms of solid chemical precursors."[22]

The inspections process, however, was beset by problems and shortcomings. Although Iraq officially welcomed the inspectors, the Hussein government also created obstacles to their effective functioning. UNSCOM "engaged Saddam in a frustrating game of cat and mouse," Scott Ritter, another inspector, later observed, "trying to hunt down the evidence of Iraq's wrongdoing" while Iraq engaged in "systematic acts of concealment." Inspectors got into a nasty pattern of interaction with the Hussein regime from the outset, Duelfer added. Because Hussein made a series of deceptive or untrue assertions, the inspectors developed "a mind-set of perpetual disbelief." The "patterns of deceit and obfuscation produced calluses of the mind, and ultimately the true status of Iraq's WMD stocks and programs became unrecognizable and unacceptable." The inability of the inspection system to test for its own effectiveness raised the risk, which ultimately became reality, that Western officials would significantly overestimate Iraq's WMD capabilities.[23]

The inspections process also faced political trouble. In the eyes of U.S. officials, Russian and French representatives at the United Nations seemed overly eager to declare Iraq compliant so they could restore financial relations with Baghdad. Duelfer declined offers from France to help with inspections on the suspicion that French inspectors would be less than rigorous. Rumors that U.S. intelligence agencies were in communication with Americans working on UNSCOM also caused tension among U.N. members and the Secretary-General, who insisted that UNSCOM remain unaffiliated with any single power, and such rumors provided Hussein grounds for arguing the justice of his resistance. Ritter revealed in 1999 that the CIA had indeed used UNSCOM since 1991 to plot an assassination attempt and other covert activities against Hussein. (The charges have not been corroborated by documentary evidence.)[24]

Ultimately (as the next chapter will discuss), Western officials came to realize after the 2003 invasion of Iraq that Hussein's WMD program had largely atrophied by the middle or late 1990s. That discovery would raise retrospective questions about why Hussein did not simply come clean, allow inspectors to verify that he lacked WMD capacity, and thus earn the favor of the international community. The answer to this puzzle lay in the nature of Hussein's hold on power in Baghdad. Because of the culture of fear that Hussein had created among his military subordinates, in which a truthful report about declining capabilities might garner severe punishment, Hussein's advisers wildly inflated their reports about the status of Iraq's WMD programs. Moreover, Hussein believed that the image of possessing WMD earned him respect among Arab leaders and enhanced his international prestige, which would bolster his ability to achieve the end of sanctions and other foreign policy goals. Even if Hussein realized that his WMD programs were empty shells, he might have perpetuated the fiction because it resulted in political gains.[25]

The arms inspection process broke down in 1997–1998. Accusing the inspectors of serving U.S. intelligence agencies, Hussein began to interfere with inspections in 1997 and to insist on the removal of American nationals from UNSCOM. The Clinton Administration used diplomacy to pressure Hussein to resume inspections, but in early 1998 Hussein demanded that UNSCOM suspend surprise inspections and consider presidential sites off limits. After canvassing the globe, Albright claimed to find more than a dozen states, including Britain and France, grimly ready to consider military action against Baghdad. At home, a Gallup poll found a surge in support for war among Republicans but growing opposition among Democrats and independents. When Clinton tried to rally domestic public opinion to the military option, moreover, he found a ground-swell of opposition. Eventually, U.N. Secretary General Kofi Annan brokered a deal in which Hussein allowed inspections to resume on the condition that U.N.-appointed diplomats would accompany inspectors to presidential sites. The U.N. Security Council also reaffirmed that future Iraqi noncompliance might result in severe consequences.[26]

Despite the warning, Hussein unilaterally halted all UNSCOM inspections in December 1998, triggering a Western military reaction. Although he realized that the use of force would not reopen the door to inspectors, Clinton ordered a massive strike against Iraqi military facilities. In Operation Desert Fox, U.S. and British forces sent some 650 aircraft and 400 missiles to hit Iraqi assets over 4 days. Hussein's breaking of his promise to allow inspections justified the raids, Clinton explained. "Iraq has abused its final chance." Privately, the president figured that even if the raids did not demolish Iraq's WMD facilities, they at least weakened its overall war-making capabilities. According to the Gallup poll, three quarters of the American people approved Operation Desert Fox.[27]

The December 1998 airstrikes on Iraq shattered the foundations of the inspections system. "Little of consequence was destroyed on the ground," Duelfer noted later, "but the bombing killed UNSCOM and the illusion that the Security Council could implement its objectives. The council was in turmoil. There had been no vote authorizing force. Washington argued it [a vote] wasn't necessary. The Russians, French, and Chinese felt otherwise and were furious." Iraq skillfully exploited this wedge among its adversaries to arrange illicit oil exports, enjoying a hike in its revenues from $250 million in 1998 to $2.6 billion in 2001. Furthermore, the sudden removal of UNSCOM removed the eyes and ears of the West from Iraq, forcing U.S. officials to make policy devoid of knowledge about Iraqi weapons.[28]

Any hope among Americans that the mutlipronged containment policy would weaken Hussein's power in Baghdad soon proved fleeting. Despite his humiliating loss of 1991 and the negative effects of sanctions, Hussein remained firmly in control. He had built an enduring power structure based on kinship and clan ties and he did not entrust any one else with real power. He allied with leading Sunni tribes, calling them "the swords of the state," flattering tribal leaders, and deferring to conservative tribal customs by passing laws that limited alcohol, restricted the rights of women, and imposed harsh criminal penalties (such as amputation of the hands of thieves). Hussein encouraged religious symbolism and (falsely) claimed the mantle of a devout Muslim. He stoked nationalistic support by labeling the no-fly zones as an imperial Western plot to "partition the region to seize control over its oil wealth." Shiite dissident groups began to organize inside and outside Iraq but Hussein's forces suppressed them mercilessly, killing tens of thousands of real or suspected rebels. The eventual weakening of sanctions, moreover, enabled Hussein to begin accumulating wealth through oil sales. "At no time since the birth of the monarchical state of Iraq in 1921," the scholar Adeed Dawisha notes, "were fundamental values, rights, and beliefs so utterly subjugated to the dictates, quirks, and ramblings of the country's hero-president."[29]

The citizens of Iraq lived in terror of the Hussein regime. By the early 2000s, the state's elaborate security apparatus earned a reputation for ruthlessness in the smashing of all forms of dissent. It tortured, mutilated, or executed thousands of individuals for real and suspected offenses including voicing criticism of Hussein or even telling jokes about the dictator. Members of Hussein's inner circle were also known to rape detainees, including children, to prey sexually on women they encountered by chance, and to extort funds from shopkeepers and businesses. In his memoirs, former Iraqi Air Force General Georges Sada recorded one grisly example of Hussein's depraved brutality. After Dr. Raji al-Tikriti, a medical doctor and military officer, spoke disparagingly of Hussein, he was summoned to a presidential palace where, as Hussein looked on, he was kicked and stomped to death by a gang of henchmen and then eaten by a pack of dogs.[30]

Although Iraq's Kurdish minority enjoyed the protection of U.S. airpower patrolling the northern no-fly zone, they did not offer much of a threat to Hussein's rule. The community instead divided politically between the KDP led by Massoud Barzani and the PUK led by Jalal Talabani. In elections of May 1992, the KDP won 50.8 percent of the vote and the PUK 49.2 percent, leading to a divided regional government. Various Kurds asked the Clinton Administration to support a Kurdish-inspired insurrection against the regime in Baghdad, but Clinton declined, on the fear that such a move would lead to a debacle reminiscent of the Bay of Pigs. Gradually, the Kurds descended into internal strife, with KDP and PUK forces engaging in civil war in 1994–1998. The Hussein government backed the KDP, forcing the PUK to seek temporary sanctuary in Iran. By the time that U.S. officials brokered a truce between the two factions in 1998, the Kurds had been splintered by Hussein's crafty diplomacy and thus neutralized as a potential means to undermine Hussein's regime from within Iraq.[31]

By 1998, Clinton faced a conundrum in Iraq. The aerial enforcement of the no-fly zones in northern and southern Iraq, although financially costly, was effectively protecting Iraq's dissident communities and neighboring states from the perils of the Iraqi military. By contrast, the other pillars of Clinton's containment policy were teetering, as Hussein adroitly consolidated his domestic power, fractured the international alliance that had initially backed financial sanctions, and escaped the controls of the U.N.'s arms inspection system. In November, Clinton privately expressed bewilderment over the apparent irrationality in Hussein's decision to block arms inspections when complicity might have secured the end of sanctions. In a casual moment with friends on a golf course, the President vented his frustrations with the Iraqi leader by declaring "I hate that son of a bitch."[32]

Map 5-3
Political rivalries between two Kurdish political groups prevented the community from offering effective resistance to Saddam Hussein's rule in the 1990s. SOURCE: Central Intelligence Agency map, courtesy of the University of Texas Libraries, The University of Texas at Austin.

ORIGINS OF "REGIME CHANGE" IN IRAQ

As it pursued the containment of Iraq, the Clinton Administration faced mounting domestic pressure to overthrow Hussein by military or other means. Such a goal—identified in public discussion as "regime change"—grew in popularity among conservative elites and garnered growing support in American public opinion as the 1990s passed. Although President Clinton did not abandon his multilayered containment policy, he progressively embraced the prospect of taking action to rid the world of Saddam Hussein.

Public opinion polls revealed a seam of support for regime change in Iraq as early as the end of the Gulf War. When asked, "would you support or oppose having U.S. forces resume military action against Iraq to force Saddam Hussein from power?," 67 percent of those polled by Gallup in July 1992 answered in the affirmative, up from 51 percent in April 1991. When asked in January 1993 if they endorsed military means to enforce U.N. resolutions in Iraq, 59 percent of respondents indicated support for continuing military strikes until Hussein fell from power. After hearing reports that Iraq had tried to assassinate former President Bush in early 1993, 53 percent of Americans polled indicated that they would endorse an attempt to assassinate Hussein.[33]

Popular discourse about Iraq's alleged complicity in terrorist attacks fed public disdain for the Hussein regime. According to the *9/11 Report* of 2004, the Islamic extremists who planted a truck bomb in a parking garage beneath the World Trade Center in New York City in February 1993 were not linked to Iraq but were inspired by terrorist mastermind Osama bin Laden. (The bomb damaged the building and killed six people although it failed to demolish the structure as intended.) Judicial authorities arrested and prosecuted six perpetrators of the bombing, and no evidence of ties to Iraq was presented in court. The *9/11 Report* also concluded that bin Laden, intent on internationalizing his al-Qaeda network of Islamic, anti-Western terrorists, met a senior Iraqi official in Khartoum in 1994 or 1995 to request access to terrorist training grounds in Iraq, but that no evidence emerged that Iraq complied with the request. Indeed, Hussein had never shown sincere Islamist proclivities, and bin Laden eventually bolstered Ansar al-Islam, an anti-Hussein Islamist group in Kurdistan.[34]

These findings notwithstanding, conservative commentators suggested that the Hussein regime fostered anti-Western terrorism in general and fomented the 1993 World Trade Center bombing in particular. In 1995, publicist Laurie Mylroie alleged that Iraqi intelligence authorities masterminded the World Trade Center attack as well as a 1995 plot to detonate 11 U.S. passenger airliners. Mylroie's thesis that the Hussein regime perpetrated state-sponsored terrorism against the United States found a receptive audience among some policy insiders. Admiral R. James Woolsey, who served as Director of Central Intelligence in 1993–1995, revealed in October 2001 that he found Mylroie's thesis viable and that he further suspected Iraqi agents of having planned other violent attacks against the United States through the 1990s.[35]

Indeed, as the Clinton Administration pursued the containment of Iraq, a widening circle of conservative officials and analysts (eventually known popularly as the "Neocons," although it included some liberals) advocated the use of military force to effect regime change in Baghdad. Neocon influence gained some prominence after the 1994 U.S. midterm elections, in which Republicans captured control of the U.S. Congress. In contrast to such old-guard Republicans as former President Bush and former Secretary of State Baker, the new Republican congressional leaders tended to embrace conservative and evangelical ideology. Neocons sensed an opportunity to use the Republican Congress to achieve a platform for capturing the White House and for taking action against Iraq. Neocons organized the "Study Group on a New Israeli Strategy toward 2000" that provided advice to Benjamin Netanyahu, elected prime minister of Israel in 1996. In a paper entitled "A Clean Break: A New Strategy for Securing the Realm," they urged that Israel abandon the Clinton-led peace process, work with Turkey and Jordan to isolate and undermine Syria, and promote regime change in Iraq. They argued that containment of Iraq was a failure. They considered Operations Northern Watch and Southern Watch too costly, both in treasure and in casualties (in light of the deaths of 19 airmen, stationed in the Khobar Towers in Saudi Arabia in support of the operations in Iraq, in a terrorist bombing in June 1996). Containment, the Neocons argued, also left the Iraqi people in oppression and provided Osama bin Laden a rallying cause against the West.[36]

Neocons also pressured the Clinton Administration to embrace regime change as a goal in Baghdad. Eighteen prominent conservatives pressed for this policy in an open letter to Clinton released in January 1998. "We are convinced that current American policy toward Iraq is not succeeding," they wrote,

> and that we may soon face a threat in the Middle East more serious than any we have known since the end of the Cold War. In your upcoming State of the Union Address, you have an opportunity to chart a clear and determined course for meeting this threat. We urge you to seize that opportunity, and to enunciate a new strategy that would secure the interests of the U.S. and our friends and allies around the world. That strategy should aim, above all, at the removal of Saddam Hussein's regime from power. We stand ready to offer our full support in this difficult but necessary endeavor.

Clinton rejected the advice, using his State of the Union address to reiterate his commitment to dismantling Iraq's WMD capabilities but refraining from announcing a bold new strategy or promising regime change.[37]

Yet the Neocons demonstrated influence in a series of laws passed by Congress in 1998. An amendment to the 1998 Supplemental Appropriations and Rescissions Act (Public Law 105–174), passed on May 1, provided $5 million "for assistance to the Iraqi democratic opposition for such activities as organization, training, communication and dissemination of information, developing and implementing agreements among opposition groups, compiling information to support the indictment of Iraqi officials for war crimes, and for related purposes." Congress followed on August 14 with Public Law 105–235, which cataloged Hussein's violations of U.N. resolutions and resolved that "the Government of Iraq is in material and unacceptable breach of its international obligations, and therefore the President is urged to take appropriate action, in accordance with the Constitution and relevant laws of the United States, to bring Iraq into compliance with its international obligations."[38]

Such legislative pressure culminated in the passage of the Iraq Liberation Act of 1998 (Public Law 105–338). The law recalled unacceptable features of Iraqi foreign policy beginning with its invasion of Iran in 1980. "It should be the policy of the United States," the act declared, "to support efforts to remove the regime

Photo 5-5
U.S. Marine Corps General Anthony Zinni, commander in chief of Central Command,
speaking in Saudi Arabia in 1998. Zinni became an outspoken opponent of the push for
preemptive war against Iraq. SOURCE: DoD photo by TSGT James D. Mossman, U.S. Air Force.

headed by Saddam Hussein from power in Iraq and to promote the emergence of
a democratic government to replace that regime." The president was authorized
to grant Iraqi opposition groups $2 million for broadcasting programs and $97
million in military aid. The House approved this legislation by a bipartisan vote
of 360–38, the Senate affirmed it by unanimous consent, and Clinton signed it on
October 31. Although Clinton declared publicly his hope that the Hussein regime
would reform its ways and "rejoin the family of nations," he also expressed the
belief that "the evidence is overwhelming that such changes will not happen
under the current Iraq leadership." By late 1998, public opinion began to move
from supporting containment to favoring regime change.[39]

Some government experts on Iraq resisted the mounting pressure to seek
regime change in Baghdad. Marine Corps General Anthony Zinni, who served
as commander of the U.S. Central Command in 1997–2000, for example, argued
after the December 1998 airstrikes on Iraq that Hussein "was contained. It was a
pain in the ass, but he was contained. He had a deteriorated military. He wasn't a
threat to the region." Zinni publicly ridiculed a proposal by regime change advocate Paul Wolfowitz to send a small force into Iraq to stimulate a rebellion as a
mistake that would lead to a "Bay of Goats." The general told reporters that "I
think a weakened, fragmented, chaotic Iraq, which could happen if this isn't done
carefully, is more dangerous in the long run than a contained Saddam is now." In

an article in the *New Republic* in December 1998, Wolfowitz repudiated Zinni's critique and claimed that "toppling Saddam is the only outcome that can satisfy the vital U.S. interest in a stable and secure Gulf region."[40]

The open discussion of regime change in Iraq coincided with—and might have contributed to—Hussein's restrictions on UNSCOM activities that triggered the U.S. aerial assaults on Iraq of December 1998. Thereafter, Clinton adopted a policy toward Iraq, known as "containment plus," that essentially embraced regime change by means short of invasion. With inspections clearly suspended, the United States bolstered its military presence in the region, toughened its enforcement of the no-fly zones, and increased its strikes on Iraqi radar facilities. In the first 8 months of 1999, U.S. air power struck 400 targets in Iraq with more than 1,000 bombs. The administration also dispatched funds allocated by the Iraq Liberation Act to Iraqi opposition forces committed to ousting Hussein. The Iraqi leader threatened "the security of the world," Clinton declared. The "best way to end that threat once and for all is with a new Iraqi government."[41]

Yet Clinton's "containment plus" approach provided no more security against Iraqi WMD capability than the previous inspections approach. In December 1999, the Security Council affirmed the precedent of inspections to ensure Iraq's riddance of WMD, and it replaced the obsolete UNSCOM with the U.N. Monitoring, Verification, and Inspection Commission (UNMOVIC) with the responsibility for conducting "a reinforced system of ongoing monitoring and investigation." But UNSCOM, in a final report issued in 1999, indicated that Iraq might still possess up to 6,000 chemical bombs, 9 surface-to-surface missiles, 26,000 liters of anthrax, and 1.5 tons of VX gas. Even with a reduced mandate of arms control rather than active disarmament, UNMOVIC would be hard pressed to monitor Iraqi capabilities in the foreseeable future.[42]

CONCLUSION

President Clinton achieved his short-term goal of containing Saddam Hussein. Although the Iraqi dictator remained in power in Baghdad, he had proven unable to provoke another regional conflict, attack his own Kurdish or Shiite peoples living under the protection of Western military aircraft, or down a single one of those aircraft. The Iraqi economy remained stressed. By hindering international weapons inspections, Hussein stoked fear that he again was developing WMD, but in reality—as confirmed by Western arms inspectors after the United States occupied Iraq in 2003—Iraq's WMD program remained dysfunctional and impotent. With the advantage of hindsight, policy analysts such as former government official Richard N. Haass concluded that "the inspections and sanctions had largely worked." Writing in 2009, Haass noted that in the late 1990s "Iraq was for all intents and purposes out of the weapons of mass destruction business. Saddam was in power but not in a position to do serious harm, either to his own people or his neighbors. Containment was doing better than its detractors, and even many of its advocates, realized. The result of all this was that by the end of the Clinton administration, the Iraq situation didn't seem all that alarming."[43]

The blemish in Clinton's containment policy, however, was its undefined culmination. The president failed to conceive or articulate a viable end-game, an ultimate outcome to the standoff with Hussein that would ensure U.S. security interests on a long-term basis. Cracks in the foundation of containment pointed toward a steady deterioration of that approach in the near future. Maintenance of the no-fly zones had become politically problematic, as Hussein exploited the attacks on his country to bolster his domestic political authority and to win world sympathy for the civilian victims of Western airstrikes. He might even have provoked incidents in the no-fly zones as a means to counter pressure to accept arms inspectors; indeed, effective arms inspections ended in December 1998. Hussein also exploited the suffering of his people under economic sanctions to consolidate his political power at home, and, when sanctions were eased under the Oil-for-Food program, he used the fresh revenue streams further to bolster his domestic authority. The U.S. policy toward Iraq also faced trouble in the global realm. The international commitment to sanctions against Iraq wavered as Russia and France pressed for the resumption of commerce and civilian air traffic to Baghdad. In 1998, the obscure terrorist Osama bin Laden cited the U.S. assaults on Iraq from airbases in Saudi Arabia as one cause of his declaration of war against the United States, which proved to be a critical milestone on the road to the terrorist attacks of September 11, 2001.[44]

By the late 1990s, Clinton thus faced an agonizing dilemma in Iraq. Containment had proved functional in the short term, but its long-term prospects were questionable. Neocons painted an alluring portrait of regime change in Baghdad, and, after the midterm elections of 1994, Clinton came under increased domestic political pressure to comply. Regime change, however, seemed fraught with perils—risk that political or covert operations to unseat Hussein would open an era of political instability in Iraq that would destabilize the region and the likelihood that a military invasion would lead to a costly and debilitating occupation of the country.

Clinton tried to resolve this dilemma by modifying his original approach to Iraq. He remained convinced that the multilayered containment policy remained a legitimate policy option and he adhered to it. As evident in his signing of the Iraq Liberation Act of 1998, however, Clinton also adopted regime change as a policy objective. Whether such an abridged version of containment—the traditional methods bolstered by pressure to collapse the Hussein regime—would have worked remains a matter of speculation. With the advantage of hindsight, however, one could reasonably conclude that the maintenance of the containment approach into the new century had a fair chance of preserving essential U.S. interests in the Middle East during the lifetime of Saddam Hussein at a small fraction of the costs incurred in the alternative approach implemented by Clinton's successor in the Oval Office.

Events did not allow a real-world testing of Clinton's abridged containment policy. In the election of 2000, George W. Bush (son of the former president George H. W. Bush) defeated Vice President Al Gore in one of the closest and most disputed presidential elections in the nation's history. Neocons saw the election as a fresh opportunity to promote an aggressive form of regime change in Iraq. Thus, as Bush took office in January 2001, national policy toward Iraq was ripe for reconsideration, and the terrorist attacks of September 11, 2001, created an opportunity for bold action. A new president in a new century would embrace a mission in Iraq fraught with opportunity and risk.

NOTES

1. Mark Thompson, "Firing Blanks," *Time*, November 8, 1999, http://www.time.com/time/magazine/article/0,9171,992467–1,00.html/ (accessed June 21, 2010).
2. Steven Lee Myers, "U.S. Wields Defter Weapon Against Iraq: Concrete Bomb," *New York Times*, October 7, 1999, http://www.nytimes.com/1999/10/07/world/us-wields-defter-weapon-against-iraq-concrete-bomb.html?pagewanted=1/ (accessed June 21, 2010); Terry Boyd, "Operation Northern Watch: Mission Complete," *Stars and Stripes*, March 31, 2003, http://www.stripes.com/news/operation-northern-watch-mission-complete-1.3658/ (accessed June 21, 2010); U.S. Air Force, "Incirlik Air Base History," http://www.incirlik.af.mil/library/factsheets/factsheet.asp?id=5344/ (accessed June 21, 2010); U.S. Air Force, "Operation Southern Watch," http://www.af.mil/information/heritage/spotlight.asp?id=123112876/ (accessed June 21, 2010).
3. U.S. Department of Defense, "Defense Strategy for the 1990s: The Regional Defense Strategy," January 15, 1993, http://www.gwu.edu/~nsarchiv/nukevault/ebb245/doc15.pdf/ (accessed November 30, 2010) (quotation); Patrick E. Tyler, "U.S. Strategy Plans," *New York Times*, March 8, 1992.
4. U.S. Department of Defense, "Defense Strategy for the 1990s: The Regional Defense Strategy," January 15, 1993, http://www.gwu.edu/~nsarchiv/nukevault/ebb245/doc15.pdf/ (accessed November 30, 2010); Leffler, "Dreams of Freedom," 142–51.
5. Baker, *Politics of Diplomacy*, 441.
6. Duelfer, *Hide and Seek*, 68–72 (quotation); U.N. Security Council Resolution 687, April 8, 1991, http://www.un.org/docs/scres/1991/scres91.htm/ (accessed September 13, 2004); *Gallup Poll Monthly*, June 1991, July 1991.
7. Baker, *Politics of Diplomacy*, 434 (quotation); Malone, *International Struggle*, 85–97.
8. Brattebo, "No-Fly Zones," 209–10; Malone, *International Struggle*, 97–104; "Operation Northern Watch Stand Down," May 1, 2003, http://www.navy.mil/search/display.asp?story_id=7207/ (accessed August 1, 2009); "Containment: The Iraqi No-Fly Zones," http://news.bbc.co.uk/2/hi/events/crisis_in_the_gulf/forces_and_firepower/244364.stm/ (accessed August 1, 2009).
9. Brattebo, "No-Fly Zones," 210–16 (quotation); Woodward, *Plan of Attack*, 9–10.
10. Brattebo, "No-Fly Zones," 211–16 (quotation 213).
11. Brattebo, "No-Fly Zones," 213–16; "Containment: The Iraqi No-Fly Zones," http://news.bbc.co.uk/2/hi/events/crisis_in_the_gulf/forces_and_firepower/244364.stm/ (accessed August 1, 2009); *Gallup Poll Monthly*, January 1993.
12. Baker, *Politics of Diplomacy*, 442.

13. Freedman, *Choice of Enemies*, 287 (quotation); Albright, *Madam Secretary*, 272–76 (quotation 276); Clinton, *My Life*, 472.

14. Indyk, *Innocent Abroad*, 214; Cleveland and Bunton, *History of the Modern Middle East*, 561.

15. Brattebo, "No-Fly Zones," 216–24; Woodward, *Plan of Attack*, 9–10; "Containment: The Iraqi No-Fly Zones," http://news.bbc.co.uk/2/hi/events/crisis_in_the_gulf/forces_and_firepower/244364.stm/ (accessed August 1, 2009).

16. Christopher, *In the Stream of History*, 193 94 (quotation 194); Kaufman, *Arab Middle East*, 183 (quotation); address by Warren Christopher, October 24, 1994, *In the Stream of History*, 195–202 (quotation 201); Clinton, *My Life*, 525–26, 624, 728; Christopher, *Chances of a Lifetime*, 232–35; *Gallup Poll Monthly*, June 1993; Freedman, *Choice of Enemies*, 288; Brattebo, "No-Fly Zones," 216–24; U.N. Security Council Resolution 949, October 15, 1994, http://www.un.org/Docs/scres/1994/scres94.htm/ (accessed November 17, 2010).

17. Marr, "Iraq after the Gulf War," 213–34; Clawson, "Iraq's Economy," 69–83; Dawisha, *Iraq*, 227; Barbara Crossette, "Iraq Sanctions Kill Children, U.N. Reports." *New York Times*, December 1, 1995; Gordon, "Cool War."

18. Pilger, "Squeezed to Death;" Lopez and Cortright, "Containing Iraq."

19. "Oil-for-Food," http://www.un.org/Depts/oip/background/index.html (accessed August 1, 2009); Freedman, *Choice of Enemies*, 294–95.

20. Malone, *International Struggle*, 115–37.

21. "United Nations Special Committee," http://www.un.org/Depts/unscom/unscom.htm/ (accessed August 1, 2009); Ritter, Endgame, 108–9.

22. Duelfer, *Hide and Seek*, 97 (quotation); Clinton, *My Life*, 669–70; Albright, *Madam Secretary*, 272–76; Ritter, *Endgame*, 16–51, 220.

23. Ritter, *Endgame*, 16, 26; Duelfer, *Hide and Seek*, 78–79; Malone, *International Struggle*.

24. Duelfer, *Hide and Seek*, 92–93, 120; Malone, *International Struggle;* Ritter, *Endgame*, 131–45.

25. Woods, *Iraqi Perspectives Project*, 89–95.

26. Albright, *Madam Secretary*, 275–83; David W. Moore, "Support Increasing for Military Action against Iraq," February 5, 1998, http://www.gallup.com/poll/4261/Support-Increasing-Military-Action-Against-Iraq.aspx/ (accessed November 17, 2010).

27. Clinton, *My Life*, 833–34 (quotation 833); Albright, *Madam Secretary*, 283–87; David W. Moore, "Public Backs Attack on Iraq," December 19, 1998, http://www.gallup.com/poll/4114/Public-Backs-Attack-Iraq.aspx/ (accessed November 17, 2010).

28. Duelfer, *Hide and Seek*, 161–70.

29. Hussein quoted in Brattebo, "No-Fly Zones," 212; Dawisha, *Iraq*, 226–41 (quotations 237, 241); Tripp, *History of Iraq*, 259–79; Marr, "Iraq after the Gulf War," 213–34; U.S. AID, "Iraq's Legacy."

30. Braude, *New Iraq*, 48–58; Rod Nordland, "That Joke Is a Killer," *Newsweek*, May 19, 2003, 10; Sada, *Saddam's Secrets*, 90–94.

31. Freedman, *Choice of Enemies*, 288–93.

32. Branch, *Clinton Tapes*, 516–17.

33. *Gallup Poll Monthly*, July 1992, January 1993, June 1993.

34. *9/11 Report*, 88–91, 104–8.

35. Mylroie, "World Trade Center Bomb;" "Interview: R. James Woolsey," http://www.pbs.org/wgbh/pages/frontline/shows/gunning/interviews/woolsey.html/

(accessed November 17, 2010). Mylroie published a fuller version of her case in *Study of Revenge* in 2001.

36. Lesch, *Arab–Israeli Conflict*, 399–401; Davis, "Ideology," 45–47; Ricks, *Fiasco*, 18–22.

37. Letter to Clinton signed by Elliott Abrams, Richard L. Armitage, William J. Bennett, Jeffrey Bergner, John Bolton, Paula Dobriansky, Francis Fukuyama, Robert Kagan, Zalmay Khalilzad, William Kristol, Richard Perle, Peter W. Rodman, Donald Rumsfeld, William Schneider Jr., Vin Weber, Paul Wolfowitz, R. James Woolsey, and Robert B. Zoellick, January 26, 1998, http://www.newamericancentury.org/iraqclintonletter.htm/ (accessed November 15, 2007); Clinton, "State of the Union Address," January 27, 1998, http://clinton4.nara.gov/textonly/WH/SOTU98/address.html (accessed August 31, 2009).

38. Public Law 105–174, May 1, 1998, Public Law 105–235, August 14, 1998; available through http://web.lexis-nexis.com (accessed September 2, 2009).

39. Public Law 105–338, October 31, 1998; available through http://web.lexis-nexis.com (accessed September 2, 2009); White House Press Release, October 31, 1998, appended to "Clinton Signs Iraq Liberation Act, http://www.fas.org/news/iraq/1998/11/01/981101-in.htm/ (accessed September 2, 2009); Freedman, *Choice of Enemies*, 296–97.

40. Ricks, *Fiasco*, 22–23.

41. Albright, *Madam Secretary*, 283–87 (quotation 287); Brattebo, "No-Fly Zones," 224–30; Woodward, *Plan of Attack*, 9–10.

42. U.N. Security Council Resolution 1284, December 17, 1999, http://ods-dds-ny.un.org/doc/UNDOC/GEN/N99/396/09/PDF/N9939609.pdf?OpenElement/ (accessed September 20, 2004); Keegan, *Iraq War*, 110–111; Duelfer, *Hide and Seek*, 177–78.

43. Haass, *War of Necessity*, 167.

44. Brattebo, "No-Fly Zones," 208–9, 224–30.

CHAPTER 6

The Downfall of Saddam Hussein

George W. Bush and the March to War in Iraq, 2001–2003

Stationed at Camp Sayliyah in Qatar, U.S. Army General Tommy Franks was summoned to hold a video conference with President George W. Bush on March 19, 2003. Franks was the highest officer of the U.S. Central Command (CENTCOM), an administrative unit of the Pentagon responsible for U.S. military security interests in the Middle East and South Asia. Having enlisted in 1965, Franks had been commissioned as a second lieutenant in the artillery in 1967. Thrice wounded in Vietnam, he then held a variety of posts, including assistant commander of the 1st Cavalry Division during the Gulf War of 1990–1991. In 2000, Franks was promoted to four-star general and appointed to lead CENTCOM. His March 2003 video conference with the commander-in-chief would prove to be among the most momentous encounters of his long military career.

The dawn of the 21st century found the United States on the cusp of military interventions in Afghanistan and Iraq. The accession of George W. Bush to the White House in January 2001 and the political repercussions of a major terrorist attack on the United States 8 months later combined to put the United States on paths to two wars. As CENTCOM commander, Franks was in the thick of both situations. He directed the U.S. military operations in Afghanistan undertaken in late 2001 to oust the Taliban government that harbored the terrorists who had attacked the United States on September 11, 2001. When President Bush also tasked the CENTCOM commander in late 2001 to draw up plans for a military invasion of Iraq, Franks postponed his plans to retire in June 2002 and devoted himself to planning Operation Iraqi Freedom, a military invasion to demolish the regime of Iraqi dictator Saddam Hussein.[1]

As Franks readied the armed services for action in Iraq, Bush made a series of important decisions leading to hostilities against that country. Shell-shocked by the 9/11 terrorist attacks, the president feared the possibility of other such assaults and resolved to prevent them. With his sensitivity to threats heightened by the 9/11 catastrophe, Bush embraced the notion that

Photo 6-1
U.S. Army General Tommy Franks, commander in chief of Central Command, at a Pentagon news briefing on March 5, 2003. Two weeks later, President George W. Bush ordered General Franks to launch an invasion of Iraq. SOURCE: DoD photo by Helene C. Stikkel.

Hussein was not merely a nuisance to the United States but also a dire threat worthy of removal, through military invasion if necessary. Antiwar arguments by domestic and international critics failed to detract him from this mission. On March 17, 2003, the U.S. president issued an ultimatum demanding that Hussein relinquish his political power within 48 hours. When the Iraq leader failed to comply, Bush summoned his CENTCOM commander via video conference to issue an order to invade. "Mr. President, this force is ready," Franks declared. "All right," the president replied. "For the sake of peace in the world and security for our country and the rest of the free world, and for the freedom of the Iraqi people, as of this moment I will give Secretary Rumsfeld the order necessary to execute Operation Iraqi Freedom. Tommy, may God bless the troops."[2]

The war that started within hours of this conversation proved to be highly controversial. Defenders and critics of Bush's decision to invade and of the political and tactical aspects of U.S. policy in Iraq argued about the wisdom of the president's policy before, during, and after the spring 2003 invasion. On one level, the administration's approach proved to be phenomenally successful: U.S. military operations fulfilled the immediate mission of removing Hussein from power and demolishing his regime. In retrospect, however, the Bush administration created a political and military situation that would trouble the region and bedevil the United States for years to come.

THE ORIGINS OF U.S. MILITARY ACTION IN IRAQ

President Bush's path to war against Iraq originated before his inauguration to the presidency. In the late 1990s, as Chapter 5 explained, the William J. Clinton Administration had modified the policy of containment of Iraq to include the notion of "regime change" in Baghdad. When Bush took office in 2001, he appointed several political conservatives who had advocated the use of military means to overthrow the Hussein regime to key positions in his administration. In the aftermath of the 9/11 attacks and in light of his determination to protect Americans from such deadly assaults in the future, Bush soon resolved that he would use military force if necessary to remove Hussein from power.

Bush's personality and leadership style made him susceptible to the ardor of conservatives for regime change in Iraq. Close observers noted that the president provided resolve, stamina, and broad policy directions but allowed Vice President Richard Cheney, Secretary of Defense Donald Rumsfeld, and other officials to make actual policy. The president's tendency to see the world in bipolar contrasts with little nuance enabled the administration to link Iraq to the 9/11 terrorist attacks in popular understanding, despite the absence of convincing evidence. Secretary of State Colin Powell eventually noted that Bush never doubted a decision once he made it. Stephen W. Hadley, who succeeded Condoleezza Rice as National Security Advisor, remarked in January 2005 that Bush was "really a visionary. . . . He defies the conventional wisdom by his boldness. He's unapologetic. He sits there and reaffirms it, and clearly almost relishes it. . . . Those of us who are here believe in him." Former government official Leslie Gelb affirmed Hadley's observation from the opposite political perspective, noting that "Bush is the one true believer. We're talking about a guy essentially cut off from all information except the official line."[3]

Bush surrounded himself, moreover, with policy advisors who favored aggressive action against Iraq. Paul Wolfowitz, for instance, emerged as a major figure in the administration. As Under Secretary for Defense Policy in 1989–1993, Wolfowitz had endorsed the decision not to invade Iraq during the Gulf War of 1990–1991. By 1996, however, he criticized the Clinton administration's containment policy, suggesting that "the United States has virtually abandoned its commitment to protect a besieged people from a bloodthirsty dictator." By 1997, Wolfowitz argued that cooperation with Hussein was impossible, that the effectiveness of containment would erode over time, and that, therefore, regime change offered the most viable policy option. He coauthored an essay advocating "an overall political strategy that sets as its goal not merely the containment of Saddam but the liberation of Iraq from his tyranny." Wolfowitz likened Saddam Hussein to Adolf Hitler and passionately warned that appeasing Hussein would repeat the diplomatic errors of the 1930s. He believed that force was necessary to break the back of a tyrant and that democracy could be implanted in Iraq as it had been in South Korea. The Cold War, he believed, proved the importance of "demonstrating that your friends will be protected and taken care of, that your enemies will be punished, and that those who refuse to support you will live to regret having done so." In 2001, Wolfowitz was appointed Deputy Secretary of Defense.[4]

Douglas Feith, another influential Neocon, also occupied a prominent office in the Bush administration. An attorney who had worked for the NSC and the Pentagon during the Reagan Administration, Feith emerged as a leading advocate of Israeli interests while privately practicing law in the 1990s. He signed the Neocons' open letter to Clinton in 1998, contributed to the "Realm" policy paper, and outspokenly opposed the 1990s peace process as too risky for Israel. Feith emphasized Hussein's legacy of atrocities against the Iraqi people and his support for international terrorist groups, especially those fighting Israel on behalf of the Palestinians, as evidence that Hussein would emerge as a threat to American interests in the Middle East. Dealing firmly with Hussein, Feith reasoned, would earn the United States the credibility and respect it needed to achieve a viable Arab–Israeli peace settlement. Bush named Feith Deputy Under Secretary of Defense for Policy in 2001.[5]

The Bush administration featured others who had identified with the Neocon perspective in the 1990s or who would be taken in by it in the early 2000s. Vice President Cheney had opposed regime change while serving as Secretary of Defense in 1991 but had converted to the idea in the 1990s. Richard Perle, who entered politics as an adviser to Democratic Senator Henry M. Jackson but migrated to neoconservatism in the 1990s, was appointed chairman of the Pentagon's Defense Policy Board Advisory Committee in July 2001. Bush named Zalmay Khalilzad, an Afghan American and political science professor who gained experience in the Reagan administration organizing anti-Soviet resistance in Afghanistan, as a member of the presidential transition team at the Pentagon, as special assistant to the President in May 2001, and, eventually, as Ambassador to Afghanistan and Ambassador to Iraq.[6]

From the dawn of the Bush presidency, such administration officials contemplated military action to break the debilitating stalemate with Iraq that had evolved through the 1990s. At his very first NSC meeting on January 30, 2001, Bush revealed that he favored the idea of regime change in Baghdad in light of evidence that Hussein was building WMD. Vice President Cheney, according to his aides, soon developed a "fever" about overthrowing Hussein. Secretary of Defense Rumsfeld argued that enforcement of the no-fly zones was expensive as well as risky for the pilots who endured Iraqi gunfire. Deputy Secretary of Defense Wolfowitz advocated a military invasion of Iraq's southern oilfields to trigger a coup by Iraqi generals. Other officials argued that the international sanctions against Baghdad were difficult to maintain in the face of French and Russian pressure to ease them and difficult to enforce in light of tricky questions about dual-use technologies (such as hydraulic cylinders on dump trucks that could be retrofitted on missile launchers).[7]

Certain officials in the administration resisted the pressure to engage in military action. Secretary of State Powell, a former chairman of the Joint Chiefs of

Staff, cautioned the president that military operations would sour politically and urged a focus on strengthening the containment approach. State Department Policy Planning Staff Director Richard Haass advocated a tightening of the sanctions policy by concentrating on embargoes of military hardware and by trying to stifle the smuggling through Turkey and Jordan that reportedly had sustained the Hussein regime through the 1990s. In early 2001, President Bush seemingly considered a reaffirmation of containment. In February, he authorized an air-strike against new Iraqi radar stations, under construction outside the no-fly zones and featuring Chinese-supplied fiber-optic cables resistant to U.S. counterintelligence measures.[8]

While planting his feet as president during the summer of 2001, Bush refrained from affirming a more assertive policy toward Iraq although his Neocon advisers pressed for it. On July 27, Rumsfeld argued to National Security Adviser Rice, Cheney, and Powell that the containment edifice erected a decade before had reached a crisis point. He warned that Hussein had escaped the pinch of economic sanctions, displayed more assertiveness in the no-fly zones, and begun to secure his communications with Chinese-supplied fiber-optic cables. The Iraqi leader "appears to believe he is getting stronger. His general behavior and relationships with his neighbors suggest he is riding higher than a year ago." Consequently, U.S. patrols of no-fly zones were becoming quite perilous, and the U.S. options for addressing that danger were limited. A reduction of the patrols would enable Hussein to bolster his military strength and political influence; if the United States should "roll up our tents" and end the patrols, "within a few years the United States will undoubtedly have to confront a Saddam armed with nuclear weapons." U.S. effort to engage Hussein in dialogue would probably fail and would alienate friendly states in the region and generate domestic criticism in the process. Rumsfeld thus recommended a "more robust policy" of recognizing that the risks of attempting regime change in Baghdad were lower than the risks of allowing Hussein to amass power. "If Saddam's regime were ousted," Rumsfeld noted, "we would have a much-improved position in the region and elsewhere." Reports that Iraqi antiaircraft batteries downed two unmanned RQ-1B Predator spy planes in late August and early September accentuated Rumsfeld's concerns. Prior to September 11, however, Bush did not act on Rumsfeld's advice.[9]

The 9/11 terrorist attacks, by contrast, profoundly affected the Bush administration's policy in the Middle East and South Asia. The administration quickly united around the idea of using force to dismantle the Taliban regime in Afghanistan that had provided sanctuary to the al-Qaeda network that had perpetrated the 9/11 attacks. "We're at war," Bush told Vice President Cheney, minutes after learning of the attacks. "Somebody's going to pay." Together with its NATO allies, the United States launched devastating air strikes against al-Qaeda camps, airfields, and barracks in Afghanistan on October 7, thereafter coordinated attacks on Taliban strongholds with fighters of the indigenous Northern Alliance, and crushed the Taliban regime by November.[10]

In contrast to the united front on Afghanistan, the Bush Administration divided internally over the connections between 9/11 and Iraq. Wolfowitz and Feith argued that the U.S. military retaliation should also target the Hussein regime, given its legacy of supporting terrorism and its mounting danger to U.S. interests. The proper response to 9/11 involved not only striking at perpetrators, Wolfowitz declared at a Pentagon press conference on September 13, "but removing the sanctuaries, removing the support systems, ending states who support terrorism. And that's why it has to be a broad and sustained campaign." Feith later recorded that "our concerns about Iraq intensified after 9/11—but not because anyone thought Saddam had actually conspired in the 9/11 attack.... Rather the concern reflected our general recognition of the dangers posed by Saddam's regime—and Saddam's hostility to the United States." Having experienced firsthand the harrowing attacks on Washington, D.C. on 9/11, Rumsfeld and Cheney embraced this line of reasoning. Pentagon briefing books prepared for an emergency presidential planning meeting at Camp David in mid-September included plans for strikes on Iraq as well as Afghanistan.[11]

Secretary of State Powell led the opposition to a rush to war in Iraq. He and his deputy, Richard Armitage, advocated military operations exclusively against Afghanistan, emphasizing to the President the importance of the broad

Photo 6-2
President George W. Bush speaking at the Pentagon on March 25, 2003, flanked by Secretary of Defense Donald H. Rumsfeld (center) and Deputy Secretary of Defense Paul Wolfowitz (left). This photo was taken days after Bush ordered the invasion of Iraq that Wolfowitz and Rumsfeld had advocated for years. SOURCE: DoD photo by R. D. Ward.

international support for that move. "We're after ending terrorism," Powell stated at a press conference on September 17, when asked to comment on Wolfowitz's call for regime change in Baghdad. "And if there are states and regimes, nations that support terrorism, we hope to persuade them that it is in their interest to stop doing that. But I think ending terrorism is where I would like to leave it, and let Mr. Wolfowitz speak for himself." In support of Powell's cautious policy, counterterrorism expert Richard Clarke sent Bush a detailed assessment rejecting the proposition that Hussein was directly involved in the 9/11 attacks.[12]

In the immediate aftermath of 9/11, President Bush decided to limit retaliation to Afghanistan but to keep his options in Iraq open for later consideration. In his first meeting with his top aides at Camp David on September 15, he removed Iraq from consideration for early military action, although he also agreed to consider it in a future, second phase of operations. When British Prime Minister Tony Blair asked Bush about Iraq on September 20, Bush replied (as reported by the 9/11 Commission) that Iraq was "not the immediate problem. Some members of his administration, he commented, had expressed a different view, but he was the one responsible for making the decisions." Later that same day, however, in an address to Congress making the case for war in Afghanistan, the president left open the option of dealing with Iraq and other states that sponsored terrorism. "We will pursue nations that provide aid or safe haven to terrorism," he declared. "Every nation, in every region, now has a decision to make. Either you are with us, or you are with the terrorists. From this day forward, any nation that continues to harbor or support terrorism will be regarded by the United States as a hostile regime."[13]

President Bush's declaration to Congress laid the foundation of his overall foreign policy for the post-9/11 era, conveniently called the Bush Doctrine. The policy rested on such foundational beliefs as a determination to pursue goals unilaterally, an expectation that states would renounce terrorism, a readiness to wage preemptive war rather than practice deterrence against foes posing imminent dangers, and a vision of spreading democracy abroad. (Because the president articulated such policies in a series of speeches and papers, there are some discrepancies among definitions of the Bush Doctrine by journalists and scholars.) The scholar Robert Jervis sees the doctrine as "a response of an enormously powerful state without great rivals but with great fears." Robert G. Kaufman vigorously defends the Bush Doctrine as a manifestation of "moral democratic realism," a grand strategy that used power to promote democracy and freedom among individuals. Bush rightly saw the twin emergence of Islamic fundamentalism and WMD as an acute danger to the American way of life, Kaufman notes, and he grasped the futility of relying on international systems and cooperative schemes to address those concerns. Michael Lind, by contrast, critiques the Bush Doctrine for feeding ardor for a war in Iraq that was destined to prove the limits of American power and to alienate much of the world community.[14]

THE MARCH TO WAR IN IRAQ, 2001–2003

As the Bush Doctrine took shape in late 2001, the administration marched down a path toward hostilities with Iraq. Seemingly unnerved by the danger of terrorism that persisted in late 2001, the president followed the lead of his pro-war advisors and began to articulate publicly a case for a preemptive and proactive invasion of Iraq. As 2002 passed, Congress and a broad swath of the American people indicated their complicity with such a move. Bush administration officials encountered a deep grain of skepticism for an attack on Iraq among some domestic commentators, foreign powers, and U.N. leaders. But the U.S. officials proved able to secure a U.N. resolution that they subsequently used as a legal basis for war. By early 2003, Bush felt emboldened to move aggressively in Iraq despite lingering resistance at home and overseas.

President Bush crossed the threshold toward war in a context of the fear verging on panic that gripped the U.S. government and people after 9/11. "For as long as I held office, I could never forget what happened to America that day," Bush later wrote. "I would pour my heart and soul into protecting the country, whatever it took." When Prime Minister Blair visited the Oval Office on September 20, he later recorded, he found Bush "at peace with himself. He had his mission as president. He hadn't asked for it. He hadn't expected it. He hadn't found it. It had found him. But he was clear. The world had changed, and as president of the world's most powerful country, he was tasked with making sense of that change and dealing with it."[15]

The insecurity provoked by 9/11 deepened in the following months. Three weeks after 9/11, an unknown perpetrator launched a bioterror attack on the United States by mailing anthrax powder to congressional and media offices, killing five people and raising alarm that such an attack of widespread scale could claim millions of victims. Although investigators later concluded that a federal employee single-handedly had launched the attack, intelligence officials at the time suspected that Iraq, which was known to have developed anthrax as a weapon, bore responsibility. On December 22, moreover, Richard Reid, a British Muslim and member of al-Qaeda, tried without success to detonate a bomb aboard a commercial flight from Paris to Miami. "The foiled plot had a big impact on me," Bush later recorded. "Three months after 9/11, it was a vivid reminder that the threats were frighteningly real." The sense of insecurity in late 2001 was universal. "For world leaders wondering and worrying where the next hostility would come from," Prime Minister Blair later noted, "the contemplation not only of what had happened but what might happen was continuous, urgent and nerve-wracking."[16]

In the climate of insecurity that gripped him in late 2001, President Bush essentially decided that the policy of containing Iraq, which he had confirmed prior to 9/11, had become too risky. He and Cheney concluded that the passivity of President Clinton's approach to Iraq and the limits of his responses to terrorism might have encouraged the 9/11 assault and that more vigorous action was needed to send a political message to American adversaries. Intelligence reports that Pakistani scientists were supplying nuclear materials to Muslim states caused deep concern about an attack on the United States with a "dirty" bomb (a conventional explosive that distributed radioactive material) and thereby pushed the administration toward action. The CIA advised Bush that covert operations to oust Hussein would likely fail, given Hussein's rigorous security and ruthlessness against potential opponents. At about the same time, the Pentagon staff prepared a detailed contingency plan for an invasion of Iraq, which made such a move a viable option for the president. Douglas Feith developed the justification for unilateral action by noting that U.N. approval of action in Iraq was "beyond the requirement of international law" and would inhibit U.S. defense capabilities. Feith eventually articulated the so-called "three T's" case for attacking Iraq: Hussein was a *terrorism* supporter, a *threat* because of WMD, and a *tyrant* to his people. The president had exhausted all nonmilitary options for dealing with Iraq, Feith concluded, and developed an "honest, well-grounded rationale" for a war.[17]

Determined to overthrow Hussein with military force, President Bush downplayed options to address the threat of Iraq with diplomatic means. "The lesson of 9/11," Bush later explained, "was that if we waited for a danger to fully materialize, we would have waited too long. I reached a decision: We would confront the threat from Iraq, one way or another." He claimed to implement "coercive diplomacy"—threatening to overthrow Hussein with force unless "he would give up his WMD, end his support for terror, stop threatening his neighbors, and, over time, respect the human rights of his people." As the United States amassed military forces capable of conquering Iraq, Bush suggested, Hussein would be able to avoid the destruction of his regime by reforming his behavior. Yet the president also admitted that "the odds of success were long." In light of his conviction that Hussein posed a threat and his skepticism that Hussein would mend his ways, Bush invested little energy in diplomacy and clearly favored military action.[18]

In early 2002, Bush publicly announced a case for war against Iraq. In his State of the Union message on January 29, he declared,

> Iraq continues to flaunt its hostility toward America and to support terror. The Iraqi regime has plotted to develop anthrax and nerve gas and nuclear weapons for over a decade. This is a regime that has already used poison gas to murder thousands of its own citizens, leaving the bodies of mothers huddled over their dead children. This is a regime that agreed to international inspections then kicked out the inspectors. This is a regime that has something to hide from the civilized world.

Iraq, Iran, North Korea, and "their terrorist allies," Bush added, "constitute an axis of evil, arming to threaten the peace of the world.... These regimes pose a grave and growing danger. They could provide these arms to terrorists, giving them the means to match their hatred. They could attack our allies or attempt to blackmail the United States. In any of these cases, the price of indifference would be catastrophic."[19]

The president developed the case for war against Iraq during the remainder of 2002. In April, after detailing the danger of Hussein providing WMD to terrorists, Bush told members of Congress that "we're taking him out" and Cheney added "the only question was when." The president also told a journalist that "I made up my mind that Saddam needs to go." In an address at the U.S. Military Academy in May, Bush declared a doctrine of preemptive war. "The war on terror will not be won on the defensive," he asserted. "We must take the battle to the enemy, disrupt his plans, and confront the worst threats before they emerge." In September, the White House released *The National Security Strategy of the United States*, a policy statement declaring that "the United States will, if necessary, act preemptively" against "a sufficient threat to our national security" and warning that the country would "make no distinction between terrorists and those who knowingly harbor or provide aid to them." In October, the president acknowledged that Iraq might not have WMD but stressed its effort to acquire them. "Facing clear evidence of peril," he intoned, "we cannot wait for the final proof, the smoking gun, that could come in the form of a mushroom cloud."[20]

The tone and substance of Bush's rhetoric stimulated considerable debate among Americans. Shell-shocked by 9/11, a broad cross-section of the public gave the president wide latitude. But dissenters argued that a war against Iraq would lead the country down a perilous path. Brent Scowcroft, who served the first Bush presidency as National Security Adviser, noted that Saddam Hussein, a secular socialist with no record of terrorism, had no part in 9/11 and was unlikely to partner with a religious fanatic like Osama bin Laden. A war against Iraq, Scowcroft warned, would cost significant lives and treasure, distract the United States from the more important antiterrorism objectives, and destabilize the Middle East. Vice President Cheney responded to such criticism in an address to a veterans group in late August. "Simply stated, there is no doubt that Saddam Hussein now has weapons of mass destruction," he warned, and "there is no doubt that he is amassing them to use against our friends, against our allies, and against us. And there is no doubt that his aggressive regional ambitions will lead him into future confrontations with his neighbors—confrontations that will involve both the weapons he has today, and the ones he will continue to develop with his oil wealth."[21]

Undeterred by the criticism, Bush sold Congress on the case for war by stressing that such a war was winnable and necessary. "Saddam Hussein is a terrible guy who is teaming up with al-Qaeda," the president told one group of legislators. "He tortures his own people and hates Israel." Alluding to Iraq's attempt to assassinate the first President Bush in 1993, the younger Bush also told a member of Congress that Hussein "tried to kill my dad." Administration officials also argued that congressional endorsement of forceful action against Iraq would motivate the U.N. Security Council to take firm action against that country. By a 296–133 margin, the House approved a resolution on October 10 authorizing Bush "to use the Armed Forces of the United States as he determines to be necessary and appropriate in order to—(1) defend the national security of the United States against the continuing threat posed by Iraq; and (2) enforce all relevant United Nations Security Council resolutions regarding Iraq." The Senate passed the measure on the next day by a 77–23 vote. Sensitive to the abiding post-9/11 security concerns among their constituents and cognizant of the political setbacks experienced by those legislators who had opposed the Gulf War of 1990–1991, members of Congress offered little resistance to the administration.[22]

Bush also prompted the United Nations to impose firm measures against Iraq. He agreed with his conservative advisors that securing a U.N. resolution was legally unnecessary and might prolong the showdown to Hussein's advantage, but he essentially decided to seek a resolution to shore up political support among other nations. In an address to the General Assembly on September 12, 2002, the president advised the United Nations to pass new resolutions to deal with Iraq or the United States would take action. In November, after weeks of effort, Powell convinced the Security Council unanimously to pass Resolution 1441, which found Iraq in "material breach" of previous U.N. resolutions, provided it "a final opportunity" to cooperate with inspections, and warned Iraq that "it will face serious consequences" if it remained defiant. France, Russia, and other states voted for Resolution 1441 on the understanding that it did not authorize military action.[23]

Despite such reservations among other powers, Bush allowed precious little time for Resolution 1441 to work. On November 25, former Swedish Foreign Minister Hans Blix led a team of 100 inspectors from UNMOVIC to Iraq. On December 7, Iraqi officials delivered 43 binders of documents supposedly verifying that Iraq was free of WMD. Several Security Council powers favored taking time to examine these records and continue inspections, a position endorsed by Secretary of State Powell. But Bush considered the disclosure "reams of irrelevant paperwork clearly designed to deceive." He told his advisors in a private meeting that war with Iraq now seemed "inevitable," and on December 19, he publicly declared that Iraq was in material breach of Resolution 1441. As John Keegan observes, UNMOVIC perhaps faced an impossible situation: proving a negative (that Iraq did not have WMD), on the basis of inspections of a sizeable country, governed by a dictator who lacked credibility, and under pressure from a very impatient U.S. government.[24]

By late December, Bush steeled himself to launch a preemptive invasion of Iraq. On December 21, Director of Central Intelligence George Tenet assured him, using a basketball metaphor, that there was "slam dunk" evidence that Iraq harbored WMD. National Security Adviser Rice counseled the president that Iraq was stringing along UNMOVIC inspectors, that nascent antiwar movements in Europe and at home would eventually make military action difficult, that the U.N. Security Council consensus on Iraq was fragmenting, and that the United States could not sustain long term its incremental military buildup in the Middle East. Refusing to retreat and unable to delay, Bush decided to take the offensive.[25]

The Bush administration made its closing argument for war in early 2003. In his State of the Union message on January 28, the president explained that Iraq could not account for massive quantities of anthrax, botulinum toxin, sarin gas, and VX nerve agent that it once possessed. He reported that British intelligence had indicated that Hussein had tried to purchase uranium in Africa (a charge that the CIA had disputed months earlier and that was later proven false). As James Fallows notes, the President definitely emphasized Iraqi WMD in the address, devoting 18 of his 19 paragraphs about Iraq to the danger of an Iraq-originated WMD terrorist attack on the United States. (The sole other paragraph addressed the right of the Iraqi people to freedom.)[26]

In early 2003, even Secretary of State Powell overcame his reluctance about attacking Iraq. In an address to the United Nations on February 5, he summarized U.S. intelligence to argue that Hussein likely possessed WMD and had deceived UNMOVIC inspectors. When Hans Blix countered that UNMVOIC had found no smoking gun and that more inspections were needed, Powell retorted that Hussein had been given sufficient opportunity to come clean and deserved no more time. Given the secretary's credibility and trustworthiness, Powell's speech proved crucial in winning support for war among the U.S. public, media, and

Photo 6-3
Initially opposed to a preemptive invasion of Iraq, Secretary of State Colin Powell shifted his position in early 2003 and embraced the notion that war was necessary to neutralize the threat inherent in Saddam Hussein's supposed weapons of mass destruction. Here, Powell displays a model vial of anthrax to accentuate Hussein's dangers while speaking to the United Nations in early February 2003. Powell's speech was crucial in building domestic support and international tolerance for the impending U.S. invasion. SOURCE: AFP/ Getty Images.

armed service officers, especially because Powell claimed to have hard factual evidence to back up his charges regarding Iraqi WMD. Such critics as Thomas E. Ricks later concluded, by contrast, that the intelligence Powell cited proved to be inaccurate, supplied by unreliable sources in the Iraqi exile community, and inadequately vetted by the CIA. Echoing the view of war opponents, Christopher D. O'Sullivan contended that Powell "provided the administration with a moderate and realist front for policies that were quite unrealistic in the conception and incompetent in their execution."[27]

Meanwhile, the U.S. military had laid the groundwork for an invasion of Iraq. Having been directed by Bush in November 2001 to begin planning military operations in Iraq, Rumsfeld thereafter met regularly with General Tommy Franks to discuss the broad scope of such a war. In 2002, the president authorized the CIA to conduct sabotage, disinformation, and "other potential lethal activities" to depose Hussein or to facilitate a prospective invasion. He also redirected $700 million from funds appropriated to the war in Afghanistan to upgrade airfields and other facilities needed for an attack on Baghdad. U.S. military jets patrolling the no-fly zones gathered tactical intelligence, eliminated ground armor in the likely invasion route through southern Iraq, and neutralized Iraqi air defenses. In early 2003, U.S. warplanes attacked Iraqi artillery and dropped some 17 million leaflets encouraging surrender in the face of invasion.[28]

During the build-up, some controversy developed within the U.S. military over the size of the planned invasion force. Committed to a transformational doctrine of trimming U.S. combat forces in favor of high-technology alternatives such as precision-guided munitions and unmanned sensors, Secretary of Defense Rumsfeld became determined to achieve U.S. objectives in Iraq with minimal ground forces. Thus, he pressed General Franks to plan an invasion with some 150,000 ground combat troops, in contrast to the provision for an invasion by 400,000 soldiers made in CENTCOM's 1999 contingency war plan "Desert Crossing." Rumsfeld convinced the Joint Chiefs of Staff to overcome their initial reluctance about such a smaller force and sign off on Franks's new plan, COBRA II, by stressing that the speed of advance would compensate for the smaller force size.[29]

Although the Joint Chiefs of Staff approved COBRA II, not all officials in Washington were comfortable with the allocated troop strength. Secretary of State Powell, who as Chair of the Joint Chiefs of Staff during the Gulf War of 1990–1991 had concentrated massive ground forces in the theater of battle, remained unpersuaded. In February 2003, Army Chief of Staff General Eric K. Shinseki testified to the Senate Armed Services Committee that the Pentagon would need many more troops than the 100,000 designated for postinvasion occupation duty in Iraq. Citing the U.S. experience in Bosnia (which resembled Iraq in size and population) and the likelihood of Shiite–Sunni ethnic tensions, Shinseki estimated that "several hundred thousand" GIs would be needed to stabilize postwar Iraq. Two days later, in testimony to the House Budget Committee, Wolfowitz rebuked Shinseki's estimate as "wildly off the mark." He predicted that Iraqis would welcome U.S. soldiers as liberators, that Iraq would escape the ethnic violence that plagued Bosnia, and that other states, even those opposing an invasion, would help with reconstruction. "It's hard to conceive that it would take more forces to provide security in post-Saddam Iraq than it would take to conduct the war itself and to secure the surrender of Saddam's security forces and his army," Wolfowitz testified. "Hard to imagine." It would soon become clear that Wolfowitz should have invested more effort in imagination.[30]

In addition, prominent domestic political voices raised questions about the move to war. Former President Jimmy Carter, for instance, asserted that Bush's determination to invade Iraq violated a long U.S. tradition of basing military decisions on moral tenets, international law, domestic political consensus, and foreign alliances. Attacking Iraq would not meet "just war" standards because the United States had not exhausted nonviolent means, because an invasion would imperil noncombatants and worsen the international situation, because Hussein's actions had not been sufficiently egregious or perilous to U.S. security, and because the United States lacked U.N. approval. "Although there are visions of peace and democracy in Iraq, it is quite possible that the aftermath of a military invasion will destabilize the region and prompt terrorists to further jeopardize our security at home," Carter wrote. "Also, by defying overwhelming world opposition, the United States will undermine the United Nations as a viable institution for world peace."[31]

Allied powers also disputed the U.S. escalation toward hostilities. France remained a vocal opponent of U.S. belligerence. "A majority of world leaders share our determination to search for a peaceful solution to disarming Iraq," French President Jacques Chirac told a *Time* reporter. "The consequences of war would be considerable in human terms. In political terms, it would destabilize the entire region. It's very difficult to explain that one is going to spend colossal sums of money to wage war when there may be another solution." In early 2003, Turkish officials decided to prohibit U.S. forces from using bases in their country to launch a ground invasion of Iraq. Turkey apparently was concerned that complicity in such an attack would encourage separatism among its Kurdish population and strain its relations with Arab powers. When Rumsfeld visited Germany in February seeking an endorsement of a war, Foreign Minister Joschka Fischer questioned whether the situation in Iraq was sufficiently dire to warrant action. He was "not convinced" that Hussein posed a mortal threat. "You are going to have to occupy Iraq for years and years," he lectured Rumsfeld. "The idea that democracy will suddenly blossom is something that I can't share." The opposition of such friendly powers did not deter Rumsfeld from his inclination to make war on Iraq.[32]

Despite these internal quarrels and domestic and allied criticisms, the Bush Administration moved to war in March 2003. Bush considered asking the U.N. Security Council for a second resolution explicitly authorizing the use of force in light of Iraqi defiance of Resolution 1441. British Prime Minister Tony Blair, the president's most supportive ally on the world stage, advocated such a move in light of a mounting antiwar movement among his people and within his own Labour Party. When it became clear, however, that France would veto a second resolution, Bush asserted that Resolution 1441 provided sufficient legal basis for offensive action. During a summit meeting in Bermuda on March 16, Bush convinced Blair to go along with this view. The hawkish Douglas Feith later expressed regret that the president had even considered a second resolution because the backtracking in the face of France's opposition placed the U.S. operation in Iraq under a cloud.[33]

With Congress having voted approval, the Bush Administration escalated to hostilities with measured optimism. Bush placed faith in assurances from Iraqi exile and Brandeis University Professor Kanan Makiya, who, during a visit to the White House in January 2003, stressed that the Iraqi people would welcome invading GIs with "sweets and flowers." After visiting Iraqi exiles in Michigan in March 2003, Wolfowitz predicted to local reporters that "you're going to find Iraqis out cheering American troops." He also downplayed the risk of Shiite–Sunni clashes, saying that tensions between the two communities in Iraq were minimal. Subsequent events would prove that such optimism among top administration officials was clearly excessive. Skepticism about rosy predictions by anti-Hussein exiles and competence about the culture of Iraqi sectarian dynamics might have better prepared U.S. leaders for the hard reality that awaited them.[34]

Having firmed up his military partnership with Britain, Bush issued an ultimatum to Iraq on March 17, warning Saddam Hussein and his sons Uday and Qusai to leave Iraq within 48 hours or face the wrath of the American military. The ultimatum had originated in an August 2002 Defense Department paper that proposed it as a means short of war to achieve regime change. The idea was based on some hope that Hussein and his top echelon would agree to a permanent, comfortable exile or, failing that, that the effort would win political favor by seemingly seeking to avert hostilities. In any case, Hussein defied the ultimatum, as Bush had expected. Thus, Bush summoned General Franks to a video conference and ordered him to start a war.[35]

THE 500-HOUR WAR

Upon the expiration of the 48-hour ultimatum, the United States promptly initiated hostilities against Iraq. An airstrike designed to kill Saddam Hussein at the outset was followed by a massive invasion of southern Iraq and special operations elsewhere in the country. Although Hussein survived the initial blow, U.S. forces and their British and Australian partners rapidly advanced on all fronts, securing a decisive military victory over Iraq in combat operations that lasted some 500 hours.

Bush boldly signaled the start of the invasion with a "decapitation" strike against Hussein on March 19, 2003. When U.S. intelligence sources reported that Hussein and his sons had gathered at a compound in Baghdad known as Dora Farms, Bush ordered the Air Force to bomb the site. Within hours, two F-117

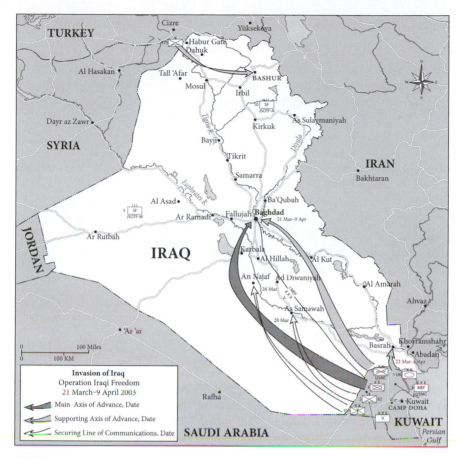

Map 6-1

This U.S. Army map shows the various axes of advance into Iraq during Operation Iraqi Freedom of March–April 2003. SOURCE: U.S. Army Center of Military History.

stealth bombers based in Kuwait delivered four "bunker-busting" bombs that demolished most of the compound. Although the attack failed to kill Hussein and his sons (either they had not been present as reported or they had left the facility before the attack), it dramatically heralded the start of the war and signaled U.S. intentions to achieve regime change in Baghdad.[36]

The next day, U.S. and Allied forces launched a major ground invasion of Iraq. Some 125,000 U.S. GIs (65,000 Army, 60,000 Marines), 20,000 British troops, and 500 Australian soldiers, backed by the air and naval strength of all three countries, invaded southern Iraq from Kuwait. A U.S. airborne task force parachuted into northern Iraq to provide guidance to Allied aircraft and to mobilize Kurdish forces to resist Hussein's authority. Other U.S. special forces swarmed into Iraq's

Photo 6-4
U.S. Army soldiers from Delta Battery, 319th Field Artillery Regiment come under enemy fire in northern Iraq during the U.S. invasion of March 2003. SOURCE: Photo by Brandon Aird, U.S. Army. *On Point: The United States Army in Operation Iraqi Freedom,* p. C-7.

western desert to capture airfields, block escape routes for Iraqi leaders, and prevent Hussein from repeating his 1991 tactic of launching Scud missiles at Israel. Iraq deployed a defensive force of some 400,000 soldiers and fielded some 4,000 tanks (compared with 500 U.S. tanks and armored Bradley fighting vehicles).[37]

Despite Iraq's numerical superiority, Western forces relatively quickly achieved key objectives in their advance on Baghdad. The U.S. Army 3rd Infantry Division captured an airfield and a Euphrates River bridgehead at an-Nasiriyah on March 23, and Marines took control of the city after heavy fighting on March 31. After an intense sandstorm forced an operational pause on March 27–30, Army forces resumed a northward advance that captured an-Najaf and Karbala while Marines occupied ad-Diwaniyah and al-Kut. Over stiffening Iraqi resistance, American forces crossed the Karbala Gap in early April, gaining a position for an assault on Baghdad. On April 7, British forces consolidated their occupation of southern Iraq by occupying Basra. In the north, Army paratroopers and special forces smashed the Kurdish terrorist group Ansar al-Islam and occupied Kirkuk on April 10.[38]

U.S. forces completed their military victory over Saddam Hussein's Iraq with a dramatic conquest of Baghdad in early April. Army commanders suspended the original plan to besiege the city and, on April 5 and 7, instead ordered two "thunder runs," fast-paced forays of armored vehicles into the heart of Baghdad designed to conquer key facilities and disorient Iraqi units arrayed in a linear defense of the city. During the first thunder run, historians

Williamson Murray and Robert H. Scales observe, Iraqi soldiers "turned out in hundreds, literally lining the route, seemingly waiting their turn to die as martyrs. The Americans obliged." Because Iraqi propaganda claimed that the withdrawal of American forces after the first foray signaled an Iraqi victory, Army Colonel David Perkins, commander of the 2nd Brigade, 3rd Infantry Division, boldly decided to remain downtown after the second thunder run. Perkins's gamble "arguably shortened the siege [of Baghdad] by weeks, if not months," Army historians concluded. "The second thunder run broke the regime's back, and any remaining political or military leaders of rank disappeared in a flash of self-preservation."[39]

In addition to inflicting massive casualties, the thunder runs led to the occupation of major symbols of the Iraqi regime's prestige: Saddam International Airport on April 3 and Hussein's presidential palaces in the city center on April 7. On the next day, Iraqi units were warned to surrender or face complete destruction as U.S. Marines occupied the eastern side of Baghdad. On April 9, the toppling of a towering statue of Saddam Hussein in Firdos Square on the east side of the Tigris River by U.S. Marines signaled the end of his regime.[40]

Photo 6-5
U.S. armored vehicles race into central Baghdad on a "thunder run," a rapid advance to the center of the city that disoriented Iraqi units and thus hastened the conquest of the capital city. SOURCE: Photo by William Glaser, U.S. Army. *On Point: The United States Army in Operation Iraqi Freedom,* p. 352.

Photo 6-6
U.S. Army Colonel David Perkins of the 2nd Brigade, 3rd Infantry Division, whose bold gamble on remaining in occupation of central Baghdad after a "thunder run" is credited by Army historians with hastening the end of combat in the city. SOURCE: Courtesy of 2nd BCT, 3rd ID. *On Point: The United States Army in Operation Iraqi Freedom*, p. 342.

In strict military terms, the conquest of Iraq was a lopsided victory by the United States and its allies. In a 21-day campaign, Allied troops completely defeated and scattered an Iraqi army of some 400,000 soldiers, occupied the country, and destroyed the government (at a cost of 139 U.S. and 33 British fatalities). The United States, military historian John Keegan notes, "achieved extraordinary results, the farthest advance at speed over distance ever recorded and the disintegration of an army twice the size of the invading force." In late April mop-up campaigns, U.S. forces captured remaining targets, including Tikrit, Hussein's hometown and the center of his political network. Bush declared an end of major combat operations in a rousing speech on May 1, while standing beneath an enormous banner proclaiming "Mission Accomplished" aboard the aircraft carrier USS *Abraham Lincoln* near San Diego.[41]

The U.S. invasion decisively demolished the Saddam Hussein regime. On July 22, U.S. soldiers from the 101st Airborne Division located Hussein's sons Uday and Qusai in Mosul and killed them in a firefight. Hussein himself was captured on December 13, when a U.S. Army unit discovered him hiding in a crude cellar on a farm near Tikrit. When soldiers lifted a trapdoor to find the fugitive dictator, he lifted his hands and declared, "I am the President of Iraq and I am ready to negotiate." An Iraqi court eventually tried and convicted Hussein of crimes against humanity and crimes against the Iraqi people. Iraqi authorities hanged the deposed dictator on December 30, 2006.[42]

The invasion also had a stabilizing effect on Iraqi Kurdistan. After the United States mediated a truce between warring Kurdish factions in 1998 (discussed in Chapter 5), Kurdish leaders had contributed to U.S. plans for regime change in Baghdad, practiced autonomy under the protection of U.S. airpower, and formed a unified parliament in 2002. The Islamic fundamentalist group Ansar al-Islam, which challenged the authority of secular leaders, was suppressed by the U.S. invasion in 2003. Ethnic turmoil, including a rivalry among Kurds, Arabs, and Turkomans for control of Kirkuk (a city that Hussein had tried to purge of Kurdish influence by replacing Kurdish citizens with Arab families), briefly threatened to complicate the U.S. occupation of Iraq. Kurds generally cooperated with U.S. objectives, however, by participating in Iraqi national politics, winning 25 percent of the vote in the national elections of 2005.[43]

The United States prevailed on the battlefields of Iraq because of its superior military forces, technology, and preparations. As Murray and Scales explain, the U.S. military was well disciplined, expertly trained, and equipped with high-tech weapons. Since the 1980s, the various armed services had coordinated tactical operations capabilities and had prepared seamlessly to integrate National Guard units. Because of prewar innovations in urban fighting, Army historians concluded, U.S. "soldiers dominated the urban terrain without significant casualties,

Photo 6-7
A bridge in Baghdad demolished by U.S. aerial bombs. Iraq's infrastructure was extensively damaged by the U.S.-led invasion that ousted Saddam Hussein from power. SOURCE: Photo by Michael Bracken, U.S. Army. *On Point: The United States Army in Operation Iraqi Freedom*, p. 340.

destruction, or collateral damage." U.S. air supremacy also gave ground forces extraordinary freedom to maneuver and close-quarter combat support, both decisive factors in the invasion. U.S. superior material resources, communications, intelligence, and planning made the fight uneven. "Moral and psychological factors" also played a role, Keegan notes. "Daring and boldness had played parts in the campaign as significant as dominance in the air, greater firepower, or greater mobility on the ground."[44]

By contrast, the Iraqi military was generally decrepit. It suffered from poor leadership, discipline, organization, equipment, logistics, and training. Fearful of internal rebellion, Hussein had regularly purged his officer corps and positioned his soldiers and supplies to safeguard against Shiite uprisings, which had undermined his Army's cohesion and fighting strength. Because Hussein had popularized the idea that the Gulf War of 1990–1991 had ended in an Iraqi victory, his officer corps, hesitant to disabuse him of the notion, exaggerated their own prowess. With the exception of the *fedayeen*—small, crack units composed of Iraq's most motivated combatants—the Iraqi army generally melted away when the Americans attacked, offering relatively little effective resistance and abandoning its equipment in the field.[45]

In addition, Hussein had made grave political miscalculations before and during the war. In light of the U.S. withdrawal from Vietnam, reluctance to invade Iraq after liberating Kuwait in 1991, withdrawal from Somalia in 1993 after eight GIs died in a battle, and reliance on airpower to achieve political objectives in Bosnia, the Iraqi leader had anticipated that the United States would limit any action against his regime to airstrikes rather than risk significant casualties in ground combat operations. The worst-case scenario in his mind was a U.S. occupation of southern Iraq that would end quickly amid mounting U.S. casualties and difficulties in governing the Shiite community. Hussein also refused to admit that he had no WMD capacity, a step that might have forestalled the American invasion, because the appearance of such capacity seemed to gain him political stature in the eyes of neighboring leaders. In short, Hussein had gambled that Bush's warnings of military invasion were bluffs or that GIs posed a hollow threat. In fact, the U.S. president was utterly sincere and the U.S. armed services were perfectly capable of destroying Hussein's regime.[46]

Hussein also stumbled badly in planning tactics for the defense of his country. In 2002, mid-rank Iraqi military officers formulated a plan for a comprehensive defense of Iraq, but on December 18, Hussein arbitrarily ordered them to concentrate their efforts on a defense of Baghdad along four concentric circles. Although Iraq's top military officers doubted the practicality of this scheme, none dared to voice any objection for fear of provoking Hussein's wrath. Nor did anyone protest when Hussein, apparently expecting a short war, ordered that his air force should be buried in sand dunes rather than resist the invasion. Hussein also accepted at face value the outrageous claims of his propaganda minister that his government was perfectly capable of bringing the American military to its knees. "Iraq is now winning…. The United States is stuck in the mud of defeat,"

Hussein declared, apparently with complete sincerity, even as U.S. tanks closed in on his capital city.[47]

The sweeping nature of the victory notwithstanding, the U.S. war effort was not without flaws. Perhaps the most glaring error was the strong pre-war suspicion among U.S. (and other Western) intelligence officials that the Hussein regime had WMD. This belief, which would be proven false in the aftermath of the war, was at the core of the Bush administration's public justi-fication for the invasion. The accentuation of the false threat led the Pentagon to adjust war plans and operations to account for Hussein's potential use of WMD against U.S. forces, resulting in misallocation of military resources, misdirection of intelligence analysis from more potent dangers, and distrac-tion from genuine threats such as the disposition of stockpiles of conventional Iraqi weapons. The postwar discovery that Hussein lacked any real WMD capacity also eroded the credibility of the Bush administration at home and abroad, despite arguments by such officials as Douglas Feith that Iraq's "*inten-tion* and *capability* to produce biological and chemical weapons" justified the decision to invade.[48]

U.S. forces also committed tactical errors. Intelligence shortcomings included the false report of Hussein's presence at Dora Farms that triggered the opening salvo of the war. Combat commanders received precious little tacti-cal intelligence about enemy forces arrayed against them, Michael R. Gordon and Bernard E. Trainor observe. They did not anticipate the deliberate destruc-tion of certain facilities like the Rumaila oil fields pumping stations, they falsely assumed that southern Shiites would rebel against the Baghdad regime, and they underestimated the determination of the *fedayeen* to resist in Nasiriyah, thus prolonging the battle there. Only gradually did U.S. commanders grasp that the *fedayeen*, rather than the Republican Guard, were their most formidable opponent. (Douglas Feith later argued that military commanders should have integrated friendly Iraqi combatants into the attacking force to create an image of internal liberation rather than foreign occupation, but this criticism is invalid given that there was no military capability in the small number of Iraqi exiles who repatriated after the start of the invasion.)[49]

The Bush Administration aggravated the challenges in Iraq by limiting the size of the invading force and failing to plan adequately for the occupation. The minimal size of the invasion force ordered by Rumsfeld compelled military com-manders to limit their presence in al-Anbar province to small numbers of special forces, which proved unable to prevent Iraqi officials from fleeing to Syria with funds, documents, and weapons. Rumsfeld's buoyant optimism that friendly Iraqis would be able to rebuild their country after the war with minimal U.S. assistance ran counter to the sense of battlefield commanders that available forces were inadequate to maintain the postwar order needed for political stabil-ity. As an anti-American insurgency took hold in Iraq in late 2003 (discussed in Chapter 7), U.S. officers concluded that it resulted from the lack of security resulting from inadequate troop strength.[50]

Indeed, signs of the insurgency materialized even before Bush's May 1 victory speech. Violence and looting plagued Baghdad and rebelliousness stirred among local peoples in other cities. A major fight erupted in Fallujah, a Sunni and Baathist stronghold west of Baghdad, on April 28 (perhaps not coincidentally Hussein's birthday), when insurgents provoked a gun battle with GIs that left 6 to 17 Iraqis dead and became a rallying cry for Sunni insurgents. Another clash 2 days later between an American convoy and a mob of 100 locals further inflamed passions. "In both image and word," war chronicler Thomas Ricks later commented about Bush's May 1 victory speech, "what Bush did was tear down the goalposts at halftime in the game."[51]

The overwhelming U.S. military victory against Iraq did little to quell criticism of the Bush administration at home or abroad. Despite the rapid military victory in Iraq, leading Democrats began to question the wisdom of the invasion as postwar problems developed. Rep. John P. Murtha (D-Pa.), a decorated Marine veteran of the Vietnam War who had voted yes on the October 2002 resolution authorizing Bush to use force in Iraq, claimed in September 2003 that false information from Pentagon officials had misled him into supporting the invasion and demanded that the president dismiss those officials who were responsible. Political groups such as the Center for Economic and Social Rights asserted that Bush's preemptive war violated international legal norms enshrined by the Nuremberg Tribunal and constituted a "crime against peace," whereas Human Rights Watch contended that U.S. treatment of prisoners and detainees violated international law and ruined goodwill toward the United States. Amnesty International protested that high civilian death rates resulted from U.S. indiscriminate use of cluster bombs in civilian areas. When questioned by a journalist in September 2004, U.N. Secretary General Kofi Annan stated that the U.S. invasion of Iraq was "not in conformity with the UN Charter…and from the Charter point of view it was illegal."[52]

Various chroniclers of the war echoed these criticisms of the Bush Administration. The war "was not worth it because of the costs involved and the lack of a threat," former Assistant Secretary of Defense Lawrence Korb observed. "We now know that the other policy—sanctions and containment—was working. He [Hussein] was in a box." Craig R. Eisendrath and Melvin A. Goodman charged that "the Bush Administration has undermined the foundations of American foreign policy, compromised the credibility of the White House, weakened the national security position of the United States, eroded civil liberties, and created greater chaos in the international arena." Former counterterrorism expert Richard A. Clarke noted that "we went off on a tangent, off after Iraq, off on a path that weakened us and strengthened the next generation of al-Qaedas. For even as we have been attriting the core al-Qaeda organization, it has metastasized." Jeffrey Record, an instructor at the Air War College, added that the war was "unnecessary because Iraq posed no measure of danger to the United States justifying war" and "damaging because the preventive, unilateralist nature of the war alienated key friends and allies and weakened the international institutions that have long served U.S. security interests."[53]

Yet the war had backers. "A regime of inspections, embargo, sanctions, no-fly zones and thousands of combat troops in Kuwait was an unstable equilibrium," conservative columnist Charles Krauthammer asserted. "The United States could have retreated and allowed Saddam Hussein free rein or it could have gone to war and removed him.... The president made the right choice, indeed the only choice." Charles A. Duelfer, a member of the U.S. Government's Iraq Survey Group, added that the decision to oust Hussein was sound despite the flaws of executing it. "The alternative future of an Iraq with Saddam in control and empowered by growing demand for its oil resources," he observed, "would have been dangerously disruptive to the region in ways that we happily no longer have to imagine."[54]

Naturally, President Bush remained the most steadfast defender of his policy. "I remembered the shattering pain of 9/11, a surprise attack from which we had received no warning," he wrote in his memoirs. "This time we had a warning like a blaring siren. Years of intelligence pointed overwhelmingly to the conclusion that Saddam had WMD.... And given his support of terror and his sworn hatred of America, there was no way to know where those weapons would end up."

Photo 6-8
Soldiers in the 54th Quartermaster Company handle the remains of a U.S. soldier killed in the invasion of Iraq. One hundred thirty-nine U.S. soldiers were killed during the invasion of Iraq in March–April 2003. Some 4,300 GIs would perish during the prolonged occupation that followed. SOURCE: Photo by 54th Quartermaster Company. *On Point: The United States Army in Operation Iraqi Freedom*, p. 338.

Although the WMD threat eventually proved false, Bush contended, the strong belief among intelligence experts worldwide that the threat existed in 2003 made his decision wise and prudent.[55]

CONCLUSION

George W. Bush led the United States on a momentous military adventure in Iraq. Motivated by a feeling of insecurity generated by 9/11, the inexperienced but decisive president committed the United States to the mission of liberating Iraq from Saddam Hussein's brutal regime. Bush believed that such drastic action was a necessary measure for the national defense against another, even more devastating terrorist attack, and he hoped that the bold step would vitalize democracy in the Middle East. So determined did Bush become to exercise the military option that he disregarded voices at home and abroad—including James Baker and Brent Scowcroft, who had served as his father's top two foreign policy advisers—cautioning about the dangers and risks in preemptive belligerence.

Once ordered into action, U.S. soldiers and their allies scored a dramatic victory on the battlefields of Iraq. They decisively defeated a numerically superior adversary that fought defensively on its own terrain. They quickly finished off the Hussein regime that had ruled Iraq for 24 years, capturing or killing its leaders who scattered in the early days of the fighting. They ensured the security of the Kurds of northern Iraq, bolstering democracy and stability in that region. In the most immediate goal of demolishing the brutal regime of Saddam Hussein, the Bush Administration accomplished its mission.

Yet the administration's decisions and methods sowed the seeds of trouble in the near future. The president based much of his rationale for war on erroneous pretenses, namely the belief that Iraq possessed dangerous quantities of WMD and the suspicion that Hussein was intent on using such weapons to attack the West in partnership with terrorists. Although many experts were fooled by the mirage of Iraq's WMD capabilities, Bush's claim that Hussein would partner with Islamic terrorists and his false association of Iraq with the 9/11 attacks muddled the justification for the war in the eyes of critics at home and overseas. Bush's decision to pursue regime change over the alternative of continuing his predecessors' containment policy generated significant criticism from observers who believed, with good reason, that war was not necessary to deal with the challenges posed by the Hussein regime and that war would cause new perils even worse than Iraq. Bush, in short, started a war that many considered unnecessary and failed accurately to anticipate the consequences of that action. The president's thin basis for action and his inadequate preparations for the aftermath of victory would soon tarnish the luster of the military achievement and the credibility of the Bush Administration.

The Bush Administration marched to war with insufficient political planning and military troop strength. Hindsight indicates clearly that the United States was ill-prepared to face the complicated political challenges that would follow the downfall of Saddam Hussein or even to restore law and order in the aftermath of wartime dislocation. The decisive victory by the soldiers and marines who crushed the Hussein regime earned for the Bush Administration the responsibility for governing a broken and dysfunctional country, the criticism of many American people, and the scorn of much of the international community. Years of trouble lay ahead.

NOTES

1. Franks, *American Soldier*, 142–431; Michael Duffy and Mark Thompson, "The General: Straight Shooter," *Time*, March 17, 2003, http://www.time.com/time/magazine/article/0,9171,1004406–3,00.html/ (accessed June 25, 2010).

2. Franks, *American Soldier*, 431.

3. Fallows, *Blind into Baghdad*, 96; Haass, *War of Necessity*, 210; Woodward, *State of Denial*, 325–26; Woodward, *War Within*, 27 (quotation); Packer, *Assassins' Gate*, 392 (quotation).

4. Mann, *Rise of the Vulcans*, 234–38 (quotation); Ricks, *Fiasco*, 17 (quotation); Packer, *Assassins' Gate*, 12–38; Haass, *War of Necessity*, 235–36.

5. Feith, *War and Decision*, 183–210.

6. Packer, *Assassins' Gate*, 12–38; Mann, *Rise of the Vulcans*, 363.

7. Woodward, *Plan of Attack*, 4, 12–23 (quotation 4); Suskind, *Price of Loyalty*, 70–75, 84–86.

8. Woodward, *Plan of Attack*, 12–23; Haass, *War of Necessity*, 171–80; Ricks, *Fiasco*, 26–28.

9. Rumsfeld to Rice, July 27, 2001, reprinted in Feith, *War and Decision*, 535–38; Brattebo, "No-Fly Zones," 231–34.

10. *9/11 Commission Report*, 38–40 (quotation 39); Franks, *American Soldier*, 283–317; Woodward, *Bush at War*, 312–16.

11. Department of Defense news transcript, September 13, 2001, http://www.defense.gov/transcripts/transcript.aspx?transcriptid=1622/ (accessed November 25, 2009) (quotation); Feith, *War and Decision*, 215 (quotation); *9/11 Commission Report*, 334–38; Feith, *War and Decision*, 48–78; Ricks, *Fiasco*, 30–32.

12. Transcript of Powell press conference, September 17, 2001, http://www.washingtonpost.com/wp-srv/nation/specials/attacked/transcripts/powelltext_091701.html/ (accessed November 25, 2009); *9/11 Commission Report*, 334.

13. *9/11 Commission Report*, 336; Bush address to Congress, September 20, 2001, http://georgewbush-whitehouse.archives.gov/news/releases/2001/09/20010920–6.html/ (accessed November 25, 2009) (quotations); Feith, *War and Decision*, 4–17.

14. Jervis, *American Foreign Policy*, 10 (quotation), 81–90; Kaufman, *In Defense*, 98–130 (quotation 127); Lind, *American Way of Strategy*, 125–70.

15. Bush, *Decision Points*, 151; Blair, *Journey*, 354.

16. Bush, *Decision Points*, 150–65 (quotation 165); Blair, *Journey*, 356.

17. Feith, *War and Decision*, 295, 222, 303–319 (quotation); Woodward, *Plan of Attack*, 24–74.

18. Bush, *Decision Points*, 229–30.

19. Bush, State of the Union Address, January 20, 2002, http://www.washingtonpost.com/wp-srv/onpolitics/transcripts/sou012902.htm/ (accessed November 10, 2009).

20. Freedman, *Choice of Enemies*, 404 (quotations); Woodward, *Plan of Attack*, 84–95, 119–20, 132, 194–202 (quotations 132, 202); Eisendrath and Goodman, *Bush League Diplomacy*, 134 (quotation).

21. Speech by Cheney, August 26, 2002, http://georgewbush-whitehouse.archives.gov/news/releases/2002/08/20020826.html/ (accessed November 25, 2009) (quotation); Brent Scowcroft, "Don't Attack Saddam," *Wall Street Journal*, August 15, 2002; Woodward, *Plan of Attack*, 159–66.

22. Woodward, *Plan of Attack*, 185–91, 203–4 (quotations 187–188); Joint Resolution on Iraq, October 11, 2002, http://www.pbs.org/newshour/bb/middle_east/july-dec02/joint_resolution_10–11-02.html/ (accessed November 10, 2009) (quotation); Ricks, *Fiasco*, 30–32, 46–64, 85–90.

23. U.N. Security Council Resolution 1441, November 8, 2002, Sifry and Cerf, *Iraq War Reader*, 648–52 (quotations); Bush, *Decision Points*, 232–42; Haass, *War of Necessity*, 231; Woodward, *Plan of Attack*, 180–85, 220–27; Fallows, *Blind into Baghdad*, 64–65.

24. Bush, *Decision Points*, 242; Feith, *War and Decision*, 341–43 (quotation 342); Keegan, *Iraq War*, 111–14.

25. Woodward, *Plan of Attack*, 247–54 (quotation 249).

26. Woodward, *Plan of Attack*, 294–95; Fallows, *Blind into Baghdad*, 9–11.

27. Woodward, *Plan of Attack*, 308–18; Ricks, *Fiasco*, 90–94; O'Sullivan, *Colin Powell*, 188.

28. William Hamilton, "Bush Began to Plan War Three Months after 9/11," *Washington Post*, April 17, 2004; Duelfer, *Hide and Seek*, 246–47 (quotation); Brattebo, "No-Fly Zones," 234–39.

29. Gordon and Trainor, *Cobra II*, 3–54, 70–74; "Post-Saddam Iraq: The War Game," http://www.gwu.edu/~nsarchiv/NSAEBB/NSAEBB207/index.htm/ (accessed Nov. 25, 2009).

30. Eric Schmitt, "Pentagon Contradicts General on Iraq Occupation Force's Size," *New York Times*, February 28, 2003 (quotations); Fallows, *Blind into Baghdad*, 97–99 (quotation); Ricks, *Fiasco*, 96–100.

31. Jimmy Carter, "Just War—Or Just a War?" *New York Times*, March 9, 2003.

32. Interview with Chirac, *Time*, February 23, 2003, http://www.time.com/time/europe/magazine/2003/0224/cover/interview.html/ (accessed November 25, 2009); Winrow, "Turkey," 197–208; Ricks, *Fiasco*, 94–95 (quotation).

33. Woodward, *Plan of Attack*, 346–79; Malone, *International Struggle*, 191–200; Feith, *War and Decision*, 353–59.

34. George Packer, "Dreaming of Democracy," http://www.nytimes.com/2003/03/02/magazine/dreaming-of-democracy.html/ (accessed November 10, 2009); Ricks, *Fiasco*, 96–97 (quotation); Packer, *Assassins' Gate*, 76–97.

35. Keegan, *Iraq War*, 114–20; Defense Department paper, August 23, 2002, reprinted in Feith, *War and Decision*, 539–40.

36. Murray and Scales, *Iraq War*, 154–56.

37. Murray and Scales, *Iraq War*, 185–95; Ricks, *Fiasco*, 118–19, 124–27.

38. Murray and Scales, *Iraq War*, 99–100, 118–28, 144–53, 190–209.

39. Murray and Scales, *Iraq War*, 209–33 (quotation 210); Fontenot, *On Point*, 336.

40. Keegan, *Iraq War*, 127–203; Gordon and Trainor, *Cobra II*, 374–89.

41. Murray and Scales, *Iraq War*, 232–35; Keegan, *Iraq War*, 193, 4 (quotations); "'Ladies and Gentlemen, We Got Him,'" *Time*, December 22, 2003, 15–19.

42. "'Ladies and Gentlemen, We Got Him,'" *Time*, December 22, 2003, 15–19; Hahn, *U.S.–Middle East Relations*, 65.

43. Packer, *Assassins' Gate*, 333–67; Rafaat, "U.S.-Kurdish Relations," 79–89.

44. Murray and Scales, *Iraq War*, 59–77; Fontenot, *On Point*, xviii (quotation); Keegan, *Iraq War*, 193 (quotation).

45. Murray and Scales, *Iraq War*, 77–84; Gordon and Trainor, *Cobra II*, 55–74; Keegan, *Iraq War*, 56–87.

46. Wood, *Iraqi Perspectives Project*, 25–32; Blair, *Journey*, 374–75.

47. Wood, *Iraqi Perspectives Project*, 32 (quotation), 39–65, 75–84.

48. Gordon and Trainor, *Cobra II*, 118–37, 327–44; Duelfer, *Hide and Seek*, 408; Ricks, *Fiasco*, 145–46; Feith, *War and Decision*, 224–27, 329–31 (quotation 227).

49. Gordon and Trainor, *Cobra II*, 182–326; Feith, *War and Decision*, 349–50, 365, 385, 398–400.

50. Ricks, *Fiasco*, 83–84, 118–23, 134–35, 146–47; Gordon and Trainor, *Cobra II*, 138–50, 497–98.

51. Ricks, *Fiasco*, 138–45 (quotation 145).

52. David Firestone, "Democratic Hawk Urges Firing of Bush Aides," *New York Times*, September 17, 2003; Center for Economic and Social Rights, "Tearing Up the Rules," in Brecher et al., *In the Name of Democracy*, 24–32; Human Rights Watch, "The Road to Abu Ghraib," in Brecher et al., *In the Name of Democracy*, 84–99; Amnesty International, "Iraq;" BBC Interview with Kofi Annan, September 16, 2004, in Brecher et al., *In the Name of Democracy*, 33 (quotation).

53. Korb quoted in "Justification for War Still Hotly Debated," *Columbus Dispatch*, March 19, 2004, A10; Eisendrath and Goodman, *Bush League Diplomacy*, 219–20; Clarke, *Against All Enemies*, 286–87; Record, *Dark Victory*, 142–43.

54. Charles Krauthammer, "President Made the Best of Two Choices," *Columbus Dispatch*, January 30, 2004; Duelfer, *Hide and Seek*, 479.

55. Bush, *Decision Points*, 252–53.

CHAPTER 7

The Quest for Stability
The Occupation of Iraq, 2003–2010

By all accounts, Zachary Grass experienced an ordinary upbringing in the late 20th century Midwest. Born on May 22, 1985, to Frank and Patti Grass, he was raised near Beach City, Ohio, a village of about 1,000 residents and two traffic lights some 60 miles south of Cleveland. He spent time in his youth playing golf and video games with a wide circle of friends. After studying Spanish, he playfully called his parents "Madre" and "Padre" and his older brother Ben "hermano." A talented athlete, Grass played guard on the basketball team and pitcher and third baseman on the baseball team at Fairless High School, graduating in 2003. "He was a kid always willing to do whatever it took to help the team," his basketball coach later recalled, "a pretty selfless kid." Grass's high school principal remembered him as "a natural-born leader among his peers." Like thousands of young Americans who absorbed the impact of the 9/11 attacks during high school, Grass decided, in February 2005, to enlist in the U.S. Army.[1]

The Army designated Grass for the Artillery. After basic and advanced training at Fort Sill, Oklahoma, he reported in June 2005 to Fort Lewis, Washington, where he was assigned at the rank of Specialist to the 2nd Battalion, 12th Field Artillery Regiment, 4th Brigade, 2nd Infantry Division (the Stryker Brigade Combat Team). Featuring the Army's eight-wheeled armored vehicle known as the "Stryker" (in honor of two soldiers of that name who were killed in action during World War II and the Vietnam War), the brigade was trained as mobile infantry. In the field, the brigade's soldiers conducted motorized and foot patrols.[2]

In April 2007, Spc. Grass was ordered to deploy to Iraq for 15 months as part of a surge in U.S. forces there. Earlier that year, President George W. Bush had ordered an additional 40,000 troops to reinforce the 130,000 soldiers in Iraq, in the hope of quelling an armed insurgency that had bedeviled the U.S. occupation of the country. Within weeks, some 11,000 soldiers from Fort Lewis were on duty in Iraq, the highest number since the invasion of March 2003. "Madre, it's just my job I have to do and it will be OK," Grass told his mother before shipping out, she later recalled. "I'll be fine." Grass, however, encountered a dangerous situation

Photo 7-1
Army Specialist Zachary Grass of Ohio, killed in action near ar-Rashidiyah, Iraq, June 16, 2007. SOURCE: Photo courtesy of the family of Zachary Grass.

Photo 7-2
Soldiers of the Stryker Brigade Combat Team conduct a dismounted patrol near Mosul, Iraq, c. 2005. Specialist Grass was on a patrol attached to such a vehicle when he died in action in 2007. SOURCE: DOD Photo by Jeremiah Johnson. Combined Arms Research Library.

when he reached Iraq the next month, within days of his 22nd birthday. The surge initially caused a spike in U.S. casualties, with May 2007 proving to be the third deadliest month for U.S. soldiers since the start of the war.[3]

On Saturday, June 16, Grass was on a patrol east of the Tigris River near ar-Rashidiyah, about 10 miles north of Baghdad, when his vehicle was hit by an improvised explosive device. Grass and 24-year-old Sgt. Danny R. Soto of Houston, Texas, were killed in the explosion. They were the first two artillery-men from the 4th Brigade's artillery battalion to be killed in action. Before the day ended, the Army promoted Grass to Corporal and military officers in Ohio delivered the news of Grass's death to his parents. The village of Beach City joined the family in mourning their loss.[4]

Grass's supreme sacrifice—and the deaths of more than 4,400 other U.S. soldiers on duty in Iraq in the 7 years following the initial invasion—illustrated the difficulties facing the United States in Iraq after the liberation of that country from Saddam Hussein's rule.[5] Indeed, President Bush's speech aboard the USS *Abraham Lincoln* on May 1, 2003, would soon be interpreted as a premature claim of victory. Events quickly discredited his declaration of the end of major combat operations in Iraq, as well as the claim of victory implied in the "Mission Accomplished" banner suspended overhead. Before long, political instability and military insurgency swept across Iraq, imperiling U.S. control of the country and undermining hope for a satisfactory outcome. The Bush Administration would struggle to find a formula for achieving peace and stability in the country quickly occupied in the 500-Hour War.

THE CHALLENGES OF OCCUPATION

Although marking the achievement of a major U.S. objective in the war in Iraq, the collapse of the Saddam Hussein regime also left the United States facing a dangerous and difficult challenge: governing a war-torn, fractious, and unstable country. Having neglected to plan carefully for an occupation of Iraq, the Bush Administration tried to rush the transition from war to peace by establishing an independent and stable government in Baghdad. Assigned responsibility for the occupation, the Pentagon planted new bureaucracies in Baghdad and empowered friendly Iraqi exiles in the hope of transferring power to a new Iraqi government as soon as possible, ideally within 90 days. The Pentagon and its chosen local leaders would find the task of managing Iraq far more difficult than they had anticipated.

Serious trouble surfaced in Baghdad even before President Bush's "Mission Accomplished" proclamation. In fact, a wave of lawlessness swept the city in the immediate aftermath of its liberation. Thousands of looters ransacked government buildings, hospitals, museums, and private businesses, throwing parts of the city into chaos. Gunfights erupted between Sunnis and Shiites and between looters and property owners. Charities suspended operations after a Red Cross aid worker was killed in a crossfire. U.S. combat soldiers were slow to curb the violence in this so-called Second Battle of Baghdad, even as some officers sensed that the turmoil was detrimental to U.S. interests. Iraqis perceived "that 'my country is being destroyed,'" Army Major Rod Coffey noted. "The looting feeds all those myths that the Americans are here and they just want to take all our oil and they want us to be weak." Worse, Secretary of Defense Donald Rumsfeld's remarks about the violence seemed impolitic to many. "Freedom's untidy," he told a group of reporters, "and free people are free to make mistakes and commit crimes and do bad things. They're also free to live their lives and do wonderful things. And that's what's going to happen here."[6]

The Bush Administration was also slow to formulate an effective policy for postwar Iraq. President Bush had established a new government agency called the Office of Reconstruction and Humanitarian Assistance (ORHA) on January 20, 2003, about 8 weeks before the war started, and Rumsfeld appointed retired Army Lieutenant General Jay Garner to head it. From its inception, however, ORHA struggled to function efficiently. In light of the security situation, Garner and his staff were unable to arrive in Baghdad until 12 days after GIs liberated the city, and thereafter they could not travel about the city safely. Garner later claimed that Under Secretary of Defense Douglas Feith's written plans for post-war Iraq did not reach him in Baghdad in a timely manner. Nor did Garner gain access to the views of the State Department, the CIA, or the National Defense University. After rioting and looting destabilized the remnants of the Iraqi government, ORHA assigned various officers to supervise Iraqi ministries in which they had little expertise.[7]

Ironically, several U.S. government agencies had anticipated the trouble that developed. In the State Department's "Future of Iraq" initiative, 17 teams of experts and Iraqi expatriates had identified solutions to the problems that the invasion might cause in Iraq's political framework, culture, infrastructure, justice system, and other matters. The initiative's 2,500 pages of reports had recommended that U.S. forces protect and restore water, electricity, and other components of the country's infrastructure and retain the rank-and-file units of the Iraqi Army while purging the officer corps of Hussein loyalists. Although the "Future of Iraq" planners had not explicitly predicted a mass insurgency, they had anticipated that lawlessness perpetrated by common criminals would plague Iraq in the aftermath of Hussein's demise. "The period immediately after regime change," the planners had warned, "might offer these criminals the opportunity to engage in acts of killing, plunder, and looting." They had urged that the Pentagon "organize military patrols by coalition forces in all major cities to prevent lawlessness, especially against vital utilities and key government officials."[8]

Various other voices had echoed these concerns. "The possibility of the United States winning the war and losing the peace is real and serious," experts of the Strategic Studies Institute of the Army War College had warned. "Thinking about the war now and the occupation later is not an acceptable solution. Without an overwhelming effort to prepare for occupation, the United States may find itself in a radically different world over the next five years, a world in which the threat of Saddam Hussein seems like a pale shadow of new problems of America's own making." General Eric Shinseki's prediction that the number of troops dispatched to Iraq was insufficient (discussed in Chapter 6) had indicated serious reservations among top uniformed officers about Rumsfeld's plans for Iraq. Even General Garner echoed such concerns after he reached Baghdad. "There was no doubt we would win the war," Garner remarked to General David D. McKiernan, the armor officer who commanded U.S. and allied invading ground forces, "but there can be doubt we will win the peace." Moreover, the CIA had predicted that decapitation of the Hussein regime would unleash sectarian conflict. Phebe Marr, an eminent historian of Iraq, had warned the Senate Foreign Relations Committee that achieving political stability after the fall of Hussein would prove to be challenging.[9]

President Bush and the top Pentagon officials responsible for postwar Iraq, however, generally disregarded these warnings. Bush later recorded that, in light of NSC planning to address such problems as refugees and food shortages and to rebuild Iraq's infrastructure, "I felt we were well prepared" to govern Iraq after the invasion. His blaming of subsequent problems on "an old adage" that "no battle plan survives the first contact with the enemy" does not properly acknowledge that he neglected the warnings of trouble that various agencies had vocalized. Rumsfeld eschewed worst-case contingency planning because he was generally skeptical about forecasts and proud of his ability to respond quickly to events. Feith showed little interest in the recommendations by experts in other agencies and his office staff reportedly found the "Future of Iraq" reports too academic and thus impractical. Noting that the "Future of Iraq" project never conceived of a plan for postinvasion Iraq, Feith later labeled as "preposterous" the suggestion that the administration had received a "memo" predicting trouble. Reflecting on the success of small-scale U.S. forces in Afghanistan, CENTCOM Commander General Tommy Franks endorsed Rumsfeld's view that Iraqi stability could be attained with a relatively small military force.[10]

The Pentagon officials who determined postwar U.S. policy clearly failed to plan adequately for the challenges that followed the destruction of the Hussein regime. Pentagon leaders ignored clearly articulated warnings of potential trouble in Iraq and instead took steps to safeguard against threats that never emerged, such as incursions by neighboring states, retribution attacks against leaders of Hussein's regime, and massive fires to oil wells. Although "the oft-stated goal of *regime change* implied some degree of postwar steps to build a new Iraqi Government in place of the Saddam regime," Army historians later noted, "*Regime removal* might have been a more accurate description of the goal" implicit in the operations actually conducted by the Pentagon. Even President Bush conceded in his memoirs that he had erred by not responding "more quickly or aggressively when the security situation started to deteriorate after Saddam's regime fell. . . . By reducing our troop presence and focusing on training Iraqis, we inadvertently allowed the insurgency to gain momentum." Bush also acknowledged that his statement "Bring 'em on"—declared in July 2003 in reference to the fledgling insurgency, in the hope of encouraging U.S. troops and defying anti-U.S. rebels—unintentionally created an impression among the American people that the president was spoiling excessively for a fight.[11]

In addition to inadequate planning, other errors marred the Bush Administration's transition from invasion to occupation. Rumsfeld's stubborn insistence on restricting the number of GIs deployed to Iraq limited the capability of the U.S. military to achieve stability there. The Defense Secretary's expectation that General Garner—within a 1-month timeframe—could achieve progress sufficient to justify a rapid U.S. demobilization was similarly unrealistic. Nor did the Pentagon leadership adequately prepare its forces in the field to overcome the language and cultural gaps with the people of Iraq that would impede U.S. efforts to govern the country. As the journalist James Fallows charged, Rumsfeld's "embrace of 'uncertainty'" became a "reckless evasion of responsibility," whereas President Bush showed a distinct "lack of curiosity about significant details."[12]

Many military officers assigned to Iraq soon realized that the ill-fated transition from invasion to occupation amounted to a massive lost opportunity by the Pentagon leadership. "Right after we got into Baghdad," Army Col. David Perkins later noted, "there was a huge window of opportunity that if we had this well-defined plan and we were ready to come in with all these resources, we could have really grabbed ahold of the city and really started pushing things forward. By the time we got a plan together to resource everything, the insurgents had closed that window of opportunity quickly." "It is reasonable to believe," Army historians eventually concluded, "…that had better military planning…been accomplished before the war, had a more robust and effective command and control structure been rapidly put in place during the summer of 2003, and had a larger number of military forces been on the ground in 2003, the Army would have been better able to contribute to the creation of a new Iraq." Such post facto assessments call attention to the fundamental flaw in the administration's approach to Iraq: a dereliction of preparations for the era that would follow conquest.[13]

The inadequate preparations by the President and Pentagon leaders imperiled General Garner's mission in Iraq from its beginning. Garner's early announcement that he would organize popular elections within 90 days upset those Pentagon officials who favored certain Iraqi expatriates, whom they feared would be disadvantaged by a rapid transition. Perhaps under pressure from Vice President Dick Cheney, Rumsfeld blocked Garner's effort to appoint to his staff such political experts as "Future of Iraq" director Thomas Warrick and aide Meghan O'Sullivan. Hoping to utilize the remnants of the Iraqi military, its command structure, and its equipment as a foundation for a new Iraqi security force, Garner explored a scheme in which 100,000 Iraqi soldiers (about one fourth of Hussein's army) would be paid small cash stipends if they enrolled in a new force and revealed their knowledge about the security situation. Garner also considered relying on Iraqi civil servants, including members of the Baath Party, to provide continuity in the governance of the country. Rumsfeld, however, refused to sanction such actions and began searching for a replacement for Garner who was more compliant with the Pentagon's wishes.[14]

The Bush administration also reportedly rejected an initiative proposed by arms inspector Charles Duelfer to facilitate a stable transfer of power among Iraqis. Having accumulated precious knowledge about Iraqi officials while working as an inspector, Duelfer had collaborated with the CIA's Iraq Operations Group before the war to plan for regime change. By January 2003, Duelfer and the Iraq Operations Group "identified reliable individuals inside the key ministries, especially the Oil, Finance, Electricity and Trade ministries, and even Iraqi intelligence. We had established routes to communicate with them. It seemed like a useful mechanism that would help make the invasion and transition to new leadership smoother." Yet such planning for "day after" activities was suspended by National Security Advisor Condoleezza Rice, who favored Rumsfeld's plan to rely on repatriated Iraqi exiles to lead postwar Iraq. After the invasion, Duelfer ventured to Baghdad to promote his collaborationist scheme, but he soon withdrew after finding that the administration was not interested in working with the Iraqi officials he had identified as prospective collaborators.[15]

By May, steadily worsening conditions in Iraq signaled the failure of Bush's and Rumsfeld's hope for a rapid transfer of authority in Iraq to a trusted group of leaders from the Iraqi exile community. Western journalists found that the country's law enforcement, emergency medicine, electricity and telephone systems, and other crucial components of social stability had collapsed after the invasion. Sectarian violence swept the city, as did violent crime. "Baghdad nights are full of menace," *Time* reporters wrote. "The smoke of looted, burning buildings turns the sunset blood orange.... When the sun goes down, the streets empty quickly.... Gunfire punches holes in the city's eerie quiet." Hobbled by the unrealistic restrictions imposed by the Pentagon leadership, General Garner was unable to stabilize the country.[16]

His initial hopes dashed, President Bush dramatically reformed his occupation administration in Iraq, but with limited effect. In a series of decisions announced on May 6–16, he created the Coalition Provisional Authority (CPA), appointed former Ambassador L. Paul Bremer to lead it, and clarified that Bremer would report to the President through Secretary Rumsfeld. (ORHA simply ceased to function and Garner returned to the United States in June.) During an early meeting in Washington, however, the President refused Bremer's request for more troops, citing Rumsfeld's judgment that the number currently deployed would be able to maintain stability. After reaching Baghdad, Bremer sent a subsequent request for more troops to Rumsfeld but never received an answer. Rumors that General Garner had been stripped of his authority for nonperformance caused some political tension, especially because Garner lingered in Baghdad. Bremer was annoyed that U.S. military officers refused to interdict oil smuggling, which ransacked the Iraqi economy. He found the federal bureaucracy in Washington slow to respond to his needs and the international media increasingly critical of U.S. policy in Iraq. Perhaps feeling triumphant, the administration also rejected calls for the United Nations to administer the occupation of Iraq. "We fought the war," an official told one journalist, "and, besides, the U.N. is not competent to handle a complex undertaking like Iraq." The irony in this statement was considerable because the Bush Administration was showing little competence itself.[17]

Bremer also failed to develop a productive working relationship with military officers in Iraq. He reportedly put off senior officers by declaring, at his first meeting with them in Baghdad, that "you all work for me." General Ricardo Sanchez, the top U.S. military officer in Iraq from June 2003 to June 2004, later claimed that he had developed a counterinsurgency plan "that combined a strong warfighting tactical plan…with an integrated political, economic, and security approach. Through this 'hearts and minds' approach, we intended to isolate hard-core insurgents from the general population, provide economic hope, and involve as many Iraqis as possible in the process." Sanchez proposed establishment of an Iraqi Civil Defense Corps as a step in that direction, but Bremer

Photo 7-3
President George W. Bush receives L. Paul Bremer, wearing boots, at the White House. As head of the Coalition Provisional Authority (CPA), Bremer issued CPA Orders Number 1 and 2, which dissolved the Baath Party and the Iraqi government. Critics later charged that these orders gravely destabilized Iraq and thus inflated the difficulties that the United States faced in occupying the country. SOURCE: White House Photo. Combined Arms Research Library.

refused to approve the creation of any group resembling an Iraqi army. Before long, Bremer and Sanchez essentially refused to speak to each other and failed to coordinate civil and military activities.[18]

In a bold ploy to exert authority in Iraq, by contrast, Bremer announced two fateful policies within days of arriving in Baghdad. In CPA Order Number 1, signed on May 16, Bremer dismantled the Baath Party, barred senior and mid-level members from holding posts in government agencies (including hospitals and universities), and subjected leaders to criminal investigations. In CPA Order Number 2, issued on May 23, Bremer dissolved the Iraqi government, its ministry of defense and all service branches, its paramilitary and special security forces, and its intelligence system. General Garner tried to dissuade Bremer from issuing the second order, and Army War College experts warned that "to tear apart the army in the war's aftermath could lead to the destruction of one of the only forces for unity within the society." Bremer told Garner, however, that he was carrying out orders from Washington. Walter Slocombe, the CPA's director of national security and defense who supported Bremer's order, told a Garner aide that "we don't pay armies we defeated."[19]

CPA Orders Number 1 and 2 quickly became subjects of controversy. Bremer later defended the orders as part of a sweeping initiative to reform every aspect of Iraqi life and to hearten Iraq's Shiite and Kurdish peoples by clearly breaking the back of Sunni dominance. Given that Iraq's army had "vaporized" during combat operations, Slocombe told an interviewer in August 2004, "we didn't disband the army. The army disbanded itself." Reconstituting it was impossible on practical grounds, he added, in light of the ethnic divisions between the Sunni officer corps and the Shiite rank-and-file and the destruction of the military's bases and other physical assets. "Using a badly trained, ethnically unacceptable army with very dubious, politically loyal leadership to do a critical security job," Slocombe asserted, "is a formula for disaster."[20]

In retrospect, however, CPA Orders Number 1 and 2 should be faulted for eliminating instruments that U.S. forces could have employed to stabilize the country. Order Number 1 missed a golden opportunity—which Duelfer claimed to have arranged as a viable option—to achieve stability by enrolling Iraqi technocrats as partners in governance. The effect of the first order, General David Petraeus later stated, "was that tens of thousands of former party members were unemployed, without any salary, without any retirement, without any benefits, and therefore, to a large degree, without any incentive to support the new Iraq." The rapid spread of the anti-U.S. insurgency after the announcement of CPA Order Number 2, moreover, strongly suggests that the hundreds of thousands of dismissed soldiers, stripped of their jobs but not their weapons, formed the backbone of the uprising. It is plausible and reasonable to observe that Garner's proposal to enlist rank-and-file soldiers in a new security force more likely would have promoted stability in postwar Iraq than the policies Bremer implemented. Although noting that alternative policies also would have been problematic, even President Bush acknowledged in his memoirs that "the orders had a psychological impact I did not foresee" and that "the de-Baathification program turned out to cut much deeper than we expected."[21]

However flawed CPA Orders Number 1 and 2 appeared in hindsight, Bremer followed them in real time with an ambitious plan to remake Iraq on a foundational level. With an initial allocation of $18 billion, he sought to dismantle the old order of the Hussein era; to reform Iraq's government, economy, infrastructure, public works, and security system; and to devise "shock absorbers" for the Iraqi people such as "free press, trade unions, political parties, [and] professional associations." Bremer used the authority of the CPA to rebuild Iraq's infrastructure, establish a new police force, promote educational and social reform, stimulate the economy, and generate a democratic potential and sense of nationhood in Iraq. He hired hundreds of American civilians to administer and reform Iraq's police force, stock market, factory production, media, taxation, motor vehicle traffic, health care, banking, and education. Attempting to win the trust of the Iraqi people, Bremer became a public figure, routinely traveling around the country and making public appearances. By the end of 2003, some 35 countries sent troops to help the United States occupy and rebuild Iraq. By early 2005, U.S. authorities had built or repaired some 2,400 schools, medical clinics, and fire stations in Iraq.[22]

Yet the CPA effort in Iraq deserved some significant criticisms. Reportedly, CPA officers were chosen for their political or ideological beliefs rather than their professional credentials and many unwisely tried to remake Iraq on the basis of conservative political values and in ignorance of Iraqi customs and culture. Rapid personnel turnover rates created inefficiency and discontinuity in the CPA, and corruption blemished several contracts with private service providers. Because most CPA staffers never left the "Green Zone," the fortified compound in central Baghdad where the Authority was headquartered, they gained little understanding of the actual conditions in the country and they soon lost credibility among the Iraqi people. "None of us truly believed," recounted Mark Etherington, a former British paratrooper who worked for the CPA, "that the reforms we had helped institute would endure." As cynics whispered that "CPA" stood for "Can't Produce Anything," critics correctly noted that the Authority failed to stabilize Iraq before an anti-American insurgency swept the country.[23]

Perhaps the only successes of the early occupation policy pertained to economic reform. In December 2003, Bush asked former Secretary of State James Baker to lead an international initiative to restructure $120 billion in Iraqi debt inherited from the Saddam Hussein era. Baker persuaded the leaders of Britain, France, Russia, Germany, Italy, China, Japan, and various Middle East states to set aside their political disagreements about the U.S. conduct of the war and forgive Iraqi debts. Ultimately, a coalition of 19 industrialized states forgave 80 percent of Iraq's sovereign debt and the United States forgave $4.1 billion (100 percent). Iraqi Finance Minister Adil Abdel Mahdi called the concessions "the second liberation of Iraq." Debt relief and the related reform of the Iraqi dinar comprised two undeniable successes in an otherwise difficult and frustrating period of U.S. occupation.[24]

FORMING AN IRAQI GOVERNMENT

While the CPA labored to stabilize Iraq, the Bush Administration also faced the challenge of forming an Iraqi government that could exercise a permanent mantle of authority. Prewar planning on this topic was minimal and generally centered on the idea of investing authority in Ahmed Chalabi, an Iraqi exile who had developed a cooperative relationship with U.S. officials over many years. When Chalabi proved to be ineffective and unacceptable to other Iraqis, however, Bush Administration officials were forced to improvise alternatives. Their efforts were complicated by the decline of physical conditions within Iraq, the anti-U.S. political fallout of Bush's decision to invade, and the bureaucratic rivalries among U.S. officials.

Prior to the U.S. invasion, the Bush administration had contemplated the challenge of state building in a post-Hussein Iraq. In October 2002, National Security Adviser Rice identified as the U.S. objective the establishment of a state that maintained peace with its neighbors, renounced terrorism and WMD, remained unified, honored the rule of law and basic human rights, and encouraged "the building of democratic institutions." To achieve such a goal, the Bush administration would use "all instruments of U.S. national power in a coordinated fashion" and, if possible, collaborate with allies, Iraqi opposition figures, and the United Nations. Once Iraq was liberated from Hussein's rule, the United States would quickly transfer authority to an elected Iraqi government, protect the country's territorial integrity, reform its economy and bureaucracies, punish its war criminals, and provide relief to its people. President Bush later noted that he disliked the idea promoted by some members of his administration to elevate Iraqi exile leaders to positions of authority, fearing that an externally imposed leader would stimulate a nationalistic backlash. Why the president allowed his top aides to follow exactly such a course of action remains a mystery.[25]

Indeed, U.S. officials relied on Iraqi expatriates as key collaborators in postwar transition plans. The administration encouraged talks in Washington and London in 2002 among several factions of Iraqi expatriate groups interested in replacing the Hussein regime. Meeting in northern Iraq on February 24–27, 2003, to discuss a transition regime to follow the anticipated U.S. invasion, opposition leaders formed a committee of six to monitor the situation. The committee included three Shiites (Ahmed Chalabi, head of the Iraqi National Congress; Ayad Allawi, leader of the Iraqi National Accord; and Mohammad Baqr al-Hakim, leader of the Supreme Council for the Islamic Revolution in Iraq), a Sunni (former Iraqi foreign minister Adnan Pachachi), and two Kurds (PUK leader Jalal Talabani and KDP head Massoud Barzani). U.S. envoys attending these meetings discouraged the Iraqi leaders from declaring a provisional government, on the grounds that such a step would appear to signify external control of Iraq's postwar political structure.[26]

Among the Iraqi leaders, Chalabi was most favored by Pentagon elites. As exiled leader of the Iraqi National Congress, Chalabi had conspired with Western intelligence agencies against Hussein since the 1990s. One of his associates, code-named Curveball, had fed the CIA information (which later proved bogus) about the proliferation of WMD in Hussein's arsenals. Despite State Department and CIA skepticism about his credibility, Chalabi emerged under Pentagon sponsorship as the most likely successor to Hussein. Deputy Under Secretary of Defense William Luti called Chalabi the "George Washington of Iraq," and Robert Blackwill, a senior aide to Condoleezza Rice, called Chalabi "far and away the most competent Iraqi official in the country." Chalabi sat in a place of honor near First Lady Laura Bush during the president's January 2004 State of the Union address. If Bush genuinely opposed the idea of installing exiles into positions of leadership, as he later claimed, then he clearly erred in allowing the Pentagon to promote Chalabi and in honoring him during his State of the Union address.[27]

As hostilities against Iraq were initiated, State Department reservations about Chalabi triggered a modification of administration policy. Doubting the political credibility of the exile leaders, the State Department criticized the Pentagon's plans to transfer power to a coalition led by Chalabi. Before the invasion, therefore, Feith prepared the Iraqi Interim Authority (IIA) Plan, which purportedly reflected State Department concerns. "The IIA plan," Feith later wrote, "...would not give authority across the board to Iraqis right away, but it would not hoard all power in American hands either; it did not empower only externals, but it did not treat the externals as illegitimate; it built on the leadership group selected by

Photo 7-4
Secretary of State Colin Powell, at microphone, is flanked by members of the Iraq Governing Council. Ahmed Chalabi stands to Powell's left. SOURCE: State Department Photo by Michael Gross. Combined Arms Research Library.

the prewar Iraqi political conferences, but it required that group to expand itself to include internals; and it did not favor Chalabi or the Iraqi National Congress over the externals; rather, it provided neutrally that Iraqis would select their own officers."[28]

Once Bremer reached Baghdad, he moved quickly to establish an Iraqi government. In July 2003, he appointed a 25-member Iraq Governing Council (IGC) to facilitate a transition to Iraqi self-rule. Bremer appointed a diverse Council (13 Shiites, 5 Sunnis, 5 Kurds, 1 Christian, and 1 Turkoman) in the hope of achieving national unity and preventing a resurgence to power by the Sunni minority. In August, the IGC established a committee to facilitate the writing of a democratic constitution that would be submitted for popular ratification and would provide for free elections of a permanent government. In September, the Council appointed 25 ministers to begin taking responsibility for the administration of the country. Under pressure from officials in Washington, who wanted the U.S. occupation to end well before President Bush stood for reelection in November 2004, Bremer set a deadline of June 30, 2004, for the dissolution of the CPA and the transfer of sovereignty to a new Iraqi government.[29]

Numerous obstacles slowed progress toward Bremer's goal. Quarrels between Bremer and Department of Defense officials over the terms of the transition caused delays and confusion in the implementation of policy. The influential Grand Ayatollah Ali al-Sistani issued a *fatwah* in June 2003 declaring that the new constitution should be written by an elected Iraqi government, free of the influence of U.S. officials, thereby hindering Bremer's goal of a rapid transition. The IGC splintered along ethnic and other lines as it debated such divisive issues as the disbanding of militias and the role of Islam in the legal code of the new state. Local political figures, most notably the popular Shiite cleric Muqtada al-Sadr, used rhetoric and armed force to resist the U.S.-appointed IGC. News of the scandalous maltreatment of Iraqi detainees by American service personnel at the Abu Ghraib prison near Baghdad, which broke in April 2004, caused widespread criticism of U.S. occupation policies and fed a mounting anti-American armed insurgency (discussed below). "I never saw any news hit Rumsfeld so hard," Feith later wrote, with regard to Abu Ghraib. "Though he had no personal culpability, he submitted two letters of resignation over it."[30]

U.S. officials gradually concluded that Chalabi, the initial darling of the Bush Administration, was not capable of leading Iraq into a new era. Chalabi's presence on the IGC drew criticism from local Iraqis in light of his identity as a long-time expatriate. Deeply skeptical about Chalabi's credentials for leadership, State Department and CIA officials fed the media a portrait of him as a master con artist who had misled Pentagon Neocons with false intelligence about Saddam Hussein and lined his own pockets in the process. As a member of the IGC, moreover, Chalabi proved noncompliant with U.S. wishes and began to criticize U.S. occupation policies. In May 2004, U.S. forces helped Iraqi police raid Chalabi's office to search for evidence of criminal wrongdoing. Soon, the

Bush Administration denounced its former partner for having leaked sensitive intelligence information to Iran.[31]

When it became clear that Iraq would not have a new constitution by the June 30, 2004, deadline for withdrawal of the CPA, Bremer established an interim Iraqi government to preside in Baghdad. On March 8, 2004, he secured the IGC's agreement to the "Law of Administration for the State of Iraq for the Transitional Period." The law provided that an Iraqi Transitional Government would preside from the departure of the CPA in June 2004 through the end of 2005, that it would hold free elections for a national assembly by January 31, 2005, and that the national assembly would write a constitution and submit it for popular ratification. On June 28 (2 days ahead of deadline), the CPA passed control of the country to a transitional regime headed by Ayad Allawi.[32]

As interim prime minister, Allawi had the potential to stabilize Iraq on terms acceptable to the United States. Born in 1946 and trained as a neurologist, Allawi had belonged to the Baath Party before he fled Iraq in 1971. In 1978, while in exile in Britain, he survived an assassination attempt by agents of Saddam Hussein. In 1991, Allawi founded the Iraqi National Accord, a group of anti-Hussein dissidents who received funding from the CIA and who launched a failed coup against Hussein in 1996. Allawi returned to Iraq in 2003 and served on the IGC. Once elevated to interim prime minister, he immediately asserted his authority and collaborated with U.S. troops in counterinsurgency operations. "It's my great

Photo 7-5
CPA Chief L. Paul Bremer, accompanied by Deputy Prime Minister Barham Saleh, departing Iraq at Baghdad International Airport on June 28, 2004. SOURCE: DoD photo by SSGT D. Myles Cullen, U.S. Air Force.

honor...," he declared in an address to the U.S. Congress on September 23, 2004, "to thank this nation and its people for making our cause your cause, our struggle your struggle.... There are no words that can express the debt of gratitude that future generations of Iraqis will owe to Americans." Because his popularity among Iraqis was tainted by his association with Western intelligence agencies, however, Allawi would prove unable to retain a position of power after the Iraqi democratic elections of 2005.[33]

In addition to encountering problems within Iraq, U.S. leaders also faced worldwide repercussions from the invasion of Iraq. Bush's decision to wage a preemptive war over widespread international opposition strained the NATO alliance and generated a surge of anti-Americanism in many countries, including formerly pro-U.S. Muslim states such as Indonesia and Nigeria. Many world leaders criticized U.S. unilateralism, also manifest in the administration's withdrawal from the Anti-Ballistic Missile Treaty, its refusal to support the International Criminal Court, its retreat from the Kyoto Protocol and the Comprehensive Test Ban Treaty, and its refusal to heed the Geneva Conventions regulating treatment of prisoners, as a threat to the international order painstakingly constructed after World War II. News of the scandal at Abu Ghraib, the columnist Fareed Zakaria

Photo 7-6
An Iraqi woman pleads for the release of her son, who was detained by U.S. forces in An Najaf in 2004. Although most detainees were treated humanely, the detention of thousands of men tested the patience of the Iraqi people with the U.S. occupation. The grotesque abuses of prisoners at Abu Ghraib prison, which became news in 2004, triggered mass outrage across Iraq and most of the rest of the world. source: DoD photo by Tech. SGT Scott Reed, U.S. Air Force (released).

observed, made the United States appear to be "an international outlaw in the eyes of much of the world."[34]

President Bush also lost credibility when U.S. officials scouring Iraq found no evidence that Hussein had possessed an arsenal of WMD, which had been the administration's most articulated cause for war. General Tommy Franks believed that U.S. forces had found "the equivalent of a dissembled pistol, lying on a table beside neatly arranged trays of bullets." But former U.N. inspector David Kay, appointed by the White House to search for evidence of WMD, concluded in January 2004 that Hussein had abandoned his WMD years before the invasion and that Western intelligence agencies had been fooled by a mirage of deception, corruption, and mismanagement in Iraq's military–scientific complex. This verdict was confirmed in a 1,000-page report completed in October 2004 by Iraq Survey Group chief Charles Duelfer. President Bush later argued that "the absence of WMD stockpiles did not change the fact that Saddam was a threat." But even he later conceded that "I had sent American troops into combat based in large part on intelligence that proved false. That was a massive blow to our credibility—my credibility—that would shake the confidence of the American people." Criticism of Bush's miscalculation was amplified when clear evidence emerged that the president had grossly misrepresented intelligence when he charged in his 2003 State of the Union address that Iraq had attempted to acquire nuclear materials from Niger. Nor did anyone find convincing evidence of political connections between Hussein's regime and al-Qaeda.[35]

STATE BUILDING DURING THE IRAQI INSURGENCY

The Bush Administration's quest to establish a viable government in Baghdad was seriously complicated by the eruption of a massive insurgency across Iraq. As the CPA lumbered through the first year of occupation, a variety of factors triggered a multilayered rebellion against U.S. officials and soldiers and the Iraqis and foreigners who cooperated with them. The initial U.S. methods for addressing the crisis proved inadequate to stem the violence. While trying to restore order and stability through military action, President Bush also pursued the political mission of establishing a viable Iraqi government, based on free elections, in the hope that such a government would stabilize and pacify the country. With his original rationales for invading Iraq—WMD and Iraq's alleged connections to al-Qaeda—in shambles, Bush advanced a new idea—the promotion of democracy—as the foundation of his policy.

The insurgency that swept Iraq within months of Hussein's downfall posed a grave threat to the U.S. position in that country. By late 2003, suicide attacks, sniper fire, car bombs, and roadside bombs inflicted a mounting toll on U.S. soldiers and Iraqi civilians. Between May and December, more than 300 U.S. soldiers were killed on duty in Iraq (more than double the 138 who died in the original invasion). By October, insurgents had bombed the U.N., Iraqi police, and Red Cross headquarters in Baghdad as well as the Shrine of Imam Ali in

Photo 7-7
The aftermath of an improvised explosive device attack on U.S. forces in occupied Iraq in April 2007. Nearly 10,000 such attacks occurred between April 2003 and November 2004, leaving thousands of U.S. soldiers dead or wounded. The number of improvised explosive device attacks continued to climb and spiked during the "surge" in U.S. force strength in 2007. SOURCE: Photo courtesy of C-52 of 3/2 Stryker Brigade Combat Team.

Najaf. U.S. forces sought to lower their profile by confining themselves to sprawling bases near major cities, reducing their visibility among the Iraqi people and thereby ceding portions of the country to the insurgents. The rebels thus trained their fire on Iraqi Shiites, foreign contractors working for the United States, and members of the U.S.-trained Iraqi police force. By April 2004, 48 suicide bombers had killed more than 700 people. Although the new police force proved unreliable and ineffective in suppressing the insurgency, more than 800 of its officers were killed in various attacks by May 2004. The capture of Saddam Hussein in December 2003 failed to alleviate the fighting.[36]

Several factors accounted for the emergence of the insurgency. The demolition of the Hussein regime had unleashed historic tensions between the Shiite and Sunni communities, and the abrupt disbandment of the Iraqi Army left thousands of veterans unemployed and unattached to state authority in Baghdad. Sunnis who had supported the Hussein regime resented the U.S. presence in their country and felt that they had no political future in light of Bremer's de-Baathification decree. Some Shiites rallied behind such leaders as Muqtada al-Sadr, who resisted the U.S.-created interim government. Leaders in Washington also

Photo 7-8
Army Lieutenant General Ricardo S. Sanchez, who commanded U.S. forces in Iraq from June 2003 to June 2004, concluded that the policies of CPA Chief Paul Bremer and other Bush administration officials fueled the mounting insurgency in Iraq. SOURCE: DoD Photo by LCPL Andrew Williams, U.S. Marine Corps.

seemed complacent to the deteriorating conditions in Iraq. Wolfowitz denied that the situation was unstable and President Bush reportedly discouraged CIA officers in late 2003 from using the term "insurgency" with regard to Iraq.[37]

The military tactics initially employed by U.S. forces to stabilize the country actually might have fanned the flames of insurgency. Stymied by Bremer, General Sanchez failed to implement an effective general strategy for combating the rebels. Lacking such direction, field commanders used battle techniques—including the use of overwhelming force resulting in casualties among noncombatants—that aggravated the political situation. U.S. forces lacked the means to process efficiently the thousands of suspected rebels detained during operations. Encouraged by top officials in Washington—including President Bush, who declared in 2002 that the Geneva Conventions on the treatment of prisoners did not apply to suspected terrorists—some intelligence officers engaged in rigorous interrogation techniques, including torture, further eroding the goodwill of the Iraqi people. The scandal over the maltreatment of Iraqi prisoners at Abu Ghraib was an extreme but not solitary example of abusive behavior by U.S. personnel that undermined the political mission in Iraq. "The Bush guidance and the military memorandums suspending the Geneva Conventions had unleashed the hounds of hell," Sanchez later noted. "And no one seemed to have the moral courage to get the animals back in their cages."[38]

By 2004, U.S. officials contended with three distinct insurgencies in Iraq. Sunnis who had formed the foundation of the Hussein regime and had resisted the U.S. invasion reorganized into anti-U.S. combatants. On March 31, 2004, Sunni insurgents in Fallujah, a politically significant town 40 miles west of Baghdad, provoked a battle against U.S. forces by brutally murdering four U.S. civilians working for the private contractor firm Blackwater USA. The grisly killings prompted a major U.S. offensive against the rebels in Fallujah that aggravated political tensions across the country. U.S. commanders suspended their operations after members of the IGC threatened to resign in protest. Only after several months of stalemate did the United States restore effective control of Fallujah through a massive combat assault by Marines and soldiers in November 2004.[39]

A second strand of insurgency developed under the leadership of Muqtada al-Sadr, the scion of a Shiite family that had long contested the Hussein regime. Although many Shiites, under the leadership of the moderate Ayatollah al-Sistani, remained generally supportive of U.S. ambitions in Iraq, a broad cross section of poor, urbanized Shiites rallied to al-Sadr after he vowed to resist the U.S. occupation and competed with more elite Shiite rivals for political influence. Al-Sadr amassed a base of influence in Sadr City, a sprawling slum of 2 million residents near Baghdad, and fielded a militia known as the Mahdi Army. In August 2003, he organized major street demonstrations to protest the arrest of one of his deputies for a car bombing that had killed Ayatollah Muhammed Baqr al-Hakim, a political rival. By early 2004, the Mahdi Army controlled many areas

Photo 7-9
GIs advance cautiously into Fallujah during Operation New Dawn, a counterinsurgency offensive to pacify that city in November 2004. SOURCE: DoD photo by SSG Michael Nasworthy, U.S. Army (released).

within the sacred towns of Najaf and Karbala as well as Sadr City. CPA efforts to stem al-Sadr's influence by closing his newspapers and vowing to capture or kill him provoked an uprising. Fighting between al-Sadr's militia and U.S. and coalition troops flared in April–May and August 2004, before Allied forces routed al-Sadr's militiamen from most of their strongholds.[40]

Non-Iraqi Islamic fighters infiltrating Iraq constituted the third part of the anti-U.S. insurgency. The U.S. invasion of Iraq provoked widespread consternation among Muslims across the Middle East, rallying significant mass support for *jihad* against the United States. In contrast to Osama bin Laden's sputtering effort to mobilize mass resistance to U.S. power in Afghanistan, the scholar Fawaz Gerges observes, Islamic combatants flocked to Iraq to resist what they viewed as an unjustified assault on an Arab Muslim country. The U.S. invasion "alienated most of the important political secular and religious Muslim groups that had rejected and opposed al-Qaeda's global jihad," Gerges notes. "The invasion also blurred the lines among mainstream, liberal, and radical politics in the Arab world and squandered most of the empathy felt by Muslims for American victims and America itself after September 11th." Former NSC terrorism expert Richard Clarke agreed that the United States "stepped right into Bin Laden's propaganda" about U.S. predilections to invade oil-rich Arab countries. "And the result of that is that al-Qaeda and organizations like it, offshoots of it, second-generation al-Qaeda have been greatly strengthened."[41]

Abu Musab al-Zarqawi emerged as the most notorious nonnative, al-Qaeda-connected, anti-U.S. combatant in Iraq. A Jordanian-born Sunni and high school dropout, al-Zarqawi had cavorted with bin Laden in Afghanistan and Pakistan in the 1980s, inflicted terrorist attacks in Jordan in the 1990s, and, from a safe haven in Iraq, arranged the assassination of Laurence Foley, a U.S. diplomat in Amman, in October 2002. After the fall of the Hussein regime, al-Zarqawi organized in Iraq the "Unity and Jihad Group" that inflicted hundreds of terrorist attacks on U.S., allied, and Iraqi transitional government targets. Al-Zarqawi perpetrated the infamous kidnapping and videotaped beheading of U.S. businessman Nicholas Berg in May 2004, reportedly in revenge for the U.S. abuse of prisoners at Abu Ghraib. A massive manhunt for al-Zarqawi eventually succeeded. On June 7, 2006, U.S. Air Force jets dropped two 500-pound bombs on a house north of Baghdad where Zarqawi was hiding with his spiritual advisor, Sheikh Abdul Rahman, killing both men.[42]

Ironically, the anti-U.S. insurgencies deepened as U.S. officials labored to establish Iraqi government sovereignty in 2004. Al-Sadr's armed rebellion and the battles for Fallujah erupted days after the CPA unveiled the Iraqi interim constitution in March. The transfer of political authority to the Iraqi Interim Government under Prime Minister Allawi on June 28 had no immediate effect of calming the insurgency. Across the country, rather, insurgents systematically kidnapped and executed hostages from states cooperating with the U.S. occupation, attacked U.S. soldiers, filled political vacuums left by the withdrawal of U.S. forces, and defied the authority of the Allawi government. The death toll among U.S. soldiers in Iraq surpassed 1,000 by September 2004 and 1,500 by March 2005.[43]

In addition to using military force against the insurgents, President Bush responded to the mounting trouble in Iraq by elevating the cause of democracy as a major U.S. objective in the country. The absence of WMD had eviscerated his original justification for war, the downfall of Ahmed Chalabi had ended his original plan for stabilizing the country, and the Abu Ghraib scandal had gravely weakened U.S. political credibility in Iraq and elsewhere. Thus, in 2004 Bush gradually shifted his rhetoric about Iraq to emphasize the goal of a democratic state and to downplay the seriousness of the insurgency. He declared in his Inaugural Address of January 2005 that "America will not impose our style of government on the unwilling. Our goal instead is to help others find their own voice, to attain their own freedom, and to make their own way." To accentuate this approach, Secretary of State Rice declared in an address in Cairo in June 2005 that "for 60 years, my country, the United States, pursued stability at the expense of democracy in this region here in the Middle East—and we achieved neither. Now, we are taking a different course. We are supporting the democratic aspirations of all people."[44]

If Bush's emphasis on democracy in Iraq was designed in part to facilitate his own re-election bid in the United States, the ploy worked. The incumbent Republican president defeated his Democratic challenger, Senator John Kerry of Massachusetts, by a margin of 51 percent to 48 percent in popular votes and 286 to 252 in electoral votes. Exit polls indicated that the Iraq War ranked below moral values, the economy, and terrorism as an issue of concern among voters and that 53 percent of voters generally approved of Bush's performance as president. Although only 44 percent of voters thought that the Iraq War was progressing well, 51 percent indicated that they approved of the original decision to start the war, and 85 percent of the latter group supported Bush. The Republican Party also increased its majorities in both chambers of Congress.[45]

Feeling vindicated at the polls, Bush was also buoyed by political developments in Iraq in 2005. On January 30, 8 million Iraqi Shiites and Kurds, at substantial risk of retribution by Sunni insurgents, participated in national elections that determined membership of a 275-member Transitional National Assembly, which was sworn in amid tight security on March 16. Members of two leading Shiite parties occupied 71 percent of the seats; Kurds, 27 percent; and Sunnis, who had generally boycotted the election, only 2 percent. In April, the Assembly appointed Jalal Talabani (a Kurd and leader of the PUK) as president and Ibrahim al-Jaafari (a Shiite) as prime minister. A committee that was gradually expanded to include Sunnis drafted a permanent constitution that was approved by popular referendum on October 15. A second national election, conducted under the permanent constitution and held on December 15, decided the membership of a new 275-seat Council of Representatives (to replace the Transitional National Assembly). With a voter turnout rate of some 80 percent, the election eventually led to a coalition government under Prime Minister Nouri al-Maliki. The

Photo 7-10
An Iraqi women displays her ink-stained finger, a sign of having voted in the Iraqi election of January 2005. Administered by poll workers to safeguard against election fraud, the ink stains became a source of pride among millions of Iraqis who participated in a democratic election for the first time. SOURCE: CENTCOM Photo. Combined Arms Research Library.

"election generally conformed to internationally recognized electoral standards in legal framework, planning, procedures and logistics," international monitors concluded. "Furthermore, the results of the elections reflected the will of the voters." In addition, inklings of democracy appeared across the Middle East, as Saudi Arabia held municipal elections for the first time ever, Egypt agreed to schedule unprecedented secret-ballot, multiparty presidential elections, and citizens of Lebanon, through peaceful street protests, forced the resignation of Syrian-backed Prime Minister Omar Karami. Supporters of President Bush observed that U.S. action in Iraq had sparked the transregional surge of democracy.[46]

Following the U.S. invasion, Kurdistan also seemed to achieve a tenuous political stability. Kurdish leader Massoud Barzani served on the U.S.-appointed IGC and, after the Iraqi elections of 2005, 77 Kurds became members of the new parliament and Jalal Talabani became interim vice president. These symbols of political accommodation between Iraq's Kurdish and Arab communities, however, were offset by indications that the Kurdish political situation remained tense. Becoming president of the Kurdish autonomous region after the elections of 2005, Barzani demanded that Kurdistan should remain autonomous under the new Iraqi government, that the historic Kurdish identity of Kirkuk should be restored, and that Kurds should reap the profits of Kurdistan's oil industry. He also warned strongly against Turkish forces entering Iraq and he demanded that Sunni injustices against Kurds be redressed. The Arab minority of Kirkuk resisted Barzani's demands for that city, whereas Shiite leaders as well as leaders of Turkey, Syria, and Iran expressed grave concerns with Kurdish separatism. The proper place of Kurds within Iraq's political order would remain a sensitive issue throughout the U.S. occupation.[47]

THE SURGE

In contrast to the upbeat political news, the military situation in Iraq continued to decline in 2006. Violence and insurgency wracked the country as it established a democratic system. With the civil strife imperiling his fundamental objectives, President Bush embraced a new military strategy calibrated to reverse his declining fortunes. Popularly known as "the surge," the new strategy blended an increase in the size of the American military force deployed to Iraq with a tactical reorientation of U.S. forces away from killing and capturing insurgents and toward providing security for the Iraqi people. Implemented over significant domestic political opposition, the surge provided a modicum of stability in Iraq by the end of the decade.

The surge originated during the low point of the U.S. war in Iraq in 2006. Despite U.S. efforts to hold elections and establish a democratic government in Baghdad, Iraq remained rife with instability and violence. The State Department reported that terrorist attacks within Iraq increased from 3,468 in 2005 to 6,630 in 2006, a 91 percent hike, and that casualties from such attacks increased from 20,685 in 2005 to 38,813 in 2006, a jump of 88 percent. "Sectarian attacks, including car bombs, suicide vests, sniper fire, targeted assassinations, and death squad murders, occurred on a close-to-daily basis with Iraqi civilians suffering the majority of causalities," according to the Department's counterterrorism experts. "Iraq's sectarian violence furthered the terrorists' goals by creating instability and weakening the government." The country's descent into an abyss of sectarian turmoil was encouraged by landmark incidents such as the terrorist bombing that destroyed the al-Askari Mosque in Samarra on February 22, 2006, an attack that stoked the religious passions of Shiites across the country. The killing of al-Zarqawi by U.S. airpower in June 2006 seemed to have little immediate effect on stemming such violence. By 2007, the United Nations counted more than 2.6 million displaced people within Iraq and another 2.2 million Iraqi refugees in other countries.[48]

The U.S. war effort in Iraq also faced remarkable challenges. U.S. casualties mounted steadily: 1,666 soldiers died in the country in 2005 and 2006, bringing the cumulative death toll to nearly 3,000 by January 1, 2007. According to the Congressional Research Service, the annual financial costs of the war also steadily increased, from $51 billion in 2003 to $77.3 billion in 2004, $87.3 billion in 2005, and $101.8 billion in 2006. Opinion polling revealed a steady decline in public support for the U.S. military operations in Iraq and rising support for the idea of troop withdrawal. By March 2006, Americans favored a rapid departure from Iraq by a margin of 50 to 44 percent. By November 2006, an all-time low of 29 percent of Americans approved President Bush's handling of the war and a strong majority of Americans expected that the Democratic Party would end the conflict if it gained control of Congress. Indeed, in the congressional elections of that month, Democrats gained 7 seats in the Senate and 32 seats in the House of Representatives to take majorities in both chambers of 51–44 and 233–202, respectively. "The American people demonstrated in the November elections that they don't believe your current Iraq policy will lead to success and that we need a change in direction for the sake of our troops and the Iraqi people," Speaker of the House Nancy Pelosi and Senate Majority Leader Harry M. Reid wrote to Bush on January 5, 2007. "Rather than deploy additional forces to Iraq, we believe the way forward is to begin the phased redeployment of our forces in the next four to six months, while shifting the principal mission of our forces there from combat to training, logistics, force protection and counter-terror."[49]

The outcome of the 2006 elections capped mounting domestic pressure on the Bush administration to deescalate the war in Iraq. Well before the election, Congress had appointed 10 distinguished former government officials to the bipartisan Iraq Study Group (ISG) to examine the situation in Iraq and recommend a national strategy. Cochaired by Republican former Secretary of State James A. Baker and Democratic former Congressman Lee H. Hamilton, the ISG painted a stark picture of the situation in Iraq: "Violence is increasing in scope and lethality. It is fed by a Sunni Arab insurgency, Shiite militias and death squads, al-Qaeda, and widespread criminality. Sectarian conflict is the principal challenge to stability. The Iraqi people have a democratically elected government, yet it is not adequately advancing national reconciliation, providing basic security, or delivering essential services. Pessimism is pervasive." In a final report issued a month after the 2006 U.S. elections, the ISG recommended that the U.S. government engage in vigorous diplomacy across the region to mobilize neighboring powers to assist in stabilizing Iraq and that it gradually remove U.S. combat forces from Iraq and transfer responsibility for internal security to the Iraqi military, bolstered with embedded U.S. military advisors.[50]

President Bush, however, resisted these powerful domestic pressures because he calculated that withdrawal from Iraq would prove catastrophic to U.S. security interests. Defeat in Iraq would comprise "a humiliating loss for the country, a shattering blow to the military, and a dramatic setback for our interests," he later wrote. "We would leave al-Qaeda with a safe haven in a country with vast oil reserves. We would embolden a hostile Iran in its pursuit of nuclear weapons. We would shatter the hopes of peoples taking risks for freedom across the Middle East. Ultimately, our enemies could use their sanctuary to attack our homeland. We had to stop that from happening." Conceding defeat to the al-Qaeda warriors who had infiltrated Iraq would gravely compromise American security, he added. "If we were to let them drive us out of Iraq, they would not have been satisfied to stop there. They would have followed us home." Having received a delegation of Iraqis in the Oval Office, moreover, Bush noted that "they were grateful to America for their liberation. They wanted to live in freedom. And I would not give up on them." In short, the president resolved not to accept a defeat in the war in Iraq. "While many in Washington had given up on the prospect of victory in Iraq," he noted, "I had not."[51]

Rather than withdraw, Bush gambled that an escalation in the U.S. commitment to Iraq would produce a victory. He fixed on the advice of Frederick W. Kagan of the American Enterprise Institute and retired Army General Jack Keane, who advocated a sustained and sizeable increase of U.S. combat forces to quell the violence in Baghdad and surrounding areas and thereby restore "security to the people of Baghdad as quickly as possible—a traditional counter-insurgency mission." In contrast to Congress's and the ISG's calls for troop withdrawal, Kagan and Keane recommended a "surge" of some 30,000 new troops for at least 18 months, stressing that smaller markers of strength and duration would risk tactical defeat. They recognized the importance of the "diplomatic, political, economic and reconciliation initiatives" proposed by the ISG but countered that "those alone will not contain the violence." Kagan and Keane concluded that "the United States faces a dire situation in Iraq because of a history of half-measures. We have always sent 'just enough' force to succeed if everything went according to plan. So far nothing has, and there's no reason to believe that it will. Sound military planning doesn't work this way. The only 'surge' option that makes sense is both long and large."[52]

A growing awareness among military officers in Iraq of the need to reform military tactics accompanied the president's determination to persist. Battlefield commanders had reached a growing realization that widely used tactics—overwhelming force without regard for collateral damage and political impact—were counterproductive to the political goals of stability and democracy. Progressive-minded officers reflected on the legacy of Mosul, where soldiers of the 101st Airborne, under the command of General David Petraeus, had achieved a remarkable stability in 2003 by restraining their firepower, befriending locals, and promoting social development, only to see the stability vaporize after Secretary of Defense Rumsfeld replaced the 101st with the Stryker Brigade, which was too small to continue such a mission, in January 2004. By 2005, experience had taught many mid-tier officers of the Army and Marine Corps that to win the war they needed to win the trust of the Iraqi people by befriending and collaborating with them.[53]

Army General George W. Casey Jr. played a role in advancing this progressive thinking through the Army. The top U.S. commander in Iraq from June 2004 to February 2007, Casey became frustrated by the inability of U.S. and Iraqi security forces to contain sectarian violence. He set in motion the development of a comprehensive counterinsurgency (COIN) strategy. He created a COIN academy to train U.S. leaders, modified U.S. tactical policies, and relied on Iraqis to help achieve stability. Casey founded the COIN school at a military base north of Baghdad and required all U.S. combat commanders in Iraq to attend a 5-day

Photo 7-11
Major General David H. Petraeus commanded the 101st Airborne Division in Mosul in 2003. By 2006, he led an effort within the armed services to develop a new counterinsurgency strategy for Iraq that was designed to win the hearts and minds of the Iraqi people. President Bush appointed General Petraeus as commander of the "surge," a strategy launched in 2007 to gain control of Iraq by increasing the number of U.S. soldiers in Iraq and reforming their mission. SOURCE: U.S. Army photo by Staff Sgt. Bradley A. Lail (released).

seminar there in theory and tactics. The seminar emphasized the importance of restraining firepower; recognizing political repercussions of civilian casualties, detentions, and property destruction; showing concern for the common people's needs; and befriending the Iraqi people.[54]

The new COIN doctrine emerging in Iraq was institutionalized in a watershed field manual finalized by the Army and Marine Corps in December 2006. Written under the authority of General Petraeus and Marine Corps General James F. Amos, Field Manual 3–24 declared that

> a counterinsurgency campaign is…a mix of offensive, defensive, and stability operations conducted along multiple lines of operations. It requires Soldiers and Marines to employ a mix of familiar combat tasks and skills more often associated with nonmilitary agencies. The balance between them depends on the local situation. Achieving this balance is not easy. It requires leaders at all levels to adjust their approach constantly. They must ensure that their Soldiers and Marines are ready to be greeted with either a handshake or a hand grenade while taking on missions only infrequently practiced until recently at our combat training centers. Soldiers and Marines are expected to be nation builders as well as warriors. They must be prepared to help reestablish institutions and local security forces and assist in rebuilding infrastructure and basic services. They must be able to facilitate establishing local governance and the rule of law.

Petraeus also mobilized such like-minded officers as Colonels H. R. McMaster, Peter Mansoor, and Tom Greenwood, the so-called "Council of Colonels" who assisted the Joint Chiefs of Staff in rethinking the strategy for the Iraq War in the autumn of 2006.[55]

In late 2006–early 2007, President Bush settled on a new surge strategy that blended his perseverance with new COIN doctrines. In so doing he resisted an emerging consensus among the Joint Chiefs of Staff, the NSC, and the State Department that the United States should avoid sending additional forces to Iraq and should instead consider partitioning the country, adopting a passive enclave strategy, or withdrawing U.S. forces completely. During a meeting in Amman in late November, the president extracted assurances from Prime Minister al-Maliki that the Iraqi government would fully cooperate with a surge in U.S. operations. "Maliki's right when he says he doesn't have enough tools to do the job," Bush told the NSC on December 9, 2006. "We need to take that excuse away from him. We need to give him the right tools. But I will be making the decisions, and the goal is radical action to achieve victory." Bush also replaced his unpopular Secretary of Defense Donald Rumsfeld with Robert Gates, stating publicly that he sought a "fresh perspective" on Iraq and that Gates's membership on the bipartisan ISG equipped him to conceive of "new ideas on how America can achieve our goals in Iraq."[56]

Bush announced his new surge strategy in an address to the nation on January 10, 2007. Refusing to accept defeat, he declared that he would send additional forces to Iraq to work in partnership with Iraqi forces to defeat enemy combatants, promote political stability, and develop friendly relations with the Iraqi people. "A successful strategy for Iraq goes beyond military operations," the president declared, echoing the new COIN doctrine. "Ordinary Iraqi citizens must see that military operations are accompanied by visible improvements in their neighborhoods and communities." Accepting one of the major recommendations of the ISG, Bush also pledged to "use America's full diplomatic resources to rally support for Iraq from nations throughout the Middle East." "Victory will not look like the ones our fathers and grandfathers achieved," the president concluded. "There will be no surrender ceremony on the deck of a battleship. But victory in Iraq will bring something new in the Arab world: a functioning democracy that polices its territory, upholds the rule of law, respects fundamental human liberties, and answers to its people." On May 1, Bush vetoed a bill favored by Congressional Democrats mandating that the president set a troop withdrawal deadline later that year.[57]

Under the surge, bolstered U.S. forces engaged in carefully calibrated offensive operations in 2007. Bush ordered an additional 40,000 soldiers to deploy to Iraq, bringing the total U.S. forces to some 160,000 troops, and he concentrated those forces in Baghdad and al-Anbar province with the missions of quelling the sectarian violence that had rent the country and giving the fledgling government of Iraq time to gain stability. U.S. forces redeployed from major fortified bases to smaller outposts in the neighborhoods of metropolitan Baghdad and other towns, from which they conducted patrols with Iraqi forces and established friendly political ties with the populace. A high initial casualty rate in May and June of 227 soldiers killed in action—among them Spc. Grass and Sgt. Soto—raised doubts about the operations, but over the summer conditions markedly improved. The U.S. death toll of 23 soldiers in December 2007 was widely interpreted as a sign of improving overall conditions. A notable decline in Iraqi civilian deaths was another marker of success. "The casualties were agonizing," Bush later wrote. "But something felt different in 2007: America was on the offense again."[58]

Inspired by the new COIN doctrine, the surge included a calculated effort to win the support of the Iraqi people. "You cannot kill your way out of an insurgency," General Petraeus told a reporter. "You're not going to defeat everybody out there. You have to turn them." Accordingly, U.S. military officers negotiated new partnerships with Iraqi political and military groups. In the so-called "Anbar Awakening," Sunni groups that had grown frustrated by al-Qaeda terrorist strikes against Iraqi civilians partnered with U.S. forces to defeat al-Qaeda fighters. Supported by financial payments and weapons, Iraqi tribal and political leaders organized some 103,000 combatants into some 125 local militias that joined efforts with the U.S. military to stabilize the country. This so-called "other

Photo 7-12
Marine Corps Lieutenant Commander Tara Smith meeting with an Iraqi girl at Ramadi General Hospital on May 18, 2009. A clinical psychologist, Smith was part of a team devoted to enhancing mental health services in Al-Anbar Province. The provision of such humanitarian assistance, one aspect of the counterinsurgency policy adopted in 2006 and after, contributed to the relative stabilization of Iraq by the end of the decade. SOURCE: Photo by Lt. Cmdr. Tara Smith.

surge" was a crucial component of the larger American strategy. In August, more-over, al-Sadr's Mahdi Army of 60,000 unilaterally declared a ceasefire against U.S. forces, resulting in a marked decline in ad hoc attacks on U.S. soldiers. By 2008, sectarian violence had declined by 95 percent from 2006 rates. The surge had brought a modicum of stability to Baghdad—allowing restoration of some commerce and political stability—at a cost of 937 U.S. military fatalities.[59]

As with other aspects of the U.S. war in Iraq, the surge attracted criticism at home. Some observers contended that the tactical maneuver had failed to pro-mote long-term stability in Iraq. *Time* columnist Joe Klein predicted that "Bush's futile pipe dream" would fail to stem the violence in Iraq given that U.S. troops lacked the numbers, training, and time needed to fulfill the mission and that the al-Maliki government in Baghdad lacked credibility. Reporter Patrick Cockburn added that the surge neither resolved the Iraqi refugee crisis nor promoted peace-ful relations between the country's Sunnis and Shiites and that the appearance of stability resulted only from the massive and painful relocations of civilians that had completely segregated the two communities. Military affairs expert Andrew J. Bacevich contended that the surge—only the latest step in a series of Bush's mistaken policies in Iraq—would merely avert a final collapse until a new presi-dent took office.[60]

With some justification, however, other voices interpreted the surge more favorably. "Last year's success, in Anbar and elsewhere, was made possible by confidence among Iraqis that U.S. troops would stay and help protect them, that the U.S. would not abandon them to their enemies," commentator William Kristol wrote in 2008. "Because the U.S. sent more troops instead of withdraw-ing—because, in other words, President Bush won his battles in 2007 with the Democratic Congress—we have been able to turn around the situation in Iraq." Although recognizing that the war was not yet won, retired Army Colonel Peter Mansoor noted in August 2008 that "the surge has created the space and time for the competition for power and resources in Iraq to play out in the political realm, with words instead of bombs." The surge did reasonably well at "turn[ing] around a war that was nearly lost two years ago." Developments in Iraq during the 3 years following the surge confirmed these positive assessments over the contemporary critics of Bush's policy.[61]

As the military situation stabilized in late 2008, the Bush administration sought to bring political stability to Iraq by negotiating two agreements with the al-Maliki government. A Status of Forces Agreement established legal pro-visions governing U.S. military personnel in Iraq and committed the United States to withdraw all of its troops from Iraq by December 31, 2011. The Strategic Framework Agreement affirmed joint commitments to promote stability in Iraq and to cooperate on matters ranging from Iraqi security and law enforcement to communications and environmental regulations.[62]

Although the domestic debate over the surge was heated, the war in Iraq and the Bush–al-Maliki security agreements seemed to play only limited roles in determining the outcome of the U.S. election of 2008. Republican presidential

Photo 7-13
Soldiers of the Alaska National Guard assemble a swing set for the children of Al-Hillah, Iraq. Such "reconstruction" projects were a crucial part of U.S. operations to win the political support of the Iraqi people in the period after the surge of 2007. The weapons carried by the guardsmen revealed their persistent concern that Iraq remained a dangerous place. SOURCE: DoD Photo by SPC Arthur D. Hamilton. Combined Arms Research Library.

nominee Senator John McCain of Arizona had a long record of supporting Bush Administration policies in Iraq from the invasion in 2003 to the surge, and Democratic candidate Senator Barack Obama of Illinois had an equally solid record of criticizing those policies (although in mid-2008 he acknowledged that the surge had seemingly quelled violence). Public opinion polls revealed, however, that voters were more concerned about health care and the economy than the war in Iraq. Obama defeated McCain by a margin of 365–173 in electoral votes. Democrats also captured congressional majorities of 59–41 in the Senate and 257–178 in the House. Many observers interpreted the Democrats' decisive victories as the electorate's rejection of the Bush legacy at home and abroad.[63]

As distasteful as a majority of voters found the Bush legacy, President Barack Obama did not immediately end U.S. military operations in Iraq. On February 27, 2009, he announced during a speech to Marines at Camp Lejeune, North Carolina, that he would end U.S. combat operations in Iraq by August 31, 2010; thereafter limit the U.S. role to advising Iraqi forces, combating terrorism, and protecting U.S. officials; and honor the stipulation of the Status of Forces Agreement to withdraw all American troops from Iraq by December 31, 2011. He also pledged to transfer responsibility for Iraq's future to the Iraqi people and government and to engage in regional diplomacy to

Photo 7-14

Political cartoonist Jeff Stahler of the *Columbus Dispatch* aptly captured the reluctance of President Barack Obama to celebrate the stability in Iraq that enabled him to withdraw the last U.S. combat forces from that country in August 2010. SOURCE: Jeff Stahler: © Columbus Dispatch/distributed by United Feature Syndicate, Inc.

ease external pressures on the state. "This strategy is grounded in a clear and achievable goal shared by the Iraqi people and the American people," the president declared, "an Iraq that is sovereign, stable, and self-reliant." By late August 2010, the Pentagon met the target of having fewer than 50,000 U.S. soldiers in Iraq. To signal a clean break in policy, the Obama Administration announced the termination of Operation Iraqi Freedom and the start of Operation New Dawn effective September 1.[64]

Meanwhile, the government of Iraq emerged from the surge on a more stable footing. In January 2008, the government passed a law allowing some former members of Hussein's Baath party to hold office, a major concession to the Sunni community and a reversal of Bremer's de-Baathification order of 2003. By summer, Muqtada al-Sadr transformed his Mahdi Army into a nonmilitary social organization, the Momahidoun (meaning "those who prepare the way"), devoted to social and religious pursuits. Provincial elections held in January 2009 in 14 of Iraq's 18 provinces, the first national polling since 2005, were peaceful and generally signaled a decline in influence among religious Shiites, like the Supreme Islamic Iraqi Council, and a rise in popularity among more secular Shiites. In July

2009, Kurds of the semiautonomous provinces in the north reelected President Barzani of the Kurdish Democratic Party in a peaceful polling.[65]

Yet the outcome of Iraq's parliamentary elections held on March 7, 2010, served as a reminder of the country's fragility. The Iraqiya party, led by the secular Shiite and former Prime Minister Ayad Allawi, gained the overwhelming support of Sunnis and narrowly won the most seats in the Council of Representatives. Prime Minister al-Maliki, however, refused to accept these results and posed legal challenges to the vote counts, provoking a political stalemate that polarized the country for many months. Persistent sectarian violence—less intense than that experienced before the U.S. surge but nonetheless deadly and destabilizing—stoked fears that the country might recrudesce into civil war after American forces were withdrawn. The Obama Administration pressured the rival Iraqi leaders to formulate a power-sharing agreement. In November, the parliament re-elected Jalal Talabani, a Kurd, as president, and Talabani directed al-Maliki to form a government as prime minister. On December 14, 2010, Allawi and al-Maliki finally announced a breakthrough deal in which al-Maliki would remain prime minister and Allawi would chair a new government council that would manage foreign policy and security interests. The Iraqi parliament officially seated the new government on December 21.[66]

CONCLUSION

At the time President Bush left office in early 2009, his policy in Iraq garnered mixed reviews by domestic observers. "George W. Bush inherited a robust economy, a budgetary surplus, a rested military, and, even after 9/11 a world largely at peace and well-disposed to the United States," Richard Haass asserted. "He handed off to his successor a recession, a massive deficit and debt, a stretched and exhausted military, two wars, and a world marked by pronounced anti-Americanism. I am hard-pressed to find another set of back-to-back presidential transitions in which so many of the basic features of the domestic and international landscapes changed so dramatically for the worse." By contrast, the columnist Charles Krauthammer credited Bush with having had the fortitude to take measures to preserve U.S. security in the face of an increasingly vocal domestic opposition. By combating terrorism, promoting homeland security, and courageously holding the line in Iraq, Krauthammer noted, Bush achieved "the most dramatic change in the fortunes of an American War since 1864."[67] Although future historians who enjoy the luxury of hindsight might best be able to render a final verdict on Bush's policy, it is possible and necessary to assess that policy from the immediate perspective.

It is difficult to find merit in the early phases of the U.S. occupation of Iraq. As they geared up for the invasion of Iraq in 2003, President Bush and Pentagon leaders unwisely neglected postwar reconstruction planning, disregarded warnings from the State Department and other experts about the dangers they would encounter, and limited the size of the occupation force despite suggestions from respected military experts that more soldiers were needed to ensure stability. The administration's initial reliance on Chalabi to govern postwar Iraq indicated grave ignorance about political conditions within the country. President Bush lost credibility when U.S. officials found no evidence that Saddam Hussein had possessed an arsenal of WMD, which had been the administration's most articulated reason for invading the country, and when the revelations about prisoner abuse at Abu Ghraib fostered a crescendo of anti-U.S. backlash around the world. Having prematurely implied "mission accomplished" in May 2003, the President displayed an excessive idealism about his goals and an absence of leadership when problems developed. He continued to rely on Rumsfeld to manage the occupation long after the Secretary of Defense had lost control of the situation.

As a result of poor leadership in Washington, U.S. officials in Baghdad experienced tactical and operational failures. General Garner found it impossible to meet the unrealistic expectations imposed by his superiors in Washington in their initial quest to stabilize Iraq after a quick occupation. Bremer's order to disband the Iraqi military aggravated the lawlessness that had gripped the country after the military victory and eventually fed a massive anti-American insurgency. His order to shun all former officials of the Baath regime separated a cadre of experienced administrators from the U.S. efforts to stabilize the country. U.S. military units struggled to make the transition from invasion to peacekeeping duties, lacked sufficient personnel strength to conduct adequate security patrols, and were ill-prepared to deal with an onslaught of roadside and suicide bombings. U.S. civilian administrators lacked the linguistic skills, cultural competence, and ethnic identity needed to develop intelligence networks and to earn the acceptance of the Iraqi people. The CPA and its Iraqi partners failed to establish effective communications or joint planning procedures. Corruption undercut the effectiveness of the lavish public works programs.

Despite such monumental shortcomings, the Bush administration managed to achieve gains during the early occupation that eventually helped stabilize the country. The CPA rebuilt considerable portions of Iraq's infrastructure, established a new police force, promoted educational and social reform, stimulated the economy, and generated a democratic potential and sense of nationhood in Iraq. The Bush Administration also gradually founded a new Iraqi government that was shaped by democratic elections, that reflected Iraq's ethnic diversity, and that ultimately achieved a degree of political stability. The series of elections held in 2005 and after were a remarkable testament to the end of an authoritarian era in Iraqi history and the dawn of a democratic legacy. By 2010, Iraqi oil production matched 2003 levels and the country had experienced significant progress in electricity production, potable water and sewage treatment capacities, and Internet service and telecommunications.[68]

To his credit, President Bush seemed to find a way eventually to achieve a modicum of stability in Iraq. Essentially reflecting a determination not to lose, he gambled that the surge strategy of 2007 would reverse his declining fortunes in Iraq. In defiance of substantial domestic pressure to withdraw from Iraq, the president dismissed Rumsfeld, authorized the deployment of additional U.S. soldiers, and reoriented their tactical missions toward protecting Iraqi people and building local alliances. Although the death tolls of Iraqi citizens and U.S. soldiers initially mounted under the surge, the strategy eventually proved instrumental in achieving a foundation of peace and stability on which a democratic Iraq could emerge from the shadow of Saddam Hussein.

These internal achievements notwithstanding, the occupation of Iraq also worked at cross purposes with other U.S. interests and objectives. To date, it left more than 4,300 American soldiers dead and 32,000 wounded, 100,000 Iraqis killed, and 2 million Iraqis displaced. It drained nearly $1 trillion from the U.S. Treasury (by one estimate, indirect and direct costs exceeded $3 trillion), contributed to a rise in the national debt from $6.4 trillion in 2003 to $10 trillion in 2008, sparked a hike in the price of oil from $25 to $140 per barrel, aggravated the economic recession of 2008, and limited the government's ability to address that recession. From 2000 to 2010, the U.S. share of global gross domestic product fell from 32 percent to 24 percent, a rate of relative national economic decline surpassed in world history only by the collapse of the Soviet Union in 1991.[69]

The war in Iraq also diverted U.S. troops from the war in Afghanistan and the hunt for Osama bin Laden. It galvanized Islamic militants, provided a staging ground for terrorists to bloody the U.S. military, and thus rejuvenated an international terrorist network that had been on the run since the aftermath of 9/11. By empowering Iraqi Shiites, the occupation seemed to extend the political influence of the Iranian government through the Gulf region. The war did not spawn democracy across the region. Rather, by consuming the attention of U.S. officials, it prevented progress on such other foreign policy challenges as the Israeli–Palestinian conflict and nuclear proliferation in North Korea. President Bush's eventual achievement of quasi-stability within Iraq—a case of grasping progress from a perilous situation—mitigated only some of the considerable damage inflicted on U.S. interests at home and overseas by his policy over 8 years.

The challenge for Obama and future administrations will be to consolidate the positive legacies of Bush era policies in Iraq and to mend the damage done to U.S. interests worldwide. An ideal outcome in Iraq would be the emergence of a democratic, multisectarian, multiethnic government that protects the best interest of its citizens, lives in peace with its neighbors, and achieves stability sufficient to obviate the need for further external intervention. There also remains considerable work to redress the international backlash against what many nations viewed as illegal and unnecessary action in invading Iraq in the first place. Although the Bush administration stumbled and blundered down its long road in Iraq, it ultimately bequeathed a situation with considerable potential for a satisfactory outcome. Bush's successors face the challenge of consolidating his gains while repairing the residual damage of his policies.

NOTES

1. Associated Press releases posted under "Army Spc. Zachary A. Grass," n.d., http://militarytimes.com/valor/army-spc-zachary-a-grass/2847484/ (accessed June 28, 2010) (quotations); obituary for Corporal Zachary A. Grass, Canton (Ohio) *Repository*, June 23, 2007, http://www.legacy.com/obituaries/cantonrep/obituary.aspx?n=zachary-a-grass&pid=89502716/ (accessed June 28, 2010).

2. Michael Gilbert, "Bomb Claims Two More Fort Lewis Soldiers," *News Tribune*, June 19, 2007, http://www.thenewstribune.com/2007/06/19/90592/bomb-claims-two-more-fort-lewis.html/ (accessed June 28, 2010).

3. Associated Press release posted under "Army Spc. Zachary A. Grass," n.d., http://militarytimes.com/valor/army-spc-zachary-a-grass/2847484/ (accessed June 28, 2010) (quotation); Gilbert, "Bomb."

4. U.S. Department of Defense, Office of the Assistant Secretary of Defense (Public Affairs) News Release 760–07, June 18, 2007, http://www.defense.gov/Releases/Release.aspx?ReleaseID=11026/ (accessed June 28, 2010); Gilbert, "Bomb"; Associated Press release posted under "Army Spc. Zachary A. Grass," n.d., http://militarytimes.com/valor/army-spc-zachary-a-grass/2847484/ (accessed June 28, 2010).

5. On December 23, 2010, the Pentagon reported casualties rates in Operation Iraqi Freedom since March 19, 2003 of 4,421 deaths (4,408 soldiers and 13 Defense Department civilian employees) and 31,935 wounded in action. In addition, it reported 12 deaths and 66 wounded in Operation New Dawn, which succeeded Operation Iraqi Freedom on September 1, 2010. See http://www.defense.gov/news/casualty.pdf/ (accessed December 23, 2010).

6. "Baghdad Protests over Looting," April 12, 2003, http://www.news.bbc.co.uk/2/hi/middle_east/2941733.stm/ (accessed September 3, 2009); Wright and Reece, *On Point II*, 92 (quotation); Sean Loughlin, "Rumsfeld on Looting in Iraq: 'Stuff Happens,'" April 12, 2003, http://www.cnn.com/2003/US/04/11/sprj.irq.pentagon/ (last accessed September 3, 2009) (quotation).

7. Ricks, *Fiasco*, 80–81, 104–7; Chandrasekaran, *Imperial Life*, 31–37; Fallows, *Blind into Baghdad*, 93–95.

8. Eric Schmitt and Joel Brinkley, "State Dept. Study Foresaw Trouble Now Plaguing Iraq," *New York Times*, October 19, 2003 (quotation); Fallows, *Blind into Baghdad*, 53–63; Ricks, *Fiasco*, 71–74.

9. Crane and Terrill, *Reconstructing Iraq*, 42; Gordon and Trainor, *Cobra II*, 457–70 (quotation 464); Sanchez, *Wiser in Battle*, 146–48.

10. Bush, *Decision Points*, 248–49 (quotations 249, 250); Fallows, *Blind into Baghdad*, 45–47, 62–63; Ricks, *Fiasco*, 76–78; Feith, *War and Decision*, 376, 386–88 (quotations).

11. Wright and Reece, *On Point II*, 569; Bush, *Decision Points*, 260, 268.

12. Gordon and Trainor, *Cobra II*, 465; Fallows, *Blind into Baghdad*, 101, 106, 46 (quotations); Wright and Reece, *On Point II*, 215–18.

13. Wright and Reece, *On Point II*, 89, 183.

14. Packer, *Assassins' Gate*, 120–46; Chandrasekaran, *Imperial Life*, 32, 41–55; Ricks, *Fiasco*, 100–4; Fallows, *Blind into Baghdad*, 155–61; Woodward, *State of Denial*, 129–46, 156–77.

15. Duelfer, *Hide and Seek* , 246–47, 316–29.

16. Brian Bennett and Michael Weisskopf, "A Journey to the Dark Side of Baghdad," *Time*, May 26, 2003, 34 (quotation); Joshua Hammer et al., "Who's in Charge Here?," *Newsweek*, May 26, 2003, 29.

17. Bush, *Decision Points*, 258–59; Report by Congressional Research Service, April 29, 2004, http://www.fas.org/man/crs/RL32370.pdf/ (accessed December 9, 2009); Fareed Zakaria, "In Iraq, It's Time for Some Smarts," *Newsweek*, March 1, 2004, 39 (quotation).

18. Wright and Reece, *On Point II*, 154 (quotation); Sanchez, *Wiser in Battle*, 232.

19. CPA Order Number 1, May 16, 2003, http://www.iraqcoalition.org/regulations/20030516_CPAORD_1_De-Ba_athification_of_Iraqi_Society_.pdf (accessed Dec. 9, 2009); CPA Order Number 2, May 23, 2003, http://www.iraqcoalition.org/regulations/20030823_CPAORD_2_Dissolution_of_Entities_with_Annex_A.pdf (accessed Dec. 9, 2003); Fallows, *Blind into Baghdad*, 103, 155–61 (quotations 103, 161).

20. Bremer, *My Year*, 24–75; Slocombe interview, August 17, 2004, http://www.pbs.org/wgbh/pages/frontline/shows/pentagon/interviews/slocombe.html/ (accessed December 9, 2009).

21. Duelfer, *Hide and Seek*, 472–73; Wright and Reece, *On Point II*, 97 (quotation); Woodward, *State of Denial*, 185–212; Bush, *Decision Points*, 259.

22. Bremer, *My Year*, 12–19 (quotation 12); Keegan, *Iraq War*, 210–13; Chandrasekaran, *Imperial Life*, 59–79; "Racing the Clock in Iraq," *Newsweek*, February 9, 2004, 32–38; "Despite Insurgency, U.S. Has Significant Successes," *Columbus Dispatch*, January 30, 2005.

23. Chandrasekaran, *Imperial Life*, 9–25, 83–124, 136–42, 209–48, 281–83; Ricks, *Fiasco*, 203–213; Packer, *Assassins' Gate*, 180–213; Rajiv Chandrasekaran, "Ties to GOP Trumped Know-How Among Staff Sent to Rebuild Iraq," *Washington Post*, September 17, 2006; Etherington, *Revolt on the Tigris*, 150–60 (quotation 159).

24. Baker, *Work Hard*, 399–402 (quotation 402).

25. Memorandum by Rice, October 29, 2002, reprinted in Feith, *War and Decision*, 541–43; Bush *Decision Points*, 249.

26. Congressional Research Service paper, March 17, 2003, http://fpc.state.gov/documents/organization/19204.pdf/ (accessed December 9, 2009).

27. Eisendrath and Goodman, *Bush League Diplomacy*, 63 (quotation); Feith, *War and Decision*, 487 (quotation); Roston, *Man Who Pushed America to War*, 101–120, 134–70.

28. Edward Walsh, "U.S. Sketches Plan for Postwar 'Iraqi Interim Authority,'" *Washington Post*, March 15, 2003; Feith, *War and Decision*, 403 (quotation).

29. Bremer, "Iraq's Path to Sovereignty," *Washington Post*, September 3, 2003, reprinted at http://www.pbs.org/wgbh/pages/frontline/yeariniraq/documents/bremerplan.html/ (accessed November 5, 2009); Bremer, *My Year*, 78–90, Feith, *War and Decision*, 437–50; Chandrasekaran, *Imperial Life*, 185–207, 244–46.

30. Bremer, *My Year*, 163–72, 182–207; Feith, *War and Decision*, 459–70, 485 (quotation); Cleveland and Bunton, *History of the Modern Middle East*, 567–68.

31. Engel, *War Journal*, 44–48; "Chalabi's House Raided by U.S. Troops," *Washington Post*, May 20, 2004; "Bush's Mr. Wrong," *Newsweek*, May 31, 2004, 22–32; Feith, *War and Decision*, 487–90.

32. Bremer, *My Year*, 212–41, 267–308; "Law of Administration for the State of Iraq for the Transitional Period," March 8, 2004, http://law.case.edu/saddamtrial/documents/TAL.pdf (accessed June 18, 2011); "Iraq's New S.O.B.," *Newsweek*, July 26, 2004, 36–37; "Taunts, Traps, and Tests," *Newsweek*, August 23, 2004, 32–33.

33. Address by Allawi, September 23, 2004, http://www.cnn.com/2004/WORLD/meast/09/23/allawi.transcript/ (accessed January 18, 2010) (quotation); Aparisim Ghosh, "Who's Iyad Allawi, and Why Should He Run Iraq?," *Time*, June 1, 2004.

34. "Abu Ghraib and Beyond," *Newsweek*, May 17, 2004, 32–38; Fareed Zakaria, "The Price of Arrogance," *Newsweek*, May 17, 2004, 39 (quotation); "Welcome to the Real World," *Newsweek*, June 23, 2004, 28–35; Eisendrath and Goodman, *Bush League Diplomacy*, 65–69, 94–96; Leffler, "Bush's Foreign Policy."

35. Franks, *American Soldier*, 546–48 (quotation 547); Bush, *Decision Points*, 261–62 (quotations 262); "A Question of Trust," *Time*, July 21, 2003, 22–26; "What Went Wrong," *Newsweek*, February 9, 2004, 24–31; "U.S. 'Almost All Wrong' on Inspections," *Washington Post*, October 7, 2004, A1, A34; Clarke, *Against All Enemies*, 264–71; Feith, *War and Decision*, 470–78.

36. "Al-Qaeda's New Home," *Time*, September 15, 2003, 60–61; "Rough Justice in Iraq," *Newsweek*, May 10, 2004, 26–30; "The Dark Road Ahead," *Newsweek*, April 12, 2004, 28–34; "'We Are Your Martyrs,'" *Newsweek*, April 19, 2004, 36–41; "A Deadly Face-Off," *Newsweek*, April 26, 2004, 30–33; "Iraq's Repairman," *Newsweek*, July 5, 2004, 22–30; "U.S. Casualties in Iraq," http://www.globalsecurity.org/military/ops/iraq_casualties.htm/ (accessed January 28, 2010).

37. Woodward, *State of Denial*, 254–67; Packer, *Assassins' Gate*, 308–15; Ricks, *Fiasco*, 190–200.

38. Sanchez, *Wiser in Battle*, 154 (quotation); Pryer, *Fight for High Ground*; Ricks, *Fiasco*, 215–64, 270–97.

39. "Taunts, Traps, and Tests," *Newsweek*, August 23, 2004, 32–33; "It's Worse Than You Think," *Newsweek*, September 20, 2004, 30–33; Chandrasekaran, *Imperial Life*, 265–77.

40. Raphaeli, "Understanding Muqtada al-Sadr," 33–42; Bremer, *My Year*, 310–35; Feith, *War and Decision*, 480–81; Ricks, *Fiasco*, 321–62.

41. Gerges, *Far Enemy*, 183–271 (quotation 271); Bloom, *Dying to Kill*, 183 (quotation).

42. "Unity and Jihad Group," http://www.globalsecurity.org/military/world/para/zarqawi.htm/ (accessed August 31, 2009); Ellen Knickmeyer and Jonathan Finer, "Insurgent Leader Al-Zarqawi Killed in Iraq," *Washington Post*, June 8, 2006, http://www.washingtonpost.com/wp-dyn/content/article/2006/06/08/AR2006060800114.html/ (accessed August 31, 2009).

43. Bremer, *My Year*, 348–96; "Developments in Iraq," *Columbus Dispatch*, March 27, 2005, A3.

44. Ricks, *Fiasco*, 375–89; transcript of Bush Inaugural Address, January 20, 2005, *Washington Post*, January 21, 2005, http://www.washingtonpost.com/wp-dyn/articles/A23747-2005Jan20.html/ (accessed September 22, 2010).

45. CNN exit polls data, http://www.cnn.com/ELECTION/2004/pages/results/states/US/P/00/epolls.0.html/ (accessed April 1, 2010).

46. "A Vote for Hope," *Time*, February 14, 2005, 33–35; Tony Karon, "The Islamist Who Could Run Iraq," *Time*, February 17, 2005, http://www.time.com/world/printout/0,8816,1028646,00.html/ (accessed September 19, 2009); "Iraqi Predicts Accord on Government in Days," *Columbus Dispatch*, March 27, 2005, A3; Robin Wright, "Experts Cautious in Assessing Iraq Election," *Washington Post*, December 16, 2005, http://www.washingtonpost.com/wp-dyn/content/article/2005/12/15/AR2005121502018.html/ (accessed August 19, 2009); International Mission for Iraqi Elections, "Final Report on the December 15, 2005, Iraqi Council of Representatives Elections," April 12, 2006 (quotation), http://www.ihec.iq/content/file/other_reports/imie_final_report_2005_cor_elections_en.pdf/ (accessed March 30, 2010); "When History Turns a Corner," *Time*, March 14, 2005, 20–25.

47. Andrea Nusse, "The Arabs Should Leave Kurdistan Again," http://www.worldpress. org/print_article.cfm?article_id=1650&dont=yes/ (accessed October 16, 2005). "The Players in Iraq's New Sovereignty," *Time*, June 28, 2004.

48. Department of State, "Country Reports on Terrorism, 2006," http://www.state. gov/s/ct/rls/crt/2006/ (accessed April 1, 2010); "UNHCR Global Report 2007: Iraq Situation," http://www.unhcr.org/484908962.html/ (accessed April 1, 2010).

49. Department of Defense, "Global War on Terrorism: Operation Iraqi Freedom," http://siadapp.dmdc.osd.mil/personnel/CASUALTY/oif-total-by-month.pdf/ (accessed April 1, 2010); Jonathan Weisman, "Projected Iraq War Costs Soar," *Washington Post*, April 27, 2006, http://www.washingtonpost.com/wp-dyn/content/ article/2006/04/26/AR2006042601601.html/ (accessed April 1, 2010); Pew Research Center, "Public Attitudes toward the War in Iraq: 2003–2008," March 19, 2008, http://pewresearch.org/pubs/770/iraq-war-five-year-anniversary/ (accessed April 1, 2010); Adam Nagourney and Megan Thee, "With Election Driven by Iraq, Voters Want New Approach," *New York Times*, November 2, 2006, http://www.nytimes. com/2006/11/02/us/politics/02poll.html/ (accessed April 1, 2010); "Democrats Retake Congress," http://cnn.hu/ELECTION/2006/ (accessed April 1, 2010); Pelosi and Reid to Bush, January 5, 2007, http://thecaucus.blogs.nytimes.com/2007/01/05/ dem-leaders-to-bush-dont-surge/ (accessed June 18, 2011).

50. Final Report of the Iraq Study Group, December 6, 2006, http://www.bakerinstitute. org/publications/iraqstudygroup_findings.pdf/view/ (accessed April 1, 2010).

51. Bush, *Decision Points*, 367, 359, 373, 378.

52. Jack Keane and Frederick W. Kagan, "The Right Type of 'Surge,'" *Washington Post*, December 27, 2006, http://www.washingtonpost.com/wp-dyn/content/article/2006/ 12/26/AR2006122600773.html/ (accessed April 1, 2010).

53. Rod Nordland, "Iraq's Repairman," *Newsweek*, July 5, 2004; Ricks, *Fiasco*, 311–19, 363–73; Atkinson, *In the Company of Soldiers*, 302–3.

54. Ricks, *Fiasco*, 390–406; Thomas E. Ricks, "U.S. Counterinsurgency Academy Giving Officers a New Mind-Set," *Washington Post*, February 21, 2006, http://www.washing- tonpost.com/wp-dyn/content/article/2006/02/20/AR2006022001303.html/ (accessed September 3, 2009).

55. U.S. Army, FM 3–24, "Counterinsurgency," December 2006, http://www.fas.org/ irp/doddir/army/fm3–24.pdf/ (accessed April 1, 2010); Woodward, *War Within*, 129–76.

56. Bush, *Decision Points*, 373–76; Woodward, *War Within*, 194–321 (quotation 272); "Bush Replaces Rumsfeld to Get 'Fresh Perspective,'" November 9, 2006, http://www. cnn.com/2006/POLITICS/11/08/rumsfeld/ (accessed March 31, 2010).

57. Transcript of Bush address, January 10, 2007, http://www.washingtonpost.com/wp- dyn/content/article/2007/01/10/AR2007011002208.html/ (accessed March 31, 2010); Woodward, *War Within*, 344–55; Bush, *Decision Points*, 382.

58. Michael Duffy, "The Surge at Year One," *Time*, January 31, 2008, http://www.time. com/time/magazine/article/0,9171,1708843–1,00.html/ (accessed March 31, 2010); "U.S. troop level in Iraq reaches record high," *Reuters*, August 7, 2007, http://www. reuters.com/article/idUSN07328662200070807/ (accessed April 1, 2010); Bush, *Decision Points*, 380.

59. Michael Duffy, "The Surge at Year One," *Time*, January 31, 2008, http://www.time. com/time/magazine/article/0,9171,1708843–1,00.html/ (accessed March 31, 2010); Woodward, *War Within*, 356–93; Bush, *Decision Points*, 388–89.

60. Joe Klein, "Good General, Bad Mission," *Time*, January 12, 2007, http://www.time.com/time/columnist/klein/article/0,9565,1587186,00.html (accessed January 10, 2008); Patrick Cockburn, "Iraq: Violence is Down—But Not Because of America's 'Surge'," *The Independent*, September 14, 2008; Andrew J. Bacevich, "Surge to Nowhere," *Washington Post*, January 20, 2008.

61. William Kristol, "The Democrats' Fairy Tale," *New York Times*, January 14, 2008, http://www.nytimes.com/2008/01/14/opinion/14kristol.html/ (accessed April 1, 2010); Peter Mansoor, "How the Surge Worked," *Washington Post*, August 10, 2008, B7.

62. Department of State, "Background Note: Iraq," http://www.state.gov/r/pa/ei/bgn/6804.htm#relations/ (accessed April 6, 2010); Greg Bruno, "U.S. Security Agreements and Iraq," http://www.cfr.org/publication/16448/ (accessed April 6, 2010).

63. "Election Results 2008," http://elections.nytimes.com/2008/results/president/exit-polls.html/ (accessed April 6, 2010); Robert Barnes and Michael D. Shear, "Obama Makes History," *Washington Post*, November 5, 2008, http://www.washingtonpost.com/wp-dyn/content/article/2008/11/04/AR2008110404246.html/ (accessed April 6, 2010).

64. Obama address, February 27, 2009, http://www.whitehouse.gov/the_press_office/Remarks-of-President-Barack-Obama-Responsibly-Ending-the-War-in-Iraq/ (accessed April 6, 2010); BBC, "US Troops in Iraq 'Below 50,000' ahead of August Target," August 24, 2010 http://www.bbc.co.uk/news/world-middle-east-11069261/ (accessed September 3, 2010).

65. Joshua Partlow and Michael Abramowitz, "Iraq Passes Bill on Baathists," *Washington Post*, January 13, 2008, http://www.washingtonpost.com/wp-dyn/content/article/2008/01/12/AR2008011201122.html/ (accessed April 6, 2010); Stephen Farrell, "Sadr to split Iraq militia into 2 groups," *New York Times*, August 8, 2008, http://www.nytimes.com/2008/08/08/world/africa/08iht-iraq.4.15124374.html/ (accessed April 1, 2010); Patrick Cockburn, "Iraq Provincial Election Is Most Peaceful since the Fall of Saddam," *The Independent*, February 1, 2009, http://www.independent.co.uk/news/world/middle-east/iraq-provincial-election-is-most-peaceful-since-the-fall-of-saddam-1522548.html/ (accessed April 6, 2010); Brian Murphy, "Iraqi Voters May Have Cut Power to Religions Parties, *Columbus Dispatch*, February 2, 2009, A3; Sam Dagher, "High Turnout in Iraqi Kurds' Elections," *New York Times*, July 25, 2009, http://www.nytimes.com/2009/07/26/world/middleeast/26kurds.html/ (accessed April 1, 2010).

66. Leila Fadel, "Ayad Allawi, Once Seen as a U.S. Puppet, Returns to the Center of Iraqi Politics," *Washington Post*, March 26, 2010, http://www.washingtonpost.com/wp-dyn/content/article/2010/03/25/AR2010032503650.html (accessed April 6, 2010); NPR, "Sunni-Backed Politician to Join Iraqi Government," December 14, 2010, http://www.npr.org/templates/story/story.php?storyId=101795064/ (accessed December 14, 2010); "Iraq Has Cabinet 9 Months after Vote," *Columbus Dispatch*, December 22, 2010.

67. Haass, *War of Necessity*, 270; Charles Krauthammer, "Bush, Like Truman, Will Be Vindicated," *Columbus Dispatch*, September 23, 2008, A7.

68. "Iraq War Journal," *Columbus Dispatch*, September 1, 2010.

69. Georgie Anne Geyer, "Elections Are Great, But Iraq War Still a Mistake," *Columbus Dispatch*, March 10, 2010, A13; Joseph E. Stiglitz and Linda J. Bilmes, "The True Cost of the Iraq War: $3 Trillion and Beyond," *Washington Post*, September 5, 2010; Frank Rich, "Freedom's Just Another Word," *New York Times*, September 5, 2010.

Conclusion
Missions Accomplished?

President George W. Bush's speech beneath the "MISSION ACCOMPLISHED" banner aboard the USS *Abraham Lincoln* quickly became a subject of considerable controversy. Within months of the May 1, 2003 address, the smashingly successful U.S. military invasion of Iraq had given way to a debilitating insurgency that retrospectively made the president's implicit claim of fulfillment of his objectives seem prematurely triumphalist and therefore wrong-headed. Even a senior official of the administration observed, using an analogy to American football, that the president had performed a celebration dance in the end zone after clumsily spiking the ball on the 10-yard line. Even worse for his credibility, the president initially fended off criticism of his appearance on the USS *Abraham Lincoln* by asserting that the crew of the ship had erected or at least requested the banner, but then rescinded the claim after journalists questioned it. Bush's late 2003 admission that his staff had arranged the sign for public relations purposes coincided with and reinforced a rising tide of public criticism about Bush's handling of the situation in Iraq from the inception of the invasion through the wave of instability that swept the country after the fall of the Saddam Hussein regime. In his memoirs, Bush admitted that the "MISSION ACCOMPLISHED" banner had been a blunder. "My speech made clear that our work was far from done," he wrote. "But all the explaining in the world could not reverse the perception. Our stagecraft had gone awry. It was a big mistake."[1]

In a microcosm, the story of the "MISSION ACCOMPLISHED" banner reveals some of the legacies of U.S. policy toward Iraq from the foundation of that state after World War I to the present day. It speaks to the sense of purpose that guided U.S. policy toward Iraq over several decades, as officials in Washington accepted for themselves the responsibility to achieve certain objectives in Baghdad that, they calculated, would enhance U.S. interests. The staging of the president's speech aboard an aircraft carrier symbolizes the increasingly military flavor of U.S. policy toward Iraq, which evolved from remote connections prior to World War II, to political involvement that deepened during the

Cold War, to the liberal use of American military power since 1990 to shape Iraq's behavior and, ultimately, its identity. President Bush's implicit claim of success in reaching his objectives—which proved to be premature, if not erroneous—epitomized a recurrent American pattern of believing or claiming that gains in Iraq had been made but then realizing that problems remained unsolved or that new and consequential problems had emerged. The controversy that erupted over the "MISSION ACCOMPLISHED" banner represented the sharp growth of public scrutiny of official policy and of dissent from the plans and pronouncements of the government in Washington.

The U.S. relationship with Iraq experienced dramatic change during the century that followed the establishment of modern Iraq at the end of World War I. The original, distant, and disconnected relationship moved through several stages that included periods of cooperation and rapprochement but also moments of conflict and two rounds of warfare. The relationship became most complicated in the early 21st century when the United States invaded and occupied Iraq and attempted to rebirth the country on a democratic, peaceful, and progressive foundation.

The intricate relationship of the early 21st century had an inauspicious beginning. When modern Iraq was established as a British mandate after World War I, the United States generally lacked official interests in the Middle East and deferred to the British to maintain Western interests across the region. The Nazi threat to the Middle East during World War II, although successfully neutralized by Britain, awoke officials in Washington to the importance of Iraq. After 1945, when British power declined as the Soviet menace arose, U.S. officials began to pay more serious attention to Iraq's place in the international order and to the political culture within the country.

During the Cold War era, U.S.–Iraqi relations grew complex and inconsistent. The United States viewed Iraq as a country with modest importance in its two interrelated challenges in the Middle East: containing the Soviet Union and averting intraregional conflicts. A friendly partnership with the royalist regime in Baghdad emerged in the 1950s but was dashed by the Iraqi revolution of 1958. Discord characterized U.S.–Iraqi relations in the subsequent 2 decades, when chronic instability afflicted the government in Baghdad. In the 1980s, the United States embraced Iraq's new leader, Saddam Hussein, as a bastion against the geographic expansion of the Iranian revolution. Sharing a common adversary in Tehran, the two powers by mid-decade worked out a rapprochement that set the stage for increased U.S. political and military involvement in the Iran–Iraq War. The U.S. intervention helped Hussein survive the war, which he had provoked in 1980, with his country and his rule intact.

1990 marked the start of a "long decade" of severe tension and conflict in the U.S. relationship with Hussein's regime. The U.S. reaction to Iraq's August 1990 invasion of Kuwait clearly indicated the end of the 1980s reconciliation. The George H. W. Bush Administration considered Hussein's action as a dire threat to Western interests across the region and thus it resolved to reverse his conquest.

The Persian Gulf War of 1990–1991 featured the United States and its allies liberating Kuwait from Iraqi occupation by force of arms. For 12 years thereafter, U.S. leaders pursued a policy of containing Hussein's regime until it atrophied, but that task became complicated by a revival of Hussein's power within his country and a restoration of his international credibility. A new president in a new century took the United States down the path of direct military invasion of Iraq, easily conquering the country but in the process inheriting the difficult and deadly task of governing Iraq and reconstructing it for the post-Hussein era.

During the century following the establishment of modern Iraq, U.S. leaders enjoyed some successes and some failures in the various missions they embraced in that country. In World War II, U.S. officials assisted in the British success in denying Nazi inroads in Baghdad. Throughout the Cold War era, by contrast, the record of achievement was more balanced. The pro-Western monarchy that the United States embraced in the 1950s as an anti-Soviet security partner did not survive that decade, although successor regimes suppressed indigenous communists and refrained from forming formal partnerships with the Soviet Union. In the 1960s and 1970s, the United States sought to stabilize Iraq and ensure Western interests by offering the country diplomatic recognition and some foreign aid, but disputes over Iraq's oil industry, Israel, and other matters perpetuated an undercurrent of tension. The U.S. tilt toward Iraq during its war with Iran in the 1980s ensured the survival of Iraq as a bastion against Iranian expansionism and the prevention of a partnership between Baghdad and Moscow.

Although the end of the Cold War liberated U.S. officials from their preoccupation with Soviet communism, it did not simplify the U.S. mission in Iraq. Seeking to transition into a stable post-Cold War era, President George H. W. Bush sought to steer Iraq toward an era of peace and stability, but Hussein decided instead to launch a war of conquest against Kuwait. That move prompted the United States to use political pressure and, ultimately, military force against the Iraqi government. President Bush achieved his limited mission of liberating Kuwait from Iraqi occupation and damaging Hussein's prestige. By leaving Hussein in power, however, he also sowed the seeds for future conflict. Similarly, the policy of containing Iraq practiced by the United States through the 1990s worked in the short term at keeping Hussein in a cage, but his growing ability to rattle that cage presaged the re-emergence of conflict in the near future.

In the early 21st century, President George W. Bush embraced the most daring mission in the history of the U.S. experience in Iraq when he decided to use military invasion as a means of achieving "regime change" in Baghdad. In strict tactical terms, the president accomplished what he aimed for: a quick and total victory on the battlefield. In this sense, he rightfully claimed "mission accomplished" while speaking aboard the USS *Abraham Lincoln* on May 1, 2003. Yet on a deeper strategic level, the president failed to anticipate, comprehend, or clarify the mission that he would embrace after the military victory. Over time, he gradually defined a goal of building a peaceful, prosperous, and democratic Iraq through a beneficent occupation policy. Although he achieved some significant forward progress toward such goals by the end of his presidency, his larger mission in Iraq clearly remained unaccomplished, and his pursuit of that mission proved to be costly. It remains to be seen whether President Barack Obama and his successors will be able to repair the damage to American interests in the Middle East and elsewhere, salvage some form of stability in Iraq, and formulate a foreign policy toward Iraq that balances goals with means, aligns actions with American values, and accomplishes missions that advance the best interests of the United States and the world community.

NOTE

1. Bush, *Decision Points*, 257 (quotation); "Bush's 'Bannergate' Shuffle," *Time*, November 1, 2003.

Bibliography

PRIMARY SOURCES

Annan, Kofi, Interview with BBC, September 16, 2004, in Jeremy Brecher, Jill Cutler, and Brendan Smith, eds. *In the Name of Democracy: American War Crimes in Iraq and Beyond*, 33. New York: Metropolitan Books, 2005.

Crane, Conrad C., and Terrill, W. Andrew. *Reconstructing Iraq: Insights, Challenges, and Missions for Military Forces in a Post-Conflict Scenario*. Carlisle, Pa.: U.S. Army War College, 2003.

Gallup Poll Public Opinion, 1937–1997: The CD-Rom Edition. Wilmington, Del.: Scholarly Resources, ND (CD-Rom).

Sifry, Micah L., and Cerf, Christopher, eds. *The Iraq War Reader: History, Documents, Opinions*. New York: Touchstone, 2003.

U.S. Agency for International Development. *Iraq's Legacy of Terror: Mass Graves*. Washington, U.S. AID, 2004.

U.S. Department of State. *Foreign Relations of the United States, 1919*. Vol. 2. Washington, D.C.: U.S. Government Printing Office, 1934.

U.S. Department of State. *Foreign Relations of the United States, 1930*. Vol. 3. Washington, D.C.: U.S. Government Printing Office, 1945.

U.S. Department of State. *Foreign Relations of the United States, 1932*. Vol. 2: *The British Commonwealth, Europe, Near East, and Africa*. Washington, D.C.: U.S. Government Printing Office, 1947.

U.S. Department of State. *Foreign Relations of the United States, 1934*. Vol. 2: *Europe, Near East, and Africa*. Washington, D.C.: U.S. Government Printing Office, 1951.

U.S. Department of State. *Foreign Relations of the United States, 1936*. Vol. 3: *The Near East and Africa*. Washington, D.C.: U.S. Government Printing Office, 1953.

U.S. Department of State. *Foreign Relations of the United States, 1937*. Vol. 2: *The British Commonwealth, Europe, Near East and Africa*. Washington, D.C.: U.S. Government Printing Office, 1954.

U.S. Department of State. *Foreign Relations of the United States, 1938*. Vol. 2: *The British Commonwealth, Europe, Near East and Africa*. Washington, D.C.: U.S. Government Printing Office, 1955.

U.S. Department of State. *Foreign Relations of the United States, 1939*. Vol. 4: *The Far East, the Near East, and Africa*. Washington, D.C.: U.S. Government Printing Office, 1955.

U.S. Department of State. *Foreign Relations of the United States, 1940*. Vol. 3: *The British Commonwealth, the Soviet Union, the Near East, and Africa*. Washington, D.C.: U.S. Government Printing Office, 1958.

U.S. Department of State. *Foreign Relations of the United States, 1942*. Vol. 4: *The Near East and Africa*. Washington, D.C.: U.S. Government Printing Office, 1963.

U.S. Department of State. *Foreign Relations of the United States, 1943*. Vol. 4: *The Near East and Africa*. Washington, D.C.: U.S. Government Printing Office, 1964.

U.S. Department of State. *Foreign Relations of the United States, 1944*. Vol. 5: *The Near East, South Asia, and Africa, the Far East*. Washington, D.C.: U.S. Government Printing Office, 1965.

U.S. Department of State. *Foreign Relations of the United States, 1945*. Vol. 8: *The Near East and Africa*. Washington, D.C.: U.S. Government Printing Office, 1969.

U.S. Department of State. *Foreign Relations of the United States, 1946*. Vol. 7: *The Near East and Africa*. Washington, D.C.: U.S. Government Printing Office, 1969.

U.S. Department of State. *Foreign Relations of the United States, 1947*. Vol. 5: *The Near East and Africa*. Washington, D.C.: U.S. Government Printing Office, 1971.

U.S. Department of State. *Foreign Relations of the United States, 1948*. Vol. 5: *The Near East, South Asia, and Africa, Parts I and II*. Washington, D.C.: U.S. Government Printing Office, 1975–1976.

U.S. Department of State. *Foreign Relations of the United States, 1949*. Vol. 6: *The Near East, South Asia, and Africa*. Washington, D.C.: U.S. Government Printing Office, 1977.

U.S. Department of State. *Foreign Relations of the United States, 1950*. Vol. 5: *The Near East and Africa*. Washington, D.C.: U.S. Government Printing Office, 1978.

U.S. Department of State. *Foreign Relations of the United States, 1951*. Vol. 5: *The Near East and Africa*. Washington, D.C.: U.S. Government Printing Office, 1982.

U.S. Department of State. *Foreign Relations of the United States, 1958–1960*. Vol. 12: *Near East Region; Iraq; Iran; Arabian Peninsula*. Washington, D.C.: U.S. Government Printing Office, 1993.

U.S. Department of State. *Foreign Relations of the United States, 1958–1960*. Vol. 13: *Arab–Israeli Dispute; United Arab Republic; North Africa*. Washington, D.C.: U.S. Government Printing Office, 1992.

U.S. Department of State. *Foreign Relations of the United States, 1961–1963*. Vol. 17: *Near East, 1961–1962*. Washington, D.C.: U.S. Government Printing Office, 1994.

U.S. Department of State. *Foreign Relations of the United States, 1961–1963*. Vol. 18: *Near East, 1962–1963*. Washington, D.C.: U.S. Government Printing Office, 1995.

U.S. Department of State. *Foreign Relations of the United States, 1964–1968*. Vol. 18: *Arab–Israeli Dispute, 1964–1967*. Washington, D.C.: U.S. Government Printing Office, 1995.

U.S. Department of State. *Foreign Relations of the United States, 1964–1968*. Vol. 19: *Arab–Israeli Crisis and War, 1967*. Washington, D.C.: U.S. Government Printing Office, 2004.

U.S. Department of State. *Foreign Relations of the United States, 1964–1968*. Vol. 20: *Arab–Israeli Dispute, 1967–1968*. Washington, D.C.: U.S. Government Printing Office, 2001.

U.S. Department of State. *Foreign Relations of the United States, 1964–1968*. Vol. 21: *Near East Region: Arabian Peninsula*. Washington, D.C.: U.S. Government Printing Office, 2000.

U.S. Department of State. *Foreign Relations of the United States, 1969–1976*, Vol. E–4, *Documents on Iran and Iraq, 1969–1972*. Electronic source available at http://www.history.state.gov/historicaldocuments/frus1969–76ve04/.

U.S. National Commission on Terrorist Attacks upon the United States. *The 9/11 Report*. New York: St. Martin's, 2004.

U.S. War and Navy Departments. *A Short Guide to Iraq*. Reprinted as *Instructions for American Servicemen in Iraq during World War II*, ed. John A. Nagl. Chicago: University of Chicago Press, 2007.

MEMOIRS

Albright, Madeleine Korbel. *Madam Secretary*. New York: Miramax Books, 2003.

Baker, James A. *The Politics of Diplomacy: Revolution, War, and Peace, 1989–1992*. New York: Putnam's, 1995.

Baker, James A. *"Work Hard, Study…, and Keep Out of Politics!": Adventures and Lessons from an Unexpected Public Life*. New York: Putnam's, 2006.

Blair, Tony. *A Journey: My Political Life*. New York: Knopf, 2010.

Bremer, L. Paul III, with Malcolm McConnell. *My Year in Iraq: The Struggle to Build a Future of Hope*. New York: Simon & Schuster, 2006.

Brzezinski, Zbigniew. *Power and Principle: Memoirs of the National Security Adviser, 1977–1981*. New York: Farrar, Strauss, and Giroux, 1983.

Bush, George and Scowcroft, Brent. *A World Transformed*. New York: Knopf, 1998.

Bush, George W. *Decision Points*. New York: Crown, 2010.

Carter, Jimmy. *Keeping Faith: Memoirs of a President*. New York: Bantam, 1982.

Christopher, Warren. *Chances of a Lifetime*. New York: Scribner, 2001.

Christopher, Warren. *In the Stream of History: Shaping Foreign Policy for a New Era*. Stanford: Stanford University Press, 1998.

Clinton, Bill. *My Life*. New York: Knopf, 2004.

Feith, Douglas J. *War and Decision: Inside the Pentagon at the Dawn of the War on Terrorism*. New York: Harper, 2008.

Franks, Tommy. *American Soldier*. New York: Regan Books, 2004.

Gallman, Waldemar J. *Iraq under General Nuri: My Recollections of Nuri al-Said, 1954–1958*. Baltimore: Johns Hopkins, 1964.

Haig, Alexander M., Jr. *Caveat: Realism, Reagan, and Foreign Policy*. New York: Macmillan, 1984.

Haig, Alexander M., Jr. *Inner Circles: How America Changed the World: A Memoir*. New York: Warner Books, 1992.

Haldane, Aylmer L. *The Insurrection in Mesopotamia, 1920*. Edinburgh: Blackwood, 1922.

Indyk, Martin. *Innocent Abroad: An Intimate Account of American Peace Diplomacy in the Middle East*. New York: Simon & Schuster, 2009.

Powell, Colin L. *My American Journey*. New York: Random House, 1995.

Reagan, Ronald. *An American Life*. New York: Simon & Schuster, 1990.

Ritter, Scott. *Endgame: Solving the Iraq Problem*. New York: Simon & Schuster, 1999.

Sada, Georges. *Saddam's Secrets: How an Iraqi General Defied and Survived Saddam Hussein*. Brentwood, Tn.: Integrity, 2006.

Sanchez, Ricardo S. *Wiser in Battle: A Soldier's Story*. New York: HarperCollins, 2008.

Shultz, George P. *Turmoil and Triumph: My Years as Secretary of State.* New York: Scribner's, 1993.

Thatcher, Margaret. *The Downing Street Years.* New York: HarperCollins, 1993.

Vance, Cyrus. *Hard Choices: Critical Years in America's Foreign Policy.* New York: Simon & Schuster, 1983.

SECONDARY SOURCES

Abdullah, Thabit A. J. *A Short History of Iraq, From 636 to the Present.* London: Pearson Longman, 2003.

Alnasrawi, Abbas. *The Economy of Iraq: Oil, War, Destruction of Development and Prospects, 1950–2000.* Westport, Ct.: Greenwood, 1994.

Amnesty International. "Iraq: Civilians under Fire." In *In the Name of Democracy: American War Crimes in Iraq and Beyond*, ed. Jeremy Brecher, Jill Cutler, and Brendan Smith, 39–42. New York: Metropolitan Books, 2005.

Anscombe, Frederick F. *The Ottoman Gulf: The Creation of Kuwait, Saudi Arabia, and Qatar.* New York: Columbia University Press, 1997.

Ashton, Nigel John. *Eisenhower, Macmillan, and the Problem of Nasser: Anglo-American Relations and Arab Nationalism, 1955–1959.* New York: Macmillan, 1996.

Atkinson, Rick. *Crusade: The Untold Story of the Persian Gulf War.* New York: Houghton Mifflin, 1993.

Atkinson, Rick. *In the Company of Soldiers: A Chronicle of Combat.* New York: Holt, 2004.

Bakhash, Shaul. *The Reign of the Ayatollahs: Iran and the Islamic Revolution.* New York: Basic, 1984.

Baram, Amatzia. "The Iraqi Invasion of Kuwait: Decision-Making in Baghdad." In *Iraq's Road to War*, eds. Amatzia Baram and Barry Rubin, 5–36. New York: St. Martin's Press, 1993.

Baram, Amatzia. "U.S. Input into Iraqi Decisionmaking, 1988–1990." In *The Middle East and the United States: A Historical and Political Reassessment*, ed. David W. Lesch, 325–53. Boulder, Colo.: Westview Press, 1996.

Batatu, Hanna. *The Old Social Classes and the Revolutionary Movements of Iraq: A Study of Iraq's Old Landed and Commercial Classes and of Its Communists, Ba'thists, and Free Officers.* Princeton, N.J.: Princeton University Press, 1978.

Bengio, Ofra. "Iraq's Shia and Kurdish Communities: From Resentment to Revolt." In *Iraq's Road to War*, eds. Amatzia Baram and Barry Rubin, 51–66. New York: St. Martin's Press, 1993.

Blair, John M. *The Control of Oil.* New York: Pantheon Books, 1976.

Bloom, Mia. *Dying to Kill: The Allure of Suicide Terror.* New York: Columbia, 2005.

Branch, Taylor. *The Clinton Tapes: Wrestling History with the President.* New York: Simon & Schuster, 2009.

Brattebo, Douglas M. "The No-Fly Zones and Low Intensity Conflict with Iraq, 1991–2003." In *Presidential Policies and the Road to the Second Iraq War: From Forty One to Forty Three*, ed. John Davis, 208–40. Burlington, Vt.: Ashgate, 2006.

Braude, Joseph. *The New Iraq: Rebuilding the Country for Its People, the Middle East, and the World.* New York: Basic Books, 2003.

Bunter, Michael A. G. "Early Concessions in Iraq and the Middle East." *Oil, Gas, & Energy Law Intelligence* 1 (January 2003), http://www.gasandoil.com/ogel/samples/freearticles/roundup_01.htm/ (accessed March 26, 2008).

Caron, David D. "Choice and Duty in Foreign Affairs: The Reflagging of the Kuwaiti Tankers." In *The Persian Gulf War: Lessons for Strategy, Law, and Diplomacy*, ed. Christopher C. Joyner, 153–72. New York: Greenwood, 1990.

Carus, W. Seth. *Ballistic Missiles in Modern Conflict*. New York: Praeger, 1991.

Center for Economic and Social Rights. "Tearing Up the Rules: The Illegality of Invading Iraq." In *In the Name of Democracy: American War Crimes in Iraq and Beyond*, ed. Jeremy Brecher, Jill Cutler, and Brendan Smith, 24–32. New York: Metropolitan Books, 2005.

Chandrasekaran, Rajiv. *Imperial Life in the Emerald City: Inside Iraq's Green Zone*. New York: Knopf, 2006.

Citino, Nathan J. "Middle East Cold Wars: Oil and Arab Nationalism in U.S.–Iraqi Relations, 1958–1961." In *The Eisenhower Administration, the Third World, and the Globalization of the Cold War*, ed. Kathryn C. Statler and Andrew L. Johns, 245–69. Lanham, Md.: Rowman & Littlefield, 2006.

Clarke, Richard A. *Against All Enemies: Inside America's War on Terror*. New York: Free Press, 2004.

Clawson, Patrick. "Iraq's Economy and International Sanctions." In *Iraq's Road to War*, ed. Amatzia Baram and Barry Rubin, 69–83. New York: St. Martin's, 1993.

Cleveland, William, and Bunton, Martin. *A History of the Modern Middle East*, 4th ed. Philadelphia: Westview, 2009.

Dann, Uriel. *Iraq under Qassem: A Political History, 1958–1963*. New York: Praeger, 1969.

Davis, John. "The Ideology of War: The Neoconservatives and the Hijacking of US Policy toward Iraq." In *Presidential Policies and the Road to the Second Iraq War: From Forty One to Forty Three*, ed. John Davis, 29–61. Burlington, Vt.: Ashgate, 2006.

Dawisha, Adeed. *Iraq: A Political History from Independence to Occupation*. Princeton, N.J.: Princeton University Press, 2009.

DeNovo, John A. *American Interests and Policies in the Middle East, 1900–1939*. Minneapolis: University of Minnesota Press, 1963.

Dockrill, Michael L., and Goold, J. Douglas. *Peace without Promise: Britain and the Peace Conferences, 1919–23*. London: Batsford, 1981.

Duelfer, Charles. *Hide and Seek: The Search for Truth in Iraq*. New York: Public Affairs, 2009.

Eisendrath, Craig R., and Goodman, Melvin A. *Bush League Diplomacy: How the Neoconservatives are Putting the World at Risk*. Amherst, N.Y.: Prometheus Books, 2004.

Engel, Richard. *War Journal: My Five Years in Iraq*. New York: Simon & Schuster, 2008.

Eppel, Michael. *The Palestine Conflict in the History of Modern Iraq: The Dynamics of Involvement, 1928–1948*. Portland, Or.: Cass, 1994.

Etherington, Mark. *Revolt on the Tigris: The Al-Sadr Uprising and the Governing of Iraq*. Ithaca: Cornell University Press, 2005.

Fallows, James M. *Blind into Baghdad: America's War in Iraq*. New York: Vintage Books, 2006.

Farouk-Sluglett, Marion, and Sluglett, Peter. *Iraq since 1958: From Revolution to Dictatorship*. London: Tauris, 2001.

Field, James A., Jr. *From Gibraltar to the Middle East: America and the Mediterranean World, 1776–1882*. Chicago: Imprint Publications, 1991.

Fontenot, Gregory, Degen, E.J., and Tohn, David. *On Point: The United States Army in Operation Iraqi Freedom*. Annapolis, Md.: Naval Institute Press, 2005.

Francona, Rick. *Ally to Adversary: An Eyewitness Account of Iraq's Fall from Grace*. Annapolis, Md.: Naval Institute Press, 1999.

Freedman, Lawrence. *A Choice of Enemies: America Confronts the Middle East*. New York: Public Affairs, 2008.

Freedman, Lawrence, and Karsh, Efraim. *The Gulf Conflict, 1990–1991: Diplomacy and War in the New World Order*. Princeton, N.J.: Princeton University Press, 1993.

Gelvin, James. "The Ironic Legacy of the King–Crane Commission." In: *The Middle East and the United States: A Historical and Political Reassessment*, ed. David W. Lesch, 11–27. Boulder, Colo.: Westview Press, 1996.

Gendzier, Irene. *Notes from the Minefield: United States Intervention in Lebanon and the Middle East, 1945–1958*. New York: Columbia University Press, 1997.

Gerges, Fawaz A. *The Far Enemy: Why Jihad Went Global*. Cambridge: Cambridge University Press, 2005.

Gordon, Joy. "Cool War: Economic Sanctions as a Weapon of Mass Destruction." *Harper's Magazine*, November 2002.

Gordon, Michael R., and Trainor, Bernard E. *Cobra II: The Inside Story of the Invasion and Occupation of Iraq*. New York: Pantheon Books, 2006.

Greene, John Robert. *The Presidency of George Bush*. Lawrence: University Press of Kansas, 2000.

Haass, Richard. *War of Necessity: War of Choice*. New York: Simon & Schuster, 2009.

Hahn, Peter L. *Caught in the Middle East: U.S. Policy toward the Arab–Israeli Conflict, 1945–1961*. Chapel Hill: University of North Carolina Press, 2004.

Hahn, Peter L. *Crisis and Crossfire: The United States and the Middle East since 1945*. Washington: Potomac Books, 2005.

Hahn, Peter L. "Grand Strategy." In *U.S. Foreign Policy after the Cold War*, 185–214. Eds. Randall B. Ripley and James M. Lindsay. Pittsburgh: University of Pittsburgh Press, 1997.

Hahn, Peter L. *Historical Dictionary of United States-Middle East Relations*. Lanham, Md.: Rowman & Littlefield, 2007.

Hahn, Peter L. *The United States, Great Britain, and Egypt, 1945–1956: Strategy and Diplomacy in the Early Cold War*. Chapel Hill: University of North Carolina Press, 1991.

Halliday, Fred. "The Middle East, the Great Powers, and the Cold War." In *The Cold War and the Middle East,* eds. Yezid Sayigh and Avi Shlaim, 6–26. Oxford: Clarendon Press, 1997.

Hathaway, Jane. *The Arab Lands under Ottoman Rule, 1516–1800*. Harlow, UK: Pearson, 2008.

Heller, Mark A. "Iraq's Army: Military Weakness, Political Utility." In *Iraq's Road to War*, eds. Amatzia Baram and Barry Rubin, 37–50. New York: St. Martin's Press, 1993.

Hiro, Dilip. *The Longest War: The Iran-Iraq Military Conflict*. London: Paladin, 1990.

Hoganson, Kristin L. *Consumers' Imperium: The Global Production of American Domesticity, 1865–1920*. Chapel Hill: University of North Carolina Press, 2007.

Human Rights Watch. "The Road to Abu Ghraib." In *In the Name of Democracy: American War Crimes in Iraq and Beyond*, eds. Jeremy Brecher, Jill Cutler, and Brendan Smith, 84–99. New York: Metropolitan Books, 2005.

Hume, Cameron. *The United Nations, Iran, and Iraq: How Peacemaking Changed*. Bloomington: Indiana University Press, 1994.

Jasse, Richard L. "The Baghdad Pact: Cold War or Colonialism?" *Middle Eastern Studies* 27:1 (Jan. 1991): 140–156.

Jervis, Robert. *American Foreign Policy in a New Era*. New York: Routledge, 2005.

Jentleson, Bruce W. *With Friends Like These: Reagan, Bush, and Saddam, 1982–1990*. New York: Norton, 1994.

Kaufman, Burton I. *The Arab Middle East and the United States: Inter-Arab Rivalry and Superpower Diplomacy*. New York: Twayne, 1996.

Kaufman, Burton I. *The Oil Cartel Case: A Documentary Study of Antitrust Activity in the Cold War Era*. Westport, Conn.: Greenwood, 1978.

Kaufman, Robert G. *In Defense of the Bush Doctrine*. Lexington: University of Kentucky Press: 2007.

Kedourie, Elie. *England and the Middle East: The Destruction of the Ottoman Empire, 1914–1921*. Boulder, Colo.: Westview, 1956, 1987.

Keegan, John. *The Iraq War*. New York: Knopf, 2004.

Kerr, Malcolm H. *The Arab Cold War: Gamal 'abd al-Nasir and his Rivals, 1958–1970*. New York: Oxford University Press, 1971.

Khadduri, Majid. *The Gulf War: The Origins and Implications of the Iran–Iraq Conflict*. Oxford: Oxford University Press, 1988.

Khadduri, Majid. *Republican Iraq: A Study in Iraqi Politics since the Revolution of 1958*. London: Oxford University Press, 1969.

Khadduri, Majid. *Socialist Iraq: A Study in Iraqi Politics since 1968*. Washington, D.C.: The Middle East Institute, 1978.

Khadduri, Majid, and Ghareeb, Edmund. *War in the Gulf, 1990–91: The Iraq-Kuwait Conflict and its Implications*. New York: Oxford University Press, 1997.

Khalil, Samir al-. *Republic of Fear: The Inside Story of Saddam's Iraq*. New York: Pantheon, 1989.

Kingston, Paul W. T. *Britain and the Politics of Modernization in the Middle East, 1945–1958*. Cambridge: Cambridge University Press, 1996.

Klare, Michael T. *Rogue States and Nuclear Outlaws: America's Search for a New Foreign Policy*. New York: Hill and Wang, 1995.

Kostiner, Joseph. "Britain and the Northern Frontier of the Saudi State, 1922–1925." In *The Great Powers in the Middle East, 1919–1939*, ed. Uriel Dann, 29–48. New York: Holmes & Meier, 1988.

Leffler, Melvyn P. "Bush's Foreign Policy." *Foreign Policy* 144 (Sept.-Oct. 2004), 22–28.

Leffler, Melvyn P. "Dreams of Freedom, Temptations of Power." In *The Fall of the Berlin Wall: The Revolutionary Legacy of 1989*, ed. Jeffrey A. Engel, 132–69. New York: Oxford University Press, 2009.

Lesch, David W. *The Arab–Israeli Conflict: A History*. New York: Oxford University Press, 2008.

Lind, Michael. *The American Way of Strategy*. New York: Oxford University Press, 2006.

Little, Doug. "Cold War and Covert Action: The United States and Syria, 1945–1958." *Middle East Journal* 44:1 (Winter 1990): 51–75.

Lopez, George A., and Cortright, David. "Containing Iraq: Sanctions Worked." *Foreign Affairs* 83:4 (July–August 2004): 90–103.

Malone, David M. *The International Struggle over Iraq.* Oxford: Oxford University Press, 2006.

Mann, James. *Rise of the Vulcans: The History of Bush's War Cabinet.* New York: Viking, 2004.

Marr, Phebe. "Iraq after the Gulf War: The Fallen Idol." In *The Middle East and the Peace Process: The Impact of the Oslo Accords,* ed. Robert O. Freedman, 213–40. Gainesville: University Press of Florida, 1998.

Marr, Phebe. *The Modern History of Iraq.* Boulder, Colo.: Westview Press, 1985.

McDowall, David. *A Modern History of the Kurds,* 3rd ed. New York: Tauris, 2004.

Miller, Judith, and Mylroie, Laurie. *Saddam Hussein and the Crisis in the Gulf.* New York: Times Books, 1990.

Monroe, Elizabeth. *Britain's Moment in the Middle East, 1914–1971.* London: Chatto & Windus, 1981.

Murray, Williamson, and Scales, Robert H., Jr. *The Iraq War: A Military History.* Cambridge, Mass.: Harvard University Press, 2003.

Mylroie, Laurie. *Study of Revenge: The First World Trade Center Attack and Saddam Hussein's War against America.* Washington, D.C.: AEI Press, 2001.

Mylroie, Laurie. "The World Trade Center Bomb: Who Is Ramzi Yousef? And Why It Matters." *The National Interest.* Winter 1995/96. http://www.nationalinterest.org/issue/winter-1995-1996/.

Nance, Susan. *How the Arabian Nights Inspired the American Dream, 1790–1935.* Chapel Hill: University of North Carolina Press, 2009.

Oren, Michael B. *Power, Faith, and Fantasy: America in the Middle East, 1776 to the Present.* New York: Norton, 2007.

O'Sullivan, Christopher D. *Colin Powell: American Power and Intervention from Vietnam to Iraq.* Lanham, Md.: Rowman & Littlefield, 2009.

O'Sullivan, Christopher, and Damluji, Manaf. "The Origins of American Power in Iraq, 1941–1945," *Peace & Change* 34:3 (July 2009): 238–59.

Packer, George. *The Assassins' Gate: America in Iraq.* New York: Farrar, Straus, and Giroux, 2005.

Palmer, Michael A. *Guardians of the Gulf: A History of America's Expanding Role in the Persian Gulf, 1833–1992.* New York: Free Press, 1992.

Pedersen, Susan. "Getting Out of Iraq—In 1932: The League of Nations and the Road to Normative Statehood." *American Historical Review* 115 (October 2010): 975–1000.

Persson, Magnus. *Great Britain, the United States, and the Security of the Middle East: The Formation of the Baghdad Pact.* Lund: Lund University Press, 1998.

Petersen, Tore T. *The Decline of the Anglo-American Middle East, 1961–1969: A Willing Retreat.* Portland, Ore.: Sussex, 2006.

Pilger, John. "Squeezed to Death," *The Guardian.* March 4, 2000. http://www.guardian.co.uk/theguardian/2000/mar/04/weekend7.weekend9/.

Podeh, Elie. *The Quest for Hegemony in the Arab World: The Struggle over the Baghdad Pact.* Leiden: E. J. Brill, 1995.

Pryer, Douglas A. *The Fight for the High Ground: The U.S. Army and Interrogation during Operation Iraqi Freedom, May 2003–April 2004.* Fort Leavenworth, Ks.: CGSC Foundation Press, 2009.

Rafaat, Aram. "U.S.-Kurdish Relations in Post-Invasion Iraq." *Middle East Review of International Affairs* 11:4 (Dec. 2007): 79–89.

Raphaeli, Nimrod. "Understanding Muqtada al-Sadr." *Middle East Quarterly* 11:4 (Fall 2004): 33–42.

Record, Jeffrey. *Dark Victory: America's Second War against Iraq.* Annapolis, Md.: Naval Institute Press, 2004.

Ricks, Thomas E. *Fiasco: The American Military Adventure in Iraq.* New York: Penguin, 2006.

Roston, Aram. *The Man Who Pushed America to War: The Extraordinary Life, Adventures, and Obsessions of Ahmad Chalabi.* New York: Nation Books, 2008.

Rubin, Barry. "America as Junior Partner: Anglo-American Relations in the Middle East, 1919–1939." In *The Great Powers in the Middle East, 1919–1939*, ed. Uriel Dann, 238–51. New York: Holmes & Meier, 1988.

Rubin, Barry. "The United States and Iraq: From Appeasement to War." In *Iraq's Road To War*, eds. Amatzia Baram and Barry Rubin, 255–72. New York: St. Martin's Press, 1993.

Sanjian, Ara. "The Formulation of the Baghdad Pact." *Middle Eastern Studies* 33:2 (Apr. 1997): 226–266.

Schofield, Richard. *Kuwait and Iraq: Historical Claims and Territorial Disputes.* London: RIIA, 1991.

Shlaim, Avi. *The Iron Wall: Israel and the Arab World.* New York: Norton, 2000.

Shlaim, Avi. *War and Peace in the Middle East; A Critique of American Policy.* New York: Whittle Books, 1994.

Silverfarb, Daniel. *Britain's Informal Empire in the Middle East: A Case Study of Iraq, 1929–1941.* New York: Oxford University Press, 1986.

Silverfarb, Daniel. *The Twilight of British Ascendancy in the Middle East: A Case Study of Iraq, 1941–1950.* New York: St. Martin's Press, 1994.

Simons, Geoff. *Iraq: From Sumer to Saddam.* New York: St. Martin's, 1994.

Suskind, Ron. *The Price of Loyalty: George W. Bush, the White House, and the Education of Paul O'Neill.* New York: Simon & Schuster, 2004.

Thorpe, James A. "The United States and the 1940–1941 Anglo-Iraqi Crisis: American Policy in Transition." *Middle East Journal* 25 (Winter 1971), 79–89.

Tripp, Charles. *A History of Iraq*, 2nd ed. Cambridge: Cambridge University Press, 2002.

Trumpener, Ulrich. "Turkey's War." In *World War I: A History*, ed. Hew Strachen, 80–91. New York: Oxford University Press, 1998.

Weinberg, Gerhard L. *A World at Arms: A Global History of World War II.* New York: Cambridge University Press, 2005.

Winrow, Gareth. "Turkey: Recalcitrant Ally." In *The Iraq War: Causes and Consequences*, eds. Rick Fawn and Raymond Hinnebusch, 197–208. Boulder, Colo.: Lynne Rienner, 2006.

Woods, Kevin M., et al. *Iraqi Perspectives Project: A View of Operation Iraqi Freedom from Saddam's Senior Leadership.* N.p.: United States Joint Forces Command, n.d. [2006].

Woodward, Bob. *Bush at War.* New York: Simon & Schuster, 2002.

Woodward, Bob. *Plan of Attack.* New York: Simon & Schuster, 2004.

Woodward, Bob. *State of Denial: Bush at War, Part III.* New York: Simon & Schuster, 2006.

Woodward, Bob. *The War Within: A Secret White House History, 2006–2008*. New York: Simon & Schuster, 2009.

Workman, W. Thom. *The Social Origins of the Iran–Iraq War*. Boulder, Colo.: Lynne Rienner, 1994.

Wright, Donald P., and Reese, Timothy R. *On Point II: Transition to the New Campaign: the United States Army in Operation Iraqi Freedom, May 2003-January 2005*. Fort Leavenworth, Ks.: Combat Studies Institute Press, 2008.

Yaqub, Salim. *Containing Arab Nationalism: The Eisenhower Doctrine and the Middle East*. Chapel Hill: University of North Carolina Press, 2004.

Yergin, Daniel. *The Prize: The Epic Quest for Oil, Money, & Power*. New York: Simon & Schuster, 1991.

Index

Page numbers that appear in italics refer to illustrations.

Abbas, Abu, 92
Abbasid dynasty, 10
Abram (Abraham), 10
Abu Ghraib prison, 176, 178–179, *178*, 181, 183–184, 196
Aden, 41
Afghanistan, 57, 197: Taliban regime, 140; U.S. invasion of, 136, 140–142, 148
Aflaq, Michel, 41
al-Askari Mosque, Samarra, 186
Albright, Madeleine, 119, 123
Algiers Accord (1975), 58, 71, 76
Ali, Caliph, 10, 71
Allawi, Ayad, 174, 177–178, 183, 195
Amnesty International, 158
"Anbar Awakening," 191
Annan, Kofi, 125, 158
Ansar al-Islam, 128, 152, 155
Anti-Ballistic Missile Treaty, 178
"Arab Cold War," 42
Arabian-American Oil Company, 27
Arabian Nights, 17
Arab-Israeli (Arab-Zionist) conflict, 26, 30, 33, 40–41, 43, 51–52, 59–60: Six Day War (1967), 49. *See also* Zionism
Arab-Israeli peace process, 72–73, 91, 114–115, 119–120, 139
Arab-Israeli War (1948–1949), 50
Arab-Israeli War (1973), 54, 59
Arab League, 29, 47, 60
Arab oil embargo (1973–1974), 55–56
Arab Union, 31, 46
Argov, Shlomo, 75
Arif, Abdul Rahman, 49–50, 53, 55–56

Arif, Colonel Abdal Salam, 32, 42, 49–51
Armenia, 17
Armistice of Mudros, 12
Armitage, Richard, 141
Asad, Hafez al-, 60, 74
Assyrians, 10
Attlee, Clement, 25
Australia, 150–151
Austria-Hungary, 11
Aziz, Tariq, 71, 75, 77–78, 91, 97, 99, 118, 123

Baath Party, 41–44, 48, 54–57, 60, 71, 74, 169, 177, 194: coup of 1963, 49–50; coup of 1968, 52–53; dismantled, 172–173, 180
Babylonians, 10
Bacevich, Andrew J., 192
Baghdad College, 19, 28
Baghdad Pact, 28–31, 33, 43–44, 48, 61, 62 n. 13
Bahrain, 18, 41, 78, 101, 117: Gulf Cooperation Council, 74
Baker, James, 87–88, 90, 92–93, 99, 106–107, 115–116, 119, 128, 160, 173, 187
Banca Nazionale del Lavoro, 90–91
Baqr, Ahmad Hasan al-, 53–54, 57–58, 60
Baram, Amatzia, 93
Barzani, Massoud, 76, 126, 174, 185–186, 195
Barzani, Mustapha, 24, 48, 50, 54, 57–58, 76
Batatu, Hanna, 13, 48
Bazoft, Farzad, 91
Begin, Menachem, 75
Berg, Nicholas, 183
Bevin, Ernest, 25
Bey, Jamil Mardam, 21
bin Laden, Osama, 128–129, 132, 145, 183, 197

Bitar, Salahedin al-, 41
Blackwill, Robert, 175
Blair, Tony, 142–143, 149–150
Blix, Hans, 146–147
Bosnia, 148–149, 156
Boutros-Ghali, Boutros, 117
Bremer, L. Paul, 170–173, 176–177, *177*, 180:
    de-Baathification, 173, 180, *181*
Brindel, Glenn R., 67, *69*, 83 n. 1
Britain: administration of India, 12; Baghdad
    Pact, 29; British-Iraqi defense treaty
    (1930), 19, 23, 25; colonization of Kuwait,
    93; conflict with Iraq over Kuwait, 45–47;
    defense pacts with Iraq, 14; Eastern
    Question, 11; forgives Iraqi debt, 173; Gulf
    War (1990–1991), 104; Hussein, recognition
    of, 11; intervention in Iraq (1941), 21;
    intervention in Jordan (1958), 32–33; Iraqi
    anti-British rebellion (1919–1921), 12–13;
    Iraqi-Kurdish problem, 50; liberation of
    Palestine and Syria from Ottoman control,
    11; Mandate of Palestine, 26; Mesopotamia,
    11; military action against Baghdad, 7,
    12–13, 21–22, 149–154; policy in Iraq, 8–16,
    33; "no-fly" zones, 117; oil production, 18;
    Operation Northern Watch, 113; Operation
    Provide Comfort, 116; Operation Southern
    Watch, 113; post-World War II policy in
    Iraq, 23–24; presence in Egypt, 11; security
    arrangements in Middle East, 41; Suez Canal
    Crisis, 30; War in Iraq, 150–152, 154
Brubeck, William H., 49
Bull, Gerald, 91
Bunche, Ralph, 26
Bunton, Martin, 71, 120
Bush, Barbara, *98*
Bush, George H.W., 6, 87, 90, 92, *94*, 95–96,
    101, 104, 119, 128, 204–205: containment
    of Iraq (1990s), 115; Gulf War (1990–1991),
    6, 87–88, 107–110; International Atomic
    Energy Agency, 116; Iraqi conspiracy to
    assassinate, 120, 128, 145; Iraqi insurgency,
    179; Iraqi withdrawal from Kuwait, 97;
    meeting with Gorbachev, 97; opposition to
    march on Baghdad, 114; shift in Iraqi policy,
    99; United Nations Special Commission,
    116; U.N. Resolution 660, 102
Bush, George W., 1, *2, 3*, 5, 6, 88, 110, 136, 139,
    141, 143, 146, 160–161, 176, 181, 185, 187,
    195–196, 204–205: appointment of Major
    General Petraeus, *189*; case for Iraq War,
    145–146; containment policy in Iraq, 113,
    140; defense of War in Iraq, 159; election
    of, 133; invasion of Iraq, 149–150, 156–157;
    Office of Reconstruction and Humanitarian

Assistance (ORHA), 167; ousting Saddam
    Hussein, 1, 150–151; post-war Iraq, 168–170,
    172–174, 176, 179, 184, 190, 192, 195, 196;
    regime change in Iraq, 139, 205; State of
    the Union (January 29, 2002), 144; "surge"
    (2003), 164–166, 168, 186, 190. *See also*
    "Mission Accomplished" address
Bush, Laura, 175
Bush Doctrine, 142–143

Camp David Accords, 59–60
Carter, Jimmy, 57, 71, 73, 76, 149
Carter Doctrine, 72
Casey, George W., Jr., 188
Center for Economic and Social Rights, 158
Central Command, U.S. (CENTCOM),
    136–137, 148
Central Intelligence Agency (CIA), 29, 47, 49,
    57, 78, 91, 124, 144, 147–148, 167–168, 170,
    175–177, 181
Central Treaty Organization, 61 n. 13
Chalabi, Ahmed, 174–175, *175*, 176,
    184, 196
Chaldeans, 17
Chamoun, Camille, 31
Chemical weapons (CW). *See* Weapons of mass
    destruction
Cheney, Richard, 96, 101, 138–141, 143,
    145, 169
China, 17, 43, 54, 125: criticism of no-fly zones,
    119; forgives Iraqi debt, 173; sanctions on
    Iraq, 121–122
Chirac, Jacques, 149
Christopher, Warren, 121
Citino, Nathan J., 44
Clarke, Richard, 142, 158, 183
"A Clean Break: A New Strategy for Securing
    the Realm," 129, 139
Cleveland, William, 71, 120
Clinton, William J., 6, 119, 124: containment
    policy in Iraq, 113, 132, 138, 143; punitive
    air strikes on Iraq, 120–121, 125–127,
    129–131
Coalition Provisional Authority (CPA),
    170–171, 173–174, 176–177, 179, *181*, 183:
    CPA Orders 1 and 2, *171*, 172–173, 196
COBRA II (war plan), 148
Cockburn, Patrick, 192
Coffey, Rod, 167
Comprehensive Test Ban Treaty, 178
Congressional Research Service, 186–187. *See*
    also United States, public opinion toward Iraq
Cornwallis, Kinahan, 21
Council of Representatives, Iraq, 184, 195
Cox, Sir Percy, 14

Crane, Charles, 17–18
Cuellar, Perez de, 81
"Curveball" (CIA source), 175
Curzon, Lord, 14, 18
Cyrus the Great, 10

Davis, John W., 18
Da'wa Party, 71, 74
Dawisha, Adeed, 126
Declaration of the United Nations, 22
Defense Planning Guidance, 115
"Desert Crossing" (war plan), 148
Dora Farms, 150, 157
Dorsz, Edmund, 25
Douglas-Home, Alec, 47
Draper, Morris, 77
Duelfer, Charles, 116, 123–125, 159, 170,
    172, 179
Dulles, Allen W., 32, 44
Dulles, John Foster, 28–30
Duncan, Bobby, 67
Duncan, Enoch S., 52
Dwight, H.G.O., 17

Eagleburger, Lawrence, 95–96, 101
Eagleton, William, 77
East Germany, 53
Eden, Anthony, 22
Egypt, 11, 24, 27, 38, 41, 43, 49–51, 57,
    60–61, 74, 93, 117, 185: Arab-Israeli War
    (1973), 54; Baghdad Pact, 29–30; Nasser's
    rise, 32
Egyptian-Israeli peace treaty (1979), 60
Eisendrath, Craig R., 158
Eisenhower, Dwight D., 28, 30–33, 43–44
Eisenhower Doctrine, 31
Etherington, Mark, 173
Export-Import Bank, 49, 78, 91

Fahd, King of Saudi Arabia, 96
Faisal I, King of Iraq, 12–14, 16
Faisal II, King of Iraq, 7, 15, 16, 28, 31, 32
Fallows, James, 147, 169
Feith, Douglas, 139, 141, 144, 150, 157, 167–168,
    175–176
Field Manual 23, 189
Fischer, Joschka, 149
Foley, Laurence, 183
France, 12, 14, 20, 74–75, 78, 90, 124–125:
    forgives Iraqi debt, 173; Gulf War
    (1990–1991), 104; oil in Iraq, 18; Operation
    Northern Watch, 113; Operation Provide
    Comfort, 116; opposition to War in Iraq,
    149–150; "no-fly" zones, 117; sanctions on
    Iraq, 121–122, 132; Suez Crisis, 30; Syrian

struggle for independence from, 41; United
    Nations Security Council Resolution
    1441, 146
Franks, Tommy, 136, 137, 148, 150, 168, 179
Fritzlan, A. David, 38–39
"Future of Iraq" initiative, 167–169

Gailani, Rashid Ali al-, 7, 20–21, 25
Gallman, Waldemar J., 29–31, 43
Garner, Jay, 167–170, 172, 196
Gates, Robert, 190
Gelb, Leslie, 138
Geneva Conventions, 178, 181
Geneva Protocol Banning the Use of Chemical
    Weapons in War (1925), 80
Gerges, Fawaz, 183
Germany, 11, 20–21, 149, 173. See also Nazi
    Germany
Ghaffar, Hardan Abdel, 54–55
Ghazi, King of Iraq, 16, 46
Glaspie, April C., 87–89, 91–92, 110 n. 4
Goodman, Melvin A., 158
Gorbachev, Mikhail, 97–98, 101–102
Gordon, Michael R., 157
Gore, Al, 133
Grass, Zachary, 164, 165, 166, 191
Greenwood, Tom, 190
Grew, Joseph, 25
Gulbenkian, C.S., 18
Gulf Cooperation Council, 74
Gulf War (1990–1991), 6, 87–110, 113–114, 117,
    121, 123, 128, 136, 138, 146, 148, 156, 205

Haass, Richard N., 131, 140, 195
Hadley, Stephen W., 138
Haidari, Darwish, 22
Haig, Alexander, 58, 75–76
Hakim, Mohammad Baqr al-, 174, 182
Haldane, General Aylmer L., 13
Hamid, Subhi al-, 49, 51
Hamilton, Lee H., 87
Hammadi, Sa'dun, 77
Hashimi, Taha al-, 7
Holland, 18
Howe, Jonathan, 77
Hull, Cordell, 20–21
Human Rights Watch, 158
Hume, Cameron, 80
Husain (son of Ali), 10
Hussein, Emir of Iraq, 21
Hussein, grand sheriff of Mecca, 11
Hussein, King of Jordan, 31, 48, 58–59
Hussein, Qusai, 150–151, 154
Hussein, Saddam, 1, 3, 5–6, 39, 54–58, 60–62,
    69–70, 77, 80, 83, 107–108, 114–115, 117,

119–121, 124–127, 130, 132, 136–137, 140, 144, 146–147, 149–150, 152, 156, 158, 160–161, 169, 175–177, 181: attempt to kill, 150–151; biography, 53; capture and execution, 154, 180; chemical weapons (CW), 78, 90, 93, 101, 106, 145, 157, 159, 175, 179, 196; collapse of regime, 161, 166–168, 174, 179, 197, 203; debt in Iraq, 173; execution of Farzad Bazoft, 91; Gulf War (1990–1991), 87–89, 91–92, 95, 97–102, 107–110, 156, 205; invasion of Iran (1980), 5, 68, 73, 204; invasion of Kuwait (1990), 6, 87, 93, 95–96, 104, 109, 204; Iran-Iraq War (1980–1989), 73–76; Khomeini regime, 71–73; Kurdistan Democratic Party (KDP), 126; legacy of atrocities, 139; Operation Northern Watch and Operation Southern Watch, 113; political image, 124; rise to power, 5, 52, 60; September 11, 2001 (9/11 terrorist attacks), 141–142; suppression of Kurds and Shiites, 72, 74, 76, 106; UNSCOM, 131; U.N. Security Council Resolution 660, 102; U.N. Security Council Resolution 986, 122; withdrawal from Kuwait, 104

Hussein, Uday, 150–151, 154
Hussein Doctrine, 72

Ilah, Abdul (Regent to Faisal II), 7, *15*, 20–21, 25
India, 12, 13, 20
Indonesia, 178
Indyk, Martin, 119
International Atomic Energy Agency, 116, 123
International Bank for Reconstruction and Development. *See* World Bank
International Criminal Court, 178
Iran, 9, 16, 20, 24–25, 29, 32, 41, 50, 53–54, 57–58, 62 n. 13, 67, 69–70, 73–77, 89, 108, 140, 187: hostage crisis, 71–72; Iranian revolution (1979), 60, 70–71; Iran-Iraq War (1980–1988), 67–70, 73–77, 79–82; Kurdish problem, 48, 186; terrorism, 144. *See also* Persia
Iran-Iraq War (1980–1988), 67–70, 73–76, 88–89, 109, 204: aftermath, 89, 109; end of, 79–82; Iraqi economy, 121; local and regional impact of, 73–76; origins, 70–73; wartime rapprochement, 76–79; weapons of mass destruction, 75–76, 78–79
Iraq: 1958 revolution, 28, 31–32, 41; anti-British rebellion (1919–1921), 12–13; anti-U.S. insurgency, 157, 176, 179, 181, 183; Arab rivalries, 49; Baathists, 42–44, 48–49, 52–53, 55–56, 59–60, 108, 158; communism, 25, 31,

40, 44–45, 48, 50, 60–61, 83; conflict with Britain over Kuwait, 45–48; demographics, 8–10, 12; independence from Britain (1932), 14; internal politics, 16, 41–42, 60, 71–72, 74, 89, 121, 124–125, 180; international politics, 52, 60–62, 99; invasion of Kuwait (1990), 6, 87–88, 93–95, 116; Iran-Iraq War (1980–1988), 67–70, 73–77, 79–82, 88–89, 121, 204; Kurds, 9, 16, 48, 50, 53–54, 57–58, 61, 71, 73–75, 80, 106; military aid, 28; naming of, 14, 34 n. 2; nationalism, 12–14, 20, 24, 60; nuclear program, 74–75; oil industry, 26–27, 52, 56–57, 61, 67, 126, 205; political turmoil in 1941, 21; pre-1945 history, 8–14; recognition of East Germany, 53; relations with Egypt, 42, 47, 49, 57, 59–61, 72, 74; relations with Iran, 5, 57–58, 60–61, 71; relations with Israel, 29, 49–50, 53–54, 57–61, 73–75, 77–78, 89, 95, 145, 152, 205; relations with Jordan, 31, 46, 54, 58–59, 74; relations with Kuwait, 6, 45, 47, 89, 92–93, 97, 204; relations with Soviet Union, 43, 46, 48, 50, 52–53, 56–57, 60, 77, 89–90, 97; relations with Syria, 13, 27, 31, 42, 57, 59, 74–75, 89; relations with Turkey, 76; relations with United States, 1, 3, 5–8, 16, 25, 28–33, 40–43, 48, 49–52, 55–56, 61, 67–83, 87–110, 113–133, 136–161, 164–197, 204–205; Sunni-Shiite relations, 12, 14, 16; weapons of mass destruction, 75–76, 78, 80, 82, 91, 93
Iraq Governing Council (IGC), 176–177, 182, 185
Iraq Liberation Act of 1998, 129, 131–132
Iraq National Oil Company (INOC), 55–56
Iraq Operations Group, 170
Iraq Petroleum Company (IPC), 18–19, *19*, 22, 26–27, 49, 55–56
Iraq Study Group (ISG), 187–188, 190
Iraq Survey Group, 159, 179
Iraqi Interim Authority Plan, 175
Iraqi Interim Government, 183
Iraqi National Accord, 177
Iraqi Transitional Government, 177
Islam: rise of in Iraq, 10
Israel: Arab-Israeli War of 1973, 54; arming by Nixon administration, 54; Baghdad Pact, 29–30; Egypt-Israeli peace treaty (1979), 60; Gulf War (1990–1991), 101; Iraqi invasion of Kuwait, 93; Occupied Territories, 97; relations with Iraq, 49–50, 53–54, 57, 61, 73–75, 77, 95, 145, 152; relations with United States, 58; Six Day War, 52; Suez Crisis, 30; U.S. support of, 31. *See also* Arab-Israeli conflict
Israeli-Palestinian conflict, 197
Italy, 20, 74, 78, 173

Jaafari, Ibrahim al-, 184
Jackson, Henry M., 139
Japan, 173
Jarring, Gunnar, 59
Jawdat, Ali, *22*
Jentleson, Bruce, 73, 80–81, 90, 93
Jernegan, John D., 47
Jervis, Robert, 142
Johnson, Lyndon B., 49–52
Jordan (Transjordan), 11, 14, 24, 31–33, 38,
    41, 43, 49, 54, 58, 74, 90, 123, 129, 140:
    Arab-Israeli conflict, 51; Arab Union,
    46; Eisenhower Doctrine, 31; troops in
    Kuwait, 47

Kagan, Frederick W., 188
Kamal, Hussein, 123
Kamal, Saddam, 123
Kamel, Mostafa, 43
Karami, Omar, 185
Kaufman, Robert G., 142
Kay, David, 179
Keane, Jack, 187
Kedourie, Elie, 13
Keegan, John, 146, 154, 156
Kennedy, John F., 44–45, *45*, 47–51
Kerr, Malcolm, 42
Kerry, John, 184
Khadduri, Majid, 71
Khalil, Samir al-, 72, 83 n. 7
Khalilzad, Zalmay, 83, 139
Khomeini, Ayatollah Ruhollah, 62, 67, 69–73,
    82–83
Khrushchev, Nikita, 32
King, Henry Churchill, 17–18
King-Crane Commission, 18
Kissinger, Henry, 54, 58
Klein, Joe, 192
Knabenshue, Paul, 7–8, 20–21, 33
Komer, Robert, 47, 49
Korb, Lawrence, 158
Korean War, 28
Krauthammer, Charles, 159, 195
Kristol, William, 192
Kurdistan, 16–17, 155, 185
Kurdistan Democratic Party (KDP), 24–25,
    58, 126
Kurds, 9, 16, 24, 44, 53–54, 57–58, 60–61,
    72–73, 74–76, 80, 106, 108, 114, 116, 121,
    149, 151, 160, 172, 184, 186, 195: Kurdish
    rebellion in northern Iraq, 48–49, 52, 71,
    108, 110, 115; Operation Provide Comfort,
    116–117
Kuwait, 14, 18, 41, 61, 79, 88, 92, 117, 120,
    150: Anglo-Iraqi crisis (1961), 45–47; Arab

Union, 31; Gulf Cooperation Council, 74;
    Iraqi invasion, 6, 92–93, 95, 116; liberation
    of, 104, 106, 109–110, 156; U.S.-flagged oil
    tankers, 67, 80, 82; U.S. troops in, 121
Kyoto Protocol, 178
Kzar, Nadhim, 54

Lausanne Conference (1922–1923), 14
"Law of Administration for the State of Iraq for
    the Transitional Period," 177
League of Nations, 12, *13*, 17–18: Middle East
    mandates, 14, 17–18
Lebanon, 12–13, 31–32, 38, 41, 43, 77, 79, 185
Lend-Lease, 22, 25
Lind, Michael, 142
"Loose" (U.S. Air Force pilot), 113–114, *114*
Lovett, Robert, 25
Lussier, John, 1, *2*
Luti, William, 175

Madrid Conference, 115
Mahabad, Republic of, 24–25
Mahdi, Adil Abdel, 173
Mahdi Army, 182, 192, 194
Majid, Ali Hasan as- ("Chemical Ali"), 76
Makiya, Kanan, 83 n. 7, 150. *See also* al-Khalil,
    Samir
Maliki, Nouri al-, 184, 190, 192, 195
Mansoor, Peter, 190, 192
Marr, Phebe, 168
McCain, John, 193
McKiernan, David D., 168
McMaster, H.R., 190
Mesopotamia, 8–12, 17
"Mission Accomplished" address, 1, 3, 5, 154,
    158, 166, 196, 203, 205
Missionaries to Iraq, U.S., 17, 33
Moncrief, Basil E., 67, 83 n. 1
Mongols, 10, 17
Monroe, Elizabeth, 11
Morocco, 117
Mossadegh, Mohammed, 29
Muawiya, 10
Mufti of Jerusalem, 20
Muhammed, The Prophet, 10, 54
Murray, Williamson, 152–153, 155
Murtha, John P., 158
Mylroie, Laurie, 128

Nance, Susan, 17
Nasser, Gamal Abdel, 24, 29–32, 43–44, 47,
    50–51, 56, 89
National Security Council (NSC), 29, 44, 47
National Security Decision Directive 139, 78
National Security Directive 26, 90–91

National Security Strategy of the United States, 145
Nazi Germany, 7. *See also* Germany
"Neocons," 128–129, 132–133, 138–140, 176
Nestorians, 17
Nestorius, 17
Netanyahu, Benjamin, 129
"New Strategy," 95
Nicaragua, 79
Niger, 179
Nigeria, 178
Nixon, Richard M., 54, 57–58
Nixon Doctrine, 54
"no-fly" zones, 117, *118*, 121, 125–126, 132, 140, 148
North Atlantic Treaty Organization (NATO), 29, 31, 140, 178
North Korea, 144, 197

Obama, Barack, 193; policy in Iraq, 193–195, 206
Office of Reconstruction and Humanitarian Assistance (ORHA), 167, 170
Oil-for-Food program, 122–123, 132
Oil resources of the Middle East, 11–12, 16, 18, 20, 24, 27, 41, 50, 57, 73–74, 92
Oman, 74, 78
Operation Desert Fox, 125
Operation Desert Shield, 96, 115
Operation Desert Storm, 100, *102*, *103*, 110, 115
Operation Iraqi Freedom, 136–137, 194: casualties, 198 n. 5
Operation New Dawn, 194: casualties, 198 n. 5
Operation Northern Watch, 113, 117, 120, 129
Operation Provide Comfort, 116–117
Operation Southern Watch, 113, *118*, 120, 129
Organization of the Petroleum-Exporting Countries, 58, 74, 95
O'Sullivan, Christopher D., 148
O'Sullivan, Meghan, 169
Ottoman Empire, 11–12, 16, 18, 45: alliance with Germany and Austria-Hungary, 11

Pachachi, Adnan M., 51–52, 174
Pahlavi, Mohammed Reza, Shah of Iran, 71
Pakistan, 28–29, 62 n. 13
Palestine, 11–14: British Mandate of, 26; dispute over, 24, 26, 197
Palestine Liberation Front, 92
Palestine Liberation Organization, 51, 59, 90
Pan-Arab Charter, 72
Paris Peace Conference (1919), 12
Pasha, Ismet, 14

Patriotic Union of Kurdistan (PUK), 58, 126
Pell, Claiborne, 81
Pelosi, Nancy, 187
Perkins, David, 153, *154*, 169
Perle, Richard, 139
Persia, 17, 18. *See also* Iran
Pesh Merga, 58
Petraeus, David, 172, 188, *189*, 190–191
Point Four aid program, 28
Portsmouth Treaty, 25–26
Powell, Colin, 96, 101, 106, 138–142, 146–148, *147*, *175*
Public Law 105–174, 129
Public Law 105–235, 129
Public Law 105–338, 129

Qaeda, al-, 128, 140, 158, 179, 183, 187, 191
Qassim, General Abdul Karim, 32, 38–47, *40*, 50, 53
Qatar, 41, 74, 101

Rahman, Sheikh Abdul, 183
Randolph, John, 19
Reagan, Ronald, 67, 69, 75–80, 82
Record, Jeffrey, 158
"Regional Defense Strategy," 95
Reid, Harry M., 187
Reid, Richard, 143
Rice, Condoleezza, 138, 140, 146, 170, 174–175, 184
Richards, James P., 31
Ricks, Thomas E., 148, 158
Ritter, Scott, 124
Rogers, William, 54, 59
Rogers peace plan, 57, 59
Roosevelt, Franklin D., 20, 22–23
Rostow, Walt W., 50–52
Rountree, William M., 38–39, *39*, 43–44, 61
Rumsfeld, Donald, 77–78, 138–141, 148–149, 157, 167–170, 176, 188, 190, 196–197
Rusk, Dean G., 46–47, *46*, 49–52
Russia, 12, 20, 90, 117, 124–125: forgives Iraqi debt, 173; sanctions on Iraq, 121–122, 132; United Nations Security Council Resolution 1441, 146. *See also* Soviet Union

Sabahin, Jabir al-Ahmad al Jabir al-, *94*
Sada, Georges, 126
Sadat, Anwar, 72
Sadr, Muqtada al-, 176, 180, 182, 192, 194
Said, Nuri al-, *15*, 16, 20–23, 26–32, 46
Saleh, Barham, *177*
Sanchez, Ricardo, 171–172, 181, *181*
San Remo conference, 12, 18

Saudi Arabia, 14, 18, 24, 27, 32, 43, 49, 72, 75, 78, 92–93, 95–98, 108, 117, 129, 185: Baghdad Pact, 29; Gulf Cooperation Council, 74; oil fields, 94; Operation Southern Watch, 113; scud missile attacks on, 101; troops in Kuwait, 47; U.S. troops stationed in, 99

Saunders, Hal, 58

Scales, Robert H., 153, 155

Schifter, Richard, 83

Schwarzkopf, H. Norman, Jr., *98*, 106, 108–109

Scowcroft, Brent, 95, 101–102, 117, 145, 160

Seelye, Talcott, 57

September 11, 2001 (9/11 terrorist attacks), 132–133, 138, 140–145, 160, 183, 197

Shamir, Yitzhak, 101

Shatt al-Arab ("River of the Arabs"), 9, 11, 46, 71, 90

Shelton, Henry Hugh, *118*

Shinseki, Eric K., 148, 168

Shlaim, Avi, 14

Shrine of Imam Ali, 179

Shultz, George P., 76–78, 80, 83

Sistani, Grand Ayatollah Ali al-, 176, 182

Six Day War (1967), 51–53

Slocombe, Walter, 172

Smith, Eli, 17

Smith, Tara, *191*

Somalia, 156

Soto, Danny R., 166, 191

Southeast Asia Treaty Organization, 29

Soviet Union, 25, 29, 33, 43, 46–47, 54–55, 80, 99, 204: arming of Arab states, 51; Baathists, 58; collapse of, 115; encourages insurrection of Iraqi Kurds, 50; invasion of Afghanistan, 57, 72, 77; involvement in Kurdish diplomacy, 58; post–World War II policy in the Middle East, 23–24, 28, 30; relations with Iraq, 50, 52–53, 56–57, 60, 77, 89–90, 97. *See* Russia

Standard Oil of New Jersey, 18

Standard Oil of New York, 18

Status of Forces Agreement, 192–193

Stettinius, Edward R., 22

Strategic Framework Agreement, 192

Strong, Robert C., 51–52, 56

"Study Group on a New Israeli Strategy toward 2000," 129

Sudanese troops in Kuwait, 47

Suez Canal Company, 30

Suez Crisis (1956), 30, 51

Suez War (1956–1957), 32, 41

Sumerians, 10

Sunnis, 10–14; Kurdish, 12

Sununu, John, 95

Supreme Council for the Islamic Revolution in Iraq, 174

Supreme Islamic Iraqi Council, 194

Sykes-Picot agreement (1916), 12

Syria, 11–14, 16, 21, 27, 32, 41, 57, 59–60, 73–75, 97, 117, 186: Arab-Israeli War of 1973, 54; Eisenhower Doctrine, 31; hostilities with Israel, 51; United Arab Republic (UAR), 31, 42

Tabatabai, Sadegh, 73

Talabani, Jalal, 58, 76, 126, 174, 184–185, 195

Talbot, Phillips, 50

Tenet, George, 146

terrorism, 143–144, 180, 183, 186

Thatcher, Margaret, 95

"thunder runs," 152, *154*

Tikriti, Raji al-, 126

Trainor, Bernard E., 157

Transitional National Assembly, 184

Transjordan: *See* Jordan

Truman, Harry S., 23, 25–28

Turkey, 16, 20, 28–29, 32, 62 n. 13, 76, 129, 149, 185: Kurdish problem, 48, 108, 114, 186

Turkish Petroleum Company, 12

Ummayad dynasty, 10

United Arab Emirates, 74, 92, 94

United Arab Republic (UAR), 31, 42, 44, 47

United Nations, 23, 26, 52, 59, 146, 149, 158, 186. *See also* U.N. Security Council Resolutions

United Nations Monitoring, Verification, and Inspection Commission (UNMOVIC), 131, 146–147

United Nations Security Council, 47, 81, 121, 125, 131

United Nations Security Council Resolution 598, 81

United Nations Security Council Resolution 660, 97, 102

United Nations Security Council Resolution 661, 115, 121

United Nations Security Council Resolution 664, 97

United Nations Security Council Resolution 665, 97

United Nations Security Council Resolution 678, 99

United Nations Security Council Resolution 687, 115, 121–122

United Nations Security Council Resolution 688, 117

United Nations Security Council Resolution 715, 123

United Nations Security Council Resolution 949, 121
United Nations Security Council Resolution 986, 122
United Nations Security Council Resolution 1441, 146, 149–150
United Nations Special Commission (UNSCOM), 116, 123–125, 131
United States: Cold War strategy, 24, 40–41, 54, 205; Congress, 148–150, 158, 178, 184, 187–188, 190, 193; cultural views of Middle East, 17; defense treaties with Turkey, Iran, and Pakistan, 62 n. 13; intervention in Jordan (1958), 32; intervention in Lebanon (1958), 32, 43; invasion of Afghanistan, 140–142, 148, 183, 197; invasion of Iraq (2003), 1, 3, 6; Kuwaiti oil tankers, 67, 80, 82; military operations in Afghanistan, 136; policy on Kurds, 50, 58, 61, 116, 160, 172; public opinion toward Iraq, 3, 76, 93, 96–100, 104, 108–109, 116, 121, 125, 128, 145, 184, 186–187, 192–193, 203–204; relations with Iran, 67, 70–71, 73, 78–79, 82–83, 89; relations with Iraq (policy in Iraq), 5–8, 16, 25, 28–33, 40–43, 48–62, 67–83, 87–110, 113–133, 136–161, 164–197, 204; relations with Israel, 58, 97, 129; relations with Saudi Arabia, 79, 97–98, 109; relations with Soviet Union, 54, 58, 61, 99, 102, 115, 204
Unity and Jihad Group, 183
Uqair Conference (1922), 14
U.S. Army War College, 167
U.S. Chamber of Commerce, 81
U.S.-Iraq Business Forum, 81

U.S.-Iraq extradition treaty (1934), 19
U.S.-Iraq Treaty of Friendship, Commerce, and Navigation (1938), 28
USS *Abraham Lincoln*, 1, *2*, *3*, 166, 203, 205
USS *Stark*, 67–70, 80, 82–83
USS *Vincennes*, 82
Utham, Caliph, 10

Veliotes, Nicholas A., 77

Warrick, Thomas, 169
Weapons of mass destruction (WMD), 75–76, 78–79, 101–102, 106, 115–116, 121, 123–124, 131, 142–143, 145–148, 156–157, 159–160, 175, 179, 184, 196
Weinberger, Caspar, 69, 75, 80
Wilson, Arnold, 12
Wilson, Woodrow, 12, 17–18: Wilsonian rhetoric about self-determination, 16
Wolfowitz, Paul, 130–131, 138–139, 141–142, 149–150, 181
Woolsey, R. James, 128
Workman, W. Thom, 74
World Bank (International Bank for Reconstruction and Development), 25, 28
World's Fair in Chicago (1893), 17
World War I, 11, 20: British Mandates, *13*; collapse of Ottoman authority, 16; French Mandates, *13*
World War II, 16, 20, 23–24, 45, 205

Zakaria, Fareed, 178–179
Zarqawi, Abu Musab al-, 183, 186
Zinni, Anthony, 130–131, *130*
Zionism, 26, 30, 53–54